Born in the U.S.A.

STUDIES IN POPULAR CULTURE
M. Thomas Inge, General Editor

Born in the U.S.A.

*The Myth of America
in Popular Music
from Colonial Times
to the Present*

Timothy E. Scheurer

UNIVERSITY PRESS OF MISSISSIPPI
Jackson & London

94 93 92 91   4 3 2 1

The paper in this book meets the guidelines for permanence and durability of the Committee on Production Guidelines for Book Longevity of the Council on Library Resources.

Library of Congress Cataloging-in-Publication Data

Scheurer, Timothy E.
    Born in the U.S.A. : the myth of America in popular music from
Colonial times to the present / Timothy E. Scheurer.
        p.   cm. — (Studies in popular culture)
    Includes bibliographical references and index.
    ISBN 0-87805-496-0. — ISBN 0-87805-497-9 (pbk.)
    1. Popular music — United States — History and criticism.   2. United
States — Popular culture — History.   I. Title.   II. Series: Studies in popu-
lar culture (Jackson, Miss.)
    ML3477.S33   1991
    782.42164'1599 — dc20   90-29114
                                                                   CIP
                                                                   MN

British Library Cataloging-in-Publication data available

FOR MY PARENTS

RUTH A. AND ANDREW C. SCHEURER

WITH LOVE AND GRATITUDE

CONTENTS

Preface viii

Introduction 3

ONE   **"To Thee Sing Psalm Wil I":**
The Roots of the Myth
in Puritan Music 16

TWO   **"We Led Fair FREEDOM Hither":**
The Revolutionary War Era 24

THREE   **"From Every Mountainside":**
From the Revolution
to the Outbreak of the Civil War .. 39

FOUR   **"Who Shall Rule This
American Nation?":**
The Civil War Era 65

FIVE   **"A Thoroughfare for Freedom Beat":**
From the End of the
Civil War to the End
of the Great War 86

SIX   **"Of Thee I Sing, Baby":**
The Tin Pan Alley Years,
1920–1950 114

SEVEN   **"This Land Is Your Land":**
The Folk-Protest Movement
and Other Voices, 1920–1960 138

EIGHT   **"They've All Come to Look for America":** The Late 1950s and the 1960s ... 166

NINE   **"You Can't Be Forever Blessed":** The 1970s 197

TEN   **"Born in the U.S.A.":** The 1980s 219

Conclusion 248

Bibliography 254

Discography 265

Index 271

Contents   vii

PREFACE

I selected Bruce Springsteen's "Born in the U.S.A." as the title for this book for a number of reasons. First, and perhaps most simply, I admire Mr. Springsteen and his music. His songs embody much of what I love about American music, because they resonate with the sounds of our rich musical heritage. In his songs one hears echoes: from the revolutionary broadside balladeers, who proudly claimed that they were Americans, from the socially engaged words of the Hutchinson family, from the sounds of protest of Woody Guthrie and later Bob Dylan. All these songwriters/performers, moreover, wrote music that spoke simultaneously of an abiding love for our country and concern over whether America was fulfilling its "true" destiny. Mr. Springsteen is an important link in that heritage.

Second, the song "Born in the U.S.A." sums up what I am trying to say about the myth of America in popular song—at once a proud declaration of his American heritage and a critical indictment of the American way of life. It is a testament of the faith of Americans in the idea of America and how that faith has been rewarded. On the one hand, there are songs that paint a picture of us stretching our arms, like Jay Gatsby, toward an ineffable, unreachable green light of hope and possibilities; and, on the other hand, there are those songs that paint a picture of us standing there, like Gatsby outside Daisy Buchanan's house, looking out over nothing.

Springsteen's song was released at a time when America seemed to be on everyone's mind. The Reagan presidency had inspired a variety of responses about what it was to be an American ranging from old-fashioned, untrammeled, no-apologies flag waving by TV evangelists and conservative commentators, who saw us in the midst of an American Renaissance, to the sometimes critical analyses of the disadvantaged, who saw America plunging into precipitous decline.

Throughout the eighties, popular musicians—in addition to

Springsteen—chronicled the hopes and fears of a divided nation: Jackson Browne, James Brown, Lee Greenwood, Laurie Anderson, Charlie Daniels, the Dell-Lords, Los Lobos, U2, Prince, John Mellencamp, Don Henley, Public Enemy. Like the TV evangelists, out-of-control S&L managers, and military hardware manufacturers, they stood for America in the eighties.

And at the heart of their songs lies the monomyth of America —that gripping narrative about the vast, rugged, and plentiful land, whose destiny is providentially guided by the hand of God, and where, because of the noble sacrifices of pilgrims and patriots in the cause of liberty and freedom, we enjoy unlimited opportunity and freedom. Some accept the myth wholeheartedly as it came down to them from Revolutionary War times; others see it as an unrealized dream or as a failure. But whatever their viewpoint, they are not afraid to tackle the totality of the myth.

After hearing Springsteen's album *Born in the U.S.A.* and John Mellencamp's "Pink Houses," I began to look back over the history of popular song in America and how "America" has been treated in music, from pre-Revolutionary times to the present. The songs I examine reflect America's first attempts to carve out a basic mythos about itself during the colonial period, its realization of a total myth in the nineteenth century, and its "coming of age" in the twentieth century. We will see that the myth of America as embodied in popular song has shifted from hymnlike paeans extolling a shared theocratic and almost transcendental ideal to, within the last twenty-five years, introspective ruminations.

One of the most difficult aspects of doing this study was song selection. One could justifiably claim that every song ever written by an American is about America. But space requires me to limit myself to those songs that deal directly with what I call the major mythemes of America. In short, a song would have to have some allusion to manifest destiny and the land—favorable or unfavorable —for me to consider it as an expression of the myth. This nonetheless leaves me with a wide range: "The Star-Spangled Banner," "America the Beautiful," "God Bless America," "This Land Is Your Land," "America" (Paul Simon) and "America" (Prince), and "Ball of Confusion" (the Temptations), and so on. The ones I selected— based on my listening and lyric analysis—were the most prominent and most compelling expressions of the myth throughout our history. I have also tried to find wherever possible, songs that represent a large cross-section of the country, including minority voices; although the myth is largely the creation of the dominant white culture, it has been affected by those "other voices." Thus the book will show the power of song to perpetuate cultural hegemony and, simultaneously, fuel the fires of dessent.

But this book represents Americans' view of America. I have not included songs about America by songwriters from other countries: Bob Marley's "Buffalo Soldier," the Clash's "I'm So Bored With the U.S.A.," and the songs on U2's *The Joshua Tree*. This is homegrown music.

This is not primarily a musicological study. Instead the book concerns itself with song lyrics as mythico-literary texts. I wanted to keep my focus on lyrics as expression of cultural myth and value.

I try to account briefly for the role played by such factors as cultural value, historical events, developments in the media, and changes in the manufacturing/distribution system may have had on the perpetuation and changes in the treatment of the myth of America. But these are all peripheral to the main thrust of the book, for interested readers, sources in the bibliography fill in some of the details to a study of popular music.

Scholarly works are humbling experiences. An author constantly confronts his need for others in helping produce the work he has in mind. Such contacts are, of course, rewarding as well, since one is continually challenged by new issues, new ideas, and new and valuable friends. Therefore, there are a number of people I want to thank:

First Allyn Ehrhardt and the staff of the Franklin University Library, including Fred Helser, Ann Brocker, Cindy Silcott, Beau McCall, Diane Thomas, and Linda Culbertson; their encouraging cooperation enabled me to obtain much-needed research materials.

My good friend Bill Schurk of the Bowling Green Music Library and Sound Recording Archives and his assistant Michael McHugh, who found many rare recordings for me.

The staff at The Ohio State University music library, who helped me locate needed materials.

Dr. Darby Williams, Dr. John DeSando, and the late Dr. Frederick Bunte, who implemented a professional development leave program at Franklin University, and the current administration and Board of Trustees who continued it; without that needed leave time, this book would not have seen completion.

My good friend and colleague Prof. Peggy Hartshorn, who read portions of this manuscript, offered sound critical advice, and enthusiastically supported my research and writing.

My colleague Prof. Brian Maze, who made many songs available to me from his vast personal record collection.

My colleague and friend Dr. Susan Opt, who suggested much valuable material related to communication theory, read preliminary drafts of this manuscript, and backed up my work with spirited encouragement.

My good friends Shirley and Harvey Rothenbuhler, who allowed me access to sheet music of World Wars I and II in their personal collection.

I also wish to express my gratitude to three people on the publishing end of this project. First, to Prof. Thomas Inge, the general editor of the Studies in Popular Culture series, for having faith in this idea and for giving me the incentive to continue my research and writing on the topic. Second, to Ann Finlayson not only for her meticulous editing of the manuscript but also for posing some thought-provoking ideas and suggestions. Finally, to Seetha Srinivasan of the University Press of Mississippi for her concern, understanding, and firm hand in seeing this book through the publishing process.

Finally, none of this could have happened if it hadn't been for the love and encouragement of my family. My wife Pam has been a constant companion and friend for twenty years; her patience and faith in me helped make this task much easier. Without her I wouldn't be in the enviable position of being able to study, research, and write about the things I love the most.

Thanks also to my son Andy for being understanding when I needed to get some work done, for occasionally getting me away from the task at hand to play a little baseball, and, finally, for thinking it was pretty neat that I had written a book.

Born in the U.S.A.

INTRODUCTION **Culture, Myth, and Popular Song**

[Man] can adapt himself somehow to anything his imagination can cope with, but he cannot cope with chaos.
—Susanne Langer

Every mythology has to do with the wisdom of life as related to a specific culture at a specific time. It integrates the individual into his society and the society into the field of nature. It unites the field of nature with my nature. It's a harmonizing force.
—Joseph Campbell

The student of popular culture knows how important myths are in the life of a culture. They are, in a sense, its cement. They are the ideological narratives that inform and give significance to our rituals, icons, heroes, and, in general, all the products of our culture. Myths have played and continue to play vital roles in all cultures everywhere.

Too often myths have been understood to be mere stories designed to explain phenomena beyond the reach of current knowledge. But myths are much more than that. Like Daisy Buchanan's voice in *The Great Gatsby* they seem to be "deathless" songs moving through time and beyond time, inspiring and destroying, animating and eliminating. Our fascination with them is evident throughout recorded history and up to the present, where within the last thirty years we have seen major works on myth by writers such as Richard Slotkin, James Oliver Robertson, Northrop

Frye, Roland Barthes, and Claude Levi-Strauss. Most recently, the late Joseph Campbell enjoyed a sort of scholarly apotheosis, when PBS presented *The Power of Myth* as a series hosted by Bill Moyers; it enjoyed a great deal of popularity with viewers, while the book based on the series even had a brief stay on the best-seller lists. In order to understand the significance of myth in our culture and consequently its importance to popular music, let us first begin by discussing what we mean by "culture" and then let us go on to examine some definitions of "myth."

My notion of culture in popular song is based largely on the definitions provided by anthropologist Clifford Geertz and the philosopher Antonio Gramsci. Geertz states that culture "denotes an historically transmitted pattern of meanings embodied in symbols, a system of inherited conceptions expressed in symbolic forms by means of which men communicate, perpetuate and develop their knowledge about and attitudes towards life" (1973, 89). Gramsci defines culture as follows: "It is organization, discipline of one's inner self, a coming to terms with one's personality; it is the attainment of a higher awareness, with the aid of which one succeeds in understanding one's own historical value, one's own function in life, and one's own rights and obligations" (1981, 194). These definitions are in agreement on some key concepts in American culture, myth, and popular music: the role of the individual in relationship to the community; values in regard to one's own function in life, rights, and obligations; higher awareness, intellectual or religious—especially through use of symbols—and, finally, history. Let us see now how myth embodies, integrates, and ultimately perpetuates these characteristics of culture.

Traditionally, we think of myths as narratives that help explain natural phenomena, seeing it as an interpretation of reality. According to Nimmo and Combs, myth is "a credible, dramatic, socially constructed re-presentation of perceived realities that people accept as permanent, fixed knowledge of reality while forgetting (if they ever were aware of it) its tentative, imaginative, created, and perhaps fictional qualities" (1980, 16). Similarly, Richard Weiss notes of the American myth of success: "I mean [myth] to connote a complex of profoundly held attitudes and values which condition the way men view the world and understand their experience. However inaccurate as a description of American society, the success myth reflects what millions believe that society is or ought to be" (1969, 3–4).

The power of myth and its significance to cultural studies stems primarily from man's need to believe in something. Myths provide, first of all, a means to describe our world and give it and our lives meaning. Consequently, myth may not only reflect a culture's values but also be a shaping force of those same values. Second, myth calls forth from the individual an acceptance and commitment to the story and the values contained in that story. Hence, individuals do not see the story as something separate from their daily lives but as a living expression of them.

In order to "sustain and authenticate" (in Roland Barthes' words) our sense of cultural being, myth performs certain key functions. One of the dominant ones is that it enables an individual to establish a relationship with the world and life in general. Myth is constantly alive because our need to believe in something and to understand our world is constantly alive. Sylvester Stallone's *Rambo* series stands as compelling evidence of the efficacy of myth in the 1980s. Those films tell us that we could have won the war in Vietnam had we willed it and that we are still a strong and basically moral nation whose fighting men are loyal to one another and to the ideals of the soldier's duty; it tells us that as long as we have fighting men such as John Rambo, America is fundamentally strong and righteous and, when called upon, we can still win the war.

And so it is with the myth of America. I have already stated the myth of America as presented in popular song: America is a vast, rugged, and plentiful land, whose destiny is providentially guided by the hand of God, and where, because of the noble sacrifices of pilgrims and patriots in the cause of liberty and freedom, we enjoy unlimited opportunity, equality and freedom. *his focus*

This is our great national monomyth. It explains where we have come from and where we are going and why we have been favored to exist as a nation. It does this by relying on some dominant symbols and images, including images of the land (vast, bountiful), freedom/liberty, opportunity, pilgrims/patriots, and manifest destiny. These will be present in all the songs under discussion here. Some songs contain them all, others merely rely upon two or three, but most of the songs feature more than just one. They will be evoked by songwriters either to reinforce this monomyth as a positive validation of our being or as touchstones for demythologizing—perhaps repudiating the monomyth—and reifying a new myth.

The latter is especially true in the popular music of the 1960s, 1970s, and 1980s, where songwriters seem to select an anomalous aspect of the myth (i.e., it is no longer freedom but oppression, we are losing "America The Beautiful" to pollution, God no longer providentially guides our destiny, and so forth). Thus, a listener/performer, when encountering one of these songs, apprehends immediately the entire myth—even if the writer stresses the anomalous characteristics—because these elements are the constants, the modern-day equivalents of the epithet, the patronymic, the verbal formulas of classical myth and legend.

This myth of America is the expression of what *we believe* our country to represent; the myth may help explain—or at least remind us of—our democratic origins; it articulates and makes manifest the country's destiny and its reason for existence; it may help the individuals understand themselves in light of the country's great geographical and ideological opportunity and freedom; it balances historical fact with legend in a seamless narrative so that the line between the two blurs and at times fades completely. Myth enables us to frame a picture of the world, order it, and have it make sense in light of the manifold mysteries of existence. One may say, don't we have more sophisticated means of achieving this self-actualized state, this state of "higher awareness," than myth, this seeming vestige of a preliterate society? We might, but they are not likely to be as efficacious.

The efficacy of mythology in popular culture is dependent upon the functions it performs and needs it fulfills for the individual listener and, by extension, the community. By examining how myth functions in popular song, we can better determine the role popular song may play in shaping a culture's consciousness. Joseph Campbell states that there is, first, a "mystical" function, wherein myth helps us make "a connection between our waking consciousness and the whole mystery of the universe"; second, there is a cosmological function wherein "myth gives us a map or picture of the universe. It allows us to see ourselves in relationship to nature, as when we speak of Father Sky and Mother Earth. There is also a sociological function for myth, in that it supports and validates a certain social and moral order for us. . . . Lastly, myth has a psychological function, in that it offers us a way of passing through, and dealing with, the various states of life from birth to death (quoted in Kennedy 1979, 14–15).

In popular song, for instance, the role of providence conforms with Campbell's notion of the mystical function of myth and, to a lesser degree, the sociological function. The role of the patriots in our history and later of the alienated individual fulfills the sociological function. The psychological function corresponds to the mytheme of freedom and opportunity. Finally, the relationship with the land and the relationship with God as guiding force in our history fulfills the cosmological function.

For the purposes of this study I have synthesized Campbell's ideas —and others as well—and identified what I call megafunctions that myth performs in popular song. I have done this partly to demonstrate the interrelatedness of the functions in the myth. The first megafunction of myth is its role in reconciling conflicting cultural ideologies, beliefs, and philosophies. Claude Levi-Strauss noted "that mythical thought always progresses from the awareness of oppositions toward their resolution" (1963, 221). It is this ability of myth to reconcile or resolve conflict and contradiction that makes it so important to the study of popular culture. The persistence and ubiquitous presence of the same myth in many of the popular arts in a given time period speak of its ability to address the needs of the mass audience. James Oliver Robertson states:

> Myths, are the patterns—of behavior, of belief, and of perception— which people have in common. . . . They provide good, "workable" ways by which the contradictions in a society, the contrasts and conflicts which normally arise among people, among ideals, among the confusing realities, are somehow reconciled, smoothed over, or at least made manageable and tolerable. (1980, xv)

One theme that I will return to, as we survey the myth of America in popular song, is how it indeed does reconcile seemingly contradictory ideologies and philosophies in different time periods. In colonial times, for instance, the myth reconciles a secular-based philosophy (Jefferson, Franklin) with the theocratic ideals of the Puritans. In our own times a songwriter such as Jackson Browne attempts to reconcile the ideals of the founding fathers, symbolized in his allusions to "The Star Spangled Banner," with the spirit of protest of 1965–1975. Another contradiction facing songwriters throughout our history was reconciling the virtually untrammeled rights and freedom of the individual with the rigid demands and needs of the community. The myth, as we shall see, effects its reconciliation by showing the individual tacitly empowered (and therefore achieving some measure of self-actualization) through communal ideals (i.e., the individual is not free if all are not free).

Myth's other megafunction is that it fills one with a sense of transcendence. This is the traditional religious function of myth in most cultures. It is an absolutely crucial one in popular culture. Clifford Geertz (1973), in speaking of religion as a cultural system, notes that religion supports certain social values by employing symbols to formulate a world where those values are fundamental. Consequently, events don't just happen but have a meaning. Our popular myths, popular heroes, and icons all speak to our sense of the promise of life and the realization of human potential. they speak to our quest for the ideal, they lift us out of the everyday and transform our imaginings into realities.

Some would say that myth does nothing but feed fantasies and distort reality, but the crucial point about myth is that it provides a greater reality. Greil Marcus has written, "History without myth is surely a wasteland; but myths are compelling only when they are at odds with history" (1982, 140). The compelling nature of myth is that it transcends the everyday, and consequently, it transcends history, and offers one a richer view of life. The transcendent function of myth is crucial to the study of popular culture, because it shows us attempting to connect our earthbound philosophies, beliefs, attitudes, and actions with some higher purpose or meaning. Mircea Eliade addresses this function very well when he states:

> [Myth's] function is to reveal models and, in so doing, to give meaning to the World and to human life. This is why its role in the constitution of man is immense. It is through myth ... that the ideas of *reality, value, transcendence* slowly dawn. Through myth, the World can be apprehended as a perfectly articulated, intelligible, and significant Cosmos. (1963, 145)

It is through popular song—and the other popular arts as well—that our world (our country) is made articulate, intelligent, and significant. Its role is also tied to the concepts of religion discussed above. Since Harvey Cox wrote *The Secular City* back in the 1960s, there has been a growing awareness of the role of popular culture in filling the void left by the decline in organized religions. Similarly, popular culture—popular song in particular—feeds into the religious perspective, because it engages the listener on a level more compelling than a merely intellectual one. Clifford Geertz notes the distinction between the religious perspective and the scientific: "Rather than detachment, [religion's] watchword is commitment; rather than analysis, encounter" (1973, 112).

I believe the same could be applied to our popular culture. Pauline Kael noted a number of years ago that part of the popularity of films has to do with the fact that they offer an escape from the analytical responses demanded of us in our school culture. We can sit back and enjoy. This does not mean, however, that our response to films is not significant and meaningful; its significance just occurs in a different way, one closer to a religious experience. And so it is with popular culture. To quote Leszek Kolakowski (1972, 6), many of our popular myths offer a "meaning-generating faith," rather than an "explanatory science." I'm reminded of a John Ford anecdote, possibly apocryphal. When challenged by a reporter that the West really wasn't the way he showed it in his films, he replied, "Well, it should have been!" And so it is with most people's response to the myths of popular culture; they show individuals that there is a significance to events and experiences that transcends what mere reality can provide. Richard Slotkin has noted that myth transforms "secular history into a body of sacred and sanctifying legends" (1986, 19).

Popular song ties into these notions of the sacred by its use of symbol and, for that matter, other types of figurative language such as metaphor, metonymy, and synecdoche. Popular symbols—such as the flag, the bald eagle, Uncle Sam, the Capitol, the Statue of Liberty —are, I would argue, like sacred symbols, of which Clifford Geertz writes: "Their peculiar power comes from their presumed ability to identify fact with value at the most fundamental level" (127). Thus, sacred symbols and popular symbols function crucially in myth as ordering devices. The symbol becomes the site where individual and communal beliefs are made manifest and are revealed to be significant. Ernest Becker comments, Man's natural yearning or organismic activity, the pleasures of incorporation and expansion, can be fed limitlessly in the domain of symbols and so into immortality" (1973, 3).

This is similar to Gramsci's idea of an "organic ideology"—that is, a worldview which is comprehensive and enables individuals to reconcile their own quest for identity with the demands of the society at large. The symbols and images contained in our myths not only have personal significance but encourage "expansiveness," a need to look outside the self and find (or form) a community where we share beliefs with others. These myth-symbols, then, are a means whereby we articulate our desire to enjoy simultaneously personal and social integration.

Popular songs play a key role in establishing social consensus through the selection of patriotic symbols songwriters choose to employ. Popular songwriters, if they are going to achieve what impels them to undertake composition—that is, to make money or to seek fame—will choose topics, themes, and symbols which they believe will communicate readily and effectively to their audience. Thus, songwriters in the eras before rock knew instinctively what sort of reaction the image and symbol of mother or home would elicit from their audiences. If the song did not win the assumed reaction, they would reassess.

Successful songwriters know very well what will work. Consider Irving Berlin, the archetypal Tin Pan Alley songsmith. When asked to comment on the work habits of a fellow composer, who claimed that he wrote songs first to please himself and if the audience liked it, that was fine, Berlin responded: "All right, I'll tell you what I think about that. I write a song to please the public—and if the public doesn't like it in New Haven, I change it" (quoted in Wilk, 1973, 262–63).

In the last thirty years songwriters appear to have adopted an attitude we used to associate exclusively with elite artists—disregard, or even contempt, for the audience. Nonetheless, most elements in the production of popular music conspire against that attitude. The songwriter *must* consider the values of the audience as well as the other variables in the production of popular songs. Symbols, images, and themes that songwriters select—for whatever emotions they are trying to evoke—are important because they are a site where cultural consensus about values and attitudes is reaffirmed. They help define our notions of the ideal woman and the ideal man; they record and probably teach different generations of courting rituals. In antebellum America sentimental popular songs—particularly those of Stephen Foster such as "My Old Kentucky Home" and "Old Black Joe"—supported the complacent conviction of some Americans that the "darkies" didn't really want their freedom.

Popular songs are able to function so powerfully as myth-making agents because they are evocative forms, relying on fixed chord progressions, melodic patterns, lyric imagery, symbolism, and metonymy to ensure their efficacy and acceptance. Above all, song evokes memory and emotion. The lyrics of popular song are byproducts of the same literary culture that produced the great poets, utilizing the same figurative language and compressed mode of expression. At the same time, these poetic devices are adapted and/or wedded to elements derived from folk culture: simple narrative forms, plain language, universal sentiments that will assure a "clear" communication and mutual sharing of ideas between songwriter/singer and audience. The meaning of the lyrics is apprehended immediately, profoundly, and—it may be argued—almost unconsciously. Roland Barthes says, "Myth essentially aims at causing an immediate impression. . . . This means that the reading of a myth is exhausted at one stroke. . . . Time or knowledge will not make it better or worse" (1982, 117–18).

The myth of America in popular song is constructed out of seemingly discrete units employing powerful symbols. For the purposes of this study I have called these units "mythemes," a term borrowed from Claude Levi-Strauss. I chose "mytheme" because of what the term implies: The mythemes are in and of themselves myths; they have a story attached to them, and this includes an element of belief as well.* These mythemes are, moreover, the main ideas that shape and give structure to the narrative design of the myth. In the case of the myth of America in popular songs, these mythemes are presented largely through conventional images and symbols associated with America. Richard Slotkin states: "A mythic symbol such as a crucifix in a community of Christian believers, or a shot-torn American flag displayed at a patriotic gathering, has meaning and power because it refers to a history, a complete series of events, whose narrative structure is well-known to that audience, and accepted by them as representing something both true and full of meaning" (1986, 82–83).

The mytheme functions in much the same fashion. For instance,

---

*Thus, the mytheme of the sacrifice of the pilgrims and patriots suggests the stories of the landing on Plymouth Rock, of Washington crossing the Delaware, of Lincoln freeing the slaves, and so forth throughout our history. In each case, morever, some fundamental belief associated with the settling of the Republic is implied.

when a songwriter alludes to the mytheme of the land, as in "golden valley" or "rocks and rills," that image might signify not only the topological features but also the bounty of the land (and by extension the opportunity afforded us by the land). It might epitomize the journey of Americans to settle the west or, on a more personal level, private property. Consequently, when Irving Berlin says "from the mountains" in his "God Bless America," the allusion could suggest vastness, beauty, power, many interpretations. Some listeners might recall Katherine Lee Bates's "America the Beautiful" with its purple mountain majesties or the fiction of Zane Grey and Louis L'Amour; some might recall the paintings of Remington, Russell, or Bierstadt, and it might remind others of a personal journey. Whatever the association, the simple evocation of the image will recall some aspect of the physical landscape of this particular continent—from the parcels of land Crevecoeur extolled in the colonial period to the "Crabgrass frontier" of twentieth century suburbia.

I also selected the term because, like Levi-Strauss, I am examining the myth of America on two axes: One lies lengthwise of time, wherein we observe how the myth (and attendant mythemes) evolves over the decades; the other lies crosswise, allowing us to observe different perspectives on a mytheme within a given era. For instance —using the mytheme of the patriot's sacrifice once more—we see that through successive decades new heroes will be added (for different ideological reasons as well), and in some cases old ones will be dropped—Custer is a recent example of hero who has slipped in the ratings. One recent song, in fact, characterizes our heroic forbearers as a bunch of "rednecks" It is not likely that this attitude will prevail widely, but a few decades ago, the idea would have been entirely unthinkable. The mytheme is important to myth's ability to establish that social consensus.

The myth of America quite naturally contains much history. Its genesis, in fact, is tied closely to crises in the American past. For that reason the myth needs to explain the significance of disparate events within the larger scheme of history. In order to, as it were, collapse history into the mythic moment, songwriters portrayed events as being part of a larger, divine plan. Therefore, God plays a major role in the myth of the country. The songs show God's guiding hand as a force in our history and as a reason for our success in both war and peace. In early days songwriters wed an Augustinian notion that history has a direction willed by God to a Biblical one about God's chosen people and that we have been set apart to assume a special place in the world—the "last best hope" for a reconciliation between the City of God and the City of Man. Within the last thirty years this mytheme, as we shall see, has perhaps changed the most dramatically, and that change has had a profound impact on the myth of America in our own times.

Closely linked to God's providential role in our country's affairs is the notion of manifest destiny. This is the teleological dimension of the myth. The myth of America is able to explain "aberrations" in cultural behavior (war, slavery, rebellion, etc.) by showing how they are part of a large plan. This plan, moreover, helps individuals understand and have faith that the country is on the right course at that precise moment in time and is also guaranteed success in the future. Myth deals with the here and now, but in order for the here and now to have significance, it must collapse history—past, present, future—into that moment; it therefore validates the national telos by reaffirming tradition and heritage. Sacvan Bercovitch notes of Mather's myth that it is "essentially projective and elite," and it seeks to impose "prophecy upon experience" (1975, 133). The myth of America in popular song is similarly prophetic in reinforcing our belief in our manifest destiny.

The past is integrated into the myth of America when the songwriter evokes the symbol/image of the pilgrims and patriots. Particular emphasis is placed on the sacrifice that these individuals endured to secure America's special place in the world, and these achievements validate our prophetic mission and the causes for which our forefathers fought (i.e., the mythemes of freedom, opportunity, and equality). Vicki Eaklor says of the treatment of the American history in antiabolition songs: "Here one sees that preoccupation with the revolutionary past and its heroes that became central to the American self-image by 1960. Here too is the merging of Pilgrims, Puritans and rebels into one vague group—'Founders'—which telescopes all colonial history into a single experience" (1988, xxxiv).

We shall see that the presence of the "founders" is central to the myth from the Revolutionary War years up to the present. God would not have set us apart as chosen people, the myth goes, or asked the great heroes of the past to sacrifice themselves if the ideological roots for the establishment of the nation were not sound. Consequently, the myth shows us to be the bearers of particular ideals. The ideals, although sanctioned by God, are rooted in the secular ideals of the "founders." We see the songs constantly referring to liberty and freedom and—secondarily, usually by association—to opportunity and equality. They are, in short, those same ideals that we find in the Declaration of Independence and the Constitution. In time these ideals will be represented by symbols such as Old Glory, the Statue of Liberty, and work. These ideals, moreover, although interpreted differently at different times, remain constants throughout the years; terms by which we not only define who we are but how good we are. Since the myth, is concerned with validating our role in the world, what we have to offer the world must be good and must be perceived to be an ideal desired by everyone everywhere.

Finally, we have the mytheme of the land. The land has two dimensions in the myth of America. One, as we have seen, asserts the bounty, goodness, and beauty of the American landscape. The other dimension takes the land as a symbol for individual achievement. In his 1800 biography of George Washington, Parson Weems invoked "this vast continent," and God's "cloud-capt mountains . . . sea-like lakes . . . mighty rivers . . . "thundering cataracts" as proof that "great men and great deeds are designed for America" (quoted in Boorstin, 1965, 343–44). Over one hundred years later, Woody Guthrie would also make claims for the importance of the land, but with subtle differences: now the land is not for "great men," but for "you and me."

Actually, the land is the least constant mytheme in the songs. It seems to fade in and out of the songwriters' consciousness, often playing a more important role in peacetime than in war. Nonetheless, some of the most popular and enduring songs are those that implement the mytheme of the land.

Popular song—as the expression of our most deeply held beliefs and myths—orders and in some cases creates reality. The songs we will be looking at are important parts of our daily lives. Readers will immediately recognize many of them. They probably had to sing them in grade school, they most assuredly sing one when they go to a sporting event, and they probably encounter a number of them at Christian church services. And thus have such songs functioned throughout our history.

Colonel T.W. Higginson (1962, 60) recounts an episode that took place at a celebration of the just-issued Emancipation Proclamation, January 1, 1863, during which an elderly ex-slave suddenly rose and began to sing "My Country, 'Tis of thee,/ Sweet land of liberty." He was instantly joined by other freedmen and women, and when the white congregation was about to join in, Higginson halted them so the blacks could continue alone through all the verses. "I never saw anything so electric. . . ." Higginson wrote. "It seemed the choked voice of a race unloosed."

This episode demonstrates how important these songs are in defining what we believe America is. They are, to be sure, the hymns of the dominant culture, but to know them and to be able to sing them is part of being an American. We define our national character in our choice of songs about ourselves. When those African-Americans, only hours into their new freedom, sang "Sweet land of liberty," they declared their faith in the ideals of the country and their hope that they would be able to share in its promise.

And so it is for each and every one of us when we sing one of these songs or nod our head in assent to its sentiments. The song may be a vituperative screed declaring that the nation is—to paraphrase the sixties rock group Steppenwolf—a "monster," or it may be a recycling of Irving Berlin's sentiments as we ask God to "bless America." In either case the song expresses a vision of the country that we need to believe in and share with fellow Americans.

There is a good deal of debate on how effective songs actually are in shaping popular beliefs—and by extension, how effective they are in shaping changes in the culture. But the songwriter is a member of a particular community at a given time in American history, and his/her efforts are directed at providing a product that will be consumed by that community. One of the reasons the community buys that product is because it finds in that song, lyrics or air, something that answers a need or states a feeling. Myth, as I have tried to make clear, fulfills a number of functions in our lives. As a result, so do our songs.

So we begin our journey through American popular song. We are in quest of the new world and an encounter with the reality, value, and transcendence promised us in the myth. When we are finished, we will have a better sense of how Americans have tried to see their world, how they have tried to forge an articulated, intelligible, and significant vision of what it is to be an American.

CHAPTER I **"To Thee Sing Psalm Wil I"**
The Roots of the Myth in Puritan Music

On December 28, 1705, Deacon Samuel Sewall (1652–1730) recorded in his diary that he "intended to set Windsor and fell into High-Dutch, and then essaying to set another Tune, went into a key too high." There is in the passage some interesting information about the role of music in the early days of the Puritan colonies. Chiefly, the early colonist was more concerned with setting (giving the pitch) and singing music already established than in freely inventing something more congenial with their new environment and way of life. For those who survived those devastating winters in Plymouth Plantation and those who sought to carve out a "citie on the hill" in the Massachusetts Bay Colony, a series of perfectly serviceable songs were already available, taken from the one authoritative source of all art and knowledge, the Bible. These were, of course, the psalms. They also had a rich storehouse of music in Protestant anthems and hymns and in the Psalters compiled by Ainsworth and Playford. For them, that was music enough, for they were not in New England to create a new world but to re-create the old.

The early colonists of Plymouth Plantation and the Massachusetts Bay Colony were seeking to establish a New Eden, a New Jerusalem. That alone tells us much about their mythic imagination. They looked backward almost exclusively for inspiration and models. The land had not as yet inspired them to make new myths, but instead to reflect on the old ones. They saw not waving fields of grain and purple mountains majesty but, instead, to quote William Bradford, "a hideous and desolate wilderness, full of wild beasts and wild men —and what multitudes there might be of them they knew not." (In fairness to these grim early settlers, appreciation of scenery did not become fashionable until the nineteenth century.) To meet the challenges and terrors of this land the colonists cast their gaze backward to the security of the world they had just left. Bernard Bailyn notes that the colonists were, in fact, quite content with maintaining the ideals of the Elizabethan world and felt comfortable in using that model to organize their society (1977, 98–100). Additionally, they faced the great challenge of making manifest and reconciling the ideals of the Old and New Testaments with that world. Bailyn writes:

> They know themselves to be provincials in the sense that their culture was not self-contained; its sources and superior expressions were to be found elsewhere than in their own land. They must seek it from afar; it must be acquired, and once acquired, be maintained according to standards externally imposed, in the creation of which they had not shared. (153–154)

They saw no need to surpass other civilizations—except, perhaps, decadent ones. They were not driven to break with the old world, but merely to improve on it—the improvement made possible by their reliance on the word of God. One of the important legacies of the early colonists, to be expressed later in popular song, was the element of submission to the will of God, like Christ in Gethsemane: not my will, Lord, but yours. This notion that individual identity is achieved through involvement in the divine plan would become one of the most pervasive expressions of the myth in popular song.

The task of the early colonist, then, was to reconcile the worlds of the past—the Bible and the Old World—with the individual and communal exigencies of New World. They could look forward to doing this with some confidence. William Bradford wrote eloquently of the Pilgrim's terrible passage and anxious first view of the New World:

> What could now sustain them but the Spirit of God and His grace? May not and ought not the children of these fathers rightly say: "Our fathers were Englishmen which came over this great ocean, and were ready to perish in this wilderness; but they cried unto the Lord, and he heard their voice and looked on their adversity."

Indeed, if they had confidence in creating the new world, it was as the children of God, who had His Word to guide them. Daniel Boorstin notes that the early colonists had no need for Utopian visions because "In their Bible they had a blueprint for the Good Society"; the novelty and insecurity of life in the wilderness, moreover, made the people cling tenaciously to familiar institutions and led them to discover a new coincidence between the laws of God and the laws of England (1958, 29). And they took to heart that Biblical admonishment from the Psalms: "If I forget thee, O Jerusalem, let my right hand forget her cunning. If I do not remember thee, let my tongue cleave to the roof of my mouth; if I prefer not Jerusalem above my chief joy."

Thus it would seem that the early colonists exerted little influence on the creation of the myth of America, but, of course, this is not true. The stamp of the "puritan imagination" is found everywhere in the work of successive generations of artists, popular and serious alike.

The musical expression of the myth, pious and practical, sought to glorify God and show people the proper path to Him. Consequently, the obvious choice for singing among the settlers at Plymouth and in the Massachusetts Bay Colony was the Psalms, specifically that volume called the *Bay Psalm Book*, which was published in 1640. Next to the Bible, the *Bay Psalm Book* was the best selling book of the colonial era. In this sense it was part of the popular culture of the New England colonies. Its presence was ubiquitous and its influence pervasive.

Many of these psalms were set to popular tunes of the day. Waldo Selden Pratt, writing of the period when America was first being settled, says:

> One of the prime factors in the momentous shift that was taking place in all artistic music was the spontaneous vitality that was being discovered in the popular songs of several countries. It was from this general treasury of popular songs that the new Protestant movement adopted or adapted its tunes for religious use (1921, 20).

Great pains were taken not to alter the meaning of the text. To sing or re-create the Psalms would be to glorify the City of God; to look elsewhere would be to glorify the City of Man and thus, to expose the worshipper to the corruptions of the world. Nevertheless, even in these earliest times the colonists would be drawing on popular culture to create their myths and worldview.

There is some difficulty in attempting to trace the influence of *The Bay Psalm Book* on later versions of the myth. New Englanders did not seem to pick hymns and anthems selectively to express a particular feeling or celebrate a given event. There is little solid evidence that, as they encountered the wilderness, they automatically turned, for instance, to Psalm 50 which begins: "For each beast of the wood to Me perteyns/The beasts that on a thousand mountains bee." William Arms Fisher has written that "The half-dozen tunes used up to 1700 and later were repeated sometimes twice on a Sabbath, and in pious families two were sung every day in the week at family worship. In church the psalms were sung in regular rotation without regard to the preacher's text or sermon" (1930, iv). Unlike the literature—let us say, specifically of William Bradford—where one observes the mythopoeic imagination at work, in the songs much is left to speculation. None of the famous Puritan writers, like Bradford, Winthrop, Sewall, or Mather, tell us how the psalms functioned as part of daily life. They simply state, "They sang psalms," or they discuss the problems of lining out a hymn. Nonetheless, the words of the psalms resonate.

The psalms as music and literature are a vital part of the mythic vision and theocratic ideals of the early colonists. Therefore, as we examine the music and text of the *Bay Psalm Book*, we find roots of the myth of America ever so tentatively manifesting themselves, especially, the mytheme of the providential role of God.

The psalms quite naturally paint a portrait of a God who is above the material world, but whose presence is felt everywhere and who is intimately involved with the fate of "His people." Psalm 46, verses 6–7, provides a good illustration of this:

> The nations did make a noyse,
>   The kingdoms moved were;
> Give forth did He His thondring voice,
>   The earth did melt with fear.
> The God of armies is with us,
>   The everbeing Jah;
> The God of Jakob is for us!
>   A refuge hye. Selah!

The passage makes clear that this God, who has the power to "melt" the earth, is also a refuge for His people. Those who seek that refuge, moreover, find themselves on the side of the God of armies; he will be their great defense. Thus, if he wills for his people to subdue the earth and to persevere, they will. And, in fact, that is the theme that Psalm 112, verses 1–3, deals with:

O blessed man that dooth Jehovah fear,
    That greatly dooth in His commands delight.
His seed in earth shal mighty persevere;
    Blessed shal be the race of the upright.
In his house riches are and wealthy store;
His justice standeth eke for evermore.

In this passage one finds the seeds of the mytheme of manifest destiny, and, to a certain extent, the myth of success. If one obeys God's will, one will persevere and be blessed with riches and wealth. The early colonists would see this hymn as the perfect articulation of what they had achieved through their struggles and triumphs. They had indeed delighted in God's commands, and as a result they had persevered, and, better, they were storing riches and wealth as the years progressed. It did appear that God's justice would be with them evermore and that He seemed to have a place for the Americans in his eternal plan.

Another mytheme suggested in the psalms is that of the land. Sacvan Bercovitch has written:

The interpretation of the actual-yet-spiritual wilderness leads out to what might be called the genre of American natural theology—the concern with the New World landscape as a source of higher laws, a key to the golden future, and a proof-by-association of the interpreter's spiritual regeneration. (1974, 13)

The land, then, becomes the perfect complement for the mythic destiny of God's chosen people: Like the people of Moses they will wander and struggle with its forces, but ultimately it will yield riches and in enough abundance to sustain a people of destiny.

The psalms present images of the "wilderness" that reaffirm the duality of God's providential role in history. The wilderness is subject to God's power, and clearly functions as but a manifestation of that awesome power. Psalm 50, verses 9–12, states:

For each beast of the wood to Me perteyns
　　The beasts that on a thousand mountayns bee.
I know al flying fowls of the mountayns,
　　And store of wild beasts of the field with Mee.
　　　If I were hungry, thee I could not tell it,
　　　For myne the world and plenty that dooth fill it.

Note as well the theme of bounty, which closes the last line; this will be an important image in future evocations of the land and is central to the ideology of the land mytheme.

The wilderness is also a refuge. A psalm which must have provided an early New England colonist with comfort was Psalm 55, verses 4–7:

Mine hart is payned in the mids of me;
Terrours of death eke falln upon me be.
　　Fear is into me come and trembling dread,
　　And quaking horrour hath me covered.
So that I say, Who wil give me a wing
As dove, that I might flye and find dwelling?
　　Lo, wandring flight I would make farr away;
　　Lodge would I in the wilderness. Selah!

The psalm expresses the belief that these early settlers *had* to settle in America. Although the later notion of regeneration through contact with the wilderness, does not figure in this nascent version of the myth, the psalms do suggest the theme of deliverance. They were seeking refuge from oppression and found that refuge in the wilderness. Singing this psalm at a service would be yet another reminder of how their lives were being lived out according to Scripture, and how intimately their destiny was connected to that of the Israelites.

If we search for other evidence of the mythemes in the psalms —those of liberty, for example—the task becomes even more speculative. In Psalm verses 3, 5–6, for instance, one encounters:

I lay'd me down and slept;
I waking rose
For Me Jehovah Firmly up did bear
For thousands ten of folk will I not fear
Which me be setting round about enclose.

The theme of freedom from oppression is suggested here, and in fact one will observe echoes of those last two lines in the songs written during wartime. Songs of war iterate the notion that we will persevere in the fight and will not be dominated by our enemies because God is on our side. Hence, the early colonist would have seen the idea of liberty—or as he would have said, "liberties"—inextricably linked with God's plan for his people: to keep them free from their enemies. Enlightenment notions of liberty and equality do not apply here. "Liberty" was used more as synonymous with "permission" than with "political freedom". The focus is closer to the narrow sentiments of Nathaniel Ward, who wrote in 1647, "I dare . . . to proclaime to the world, in the name of our Colony, that all Familists, Antinomians, Anabaptists, and other Enthusiasts, shall have free Liberty to keep away from us, and such as will come to be gone as fast as they can, the sooner, the better" (quoted in Boorstin, 1958, 7). The Puritan wished to be "free" of those who would turn him from God's path.

Finally, there is the issue as to just how much influence the psalms exerted. One bit of evidence is provided, by the many printings and editions of the *Bay Psalm Book* (nine editions in the seventeenth century alone—that among a sparse, poor and scattered population). In the future, moreover, the texts of psalms will be used as a springboard to sound contemporary ideas and issues. Note this from the Revolutionary War period, a setting of the 137th Psalm, verses 5–6, by William Billings entitled "Lamentation over Boston" (1778); first, the original:

> Jerusalem, if I doo thee
>   Forget, forget let my right hand,
> Cleav let my tongue to my palat,
>   If I doo not in mind thee bear,
> If I Jerusalem doo not
>   Above my chiefest joy prefer.

Here is Billing's version, verses 1 plus 5–6:

> By the Rivers of Watertown we sat down and wept we wept,
>   we wept, we wept,
> When we remembered thee O Boston! . . .
> If I forget thee, yea, if I do not remember thee,
> Then let my tongue forget to move,
> And ever be confined

Let horrid jargon split the air,
And rive my nerves asunder.

As we examine the songs of the Revolutionary War period—like the one of Billings just cited—and of succeeding generations, we will hear echoes of the psalms, testimony to the power and efficacy of the mytheme. As we look to the songs of the Revolutionary War era we will indeed see just how compelling the mythic vision of America was.

CHAPTER II   "We Led Fair FREEDOM
Hither"
The Revolutionary War
Era

Love your neighbor
as yourself, and your
country more than
yourself.
—Thomas Jefferson

Had the colonies remained just that—
colonies (with the emphasis on the
plural), where each region and its people felt that they were totally free to
work out their own private destinies,
there might not have been any need to
create a monomyth for the total national experience. But that, of
course, was not to be the case. Those principles which guided the
founding of Plymouth Plantation and Massachusetts Bay and which
promised God's protection, opportunity, and property needed to be
recast in a new light for the citizens of eighteenth-century America.
Theirs was a changing world. In America as in Great Britain, it was
an Age of Reason, an age of "enlightened" thought, driven more
—at least on the surface—by the theories of Newton and Locke than
those of the Bible. The songs of the Revolutionary War era find songwriters attempting to reconcile the ideals of the Puritan theocratic
heritage with those of the emergent enlightenment. Accordingly, it
is during this era that we encounter the first and most complete
expression of the myth of America in our popular music.

The need to articulate a myth of America was born partially out
of cultural trauma. For many, England was the "Old" World, and
what we were about here was making a "New" England. It also was
the motherland, and the formation of the colonies and their govern-

24

ments owed much to English models. It was when Americans perceived that Great Britain was engaged in conspiracy to deny Americans the rights of Englishmen that the tide turned and the "idea" of America began to take root and be talked and sung about.

Historians, and average Americans today, naturally look to the Declaration of Independence as the galvanic document that sums up the discontent and the aspirations of eighteenth-century Americans. The Declaration rightly or wrongly—as historians Garry Wills (1978, xiii–xxvi) and James Oliver Robertson (1980, 65–69) have noted—stands as the symbol and embodiment of the idea of America, as proof that the nation (more exactly, the idea of the nation) was indeed invented. The Declaration, however, is only part of a larger artistic and intellectual attempt to create a myth of the New World. Music played a major role in the formation of that myth. It is in the broadsides composed from the 1760s through the 1780s that we find the fullest expression of the myth. It is these songs, moreover, which form the core of this chapter and which stand as evidence of the efficacy of the popular song to reconcile opposing ideologies, animate visions, and forge history itself.

The Puritan religious experience and vision, although outdated, was not forgotten in America. The memory of the Great Awakening led by George Whitfield in the 1740s—and made an indelible part of the American literary scene by Jonathan Edwards in the 1750s—was fresh enough to remind the eighteenth-century citizens of how close they were to their spiritual forebears of Plymouth Plantation and the Massachusetts Bay Colony. Consequently, it was no quantum leap from the attempt by the Reverend Samuel Sewall to line out a psalm properly to the efforts of the broadside balladeer to tell a new story about the country in song. The Revolutionary War era songwriter had to establish a new model for human activity, one that would incorporate religiosity with enlightenment. These songs are not mere evocations of Old World ideals. On the contrary, they celebrate the idea of the New World—with emphasis on new. The story they tell is nothing less than the saga of how and why we journeyed to this continent, and how it came to have a special place in the world.

Americans no longer see themselves reliving the story of Moses seeking the Promised Land, but instead as reconciling the troubling issues of their times and seeking an ideal that will enable them to transcend those trials and ultimately regenerate them.

The task facing the songwriter and balladeer of the Revolutionary War era was formidable. The country was hardly a unified whole, working harmoniously to achieve some utopian vision. Like their Puritan forebears, eighteenth-century citizens were practical people with a wide range of value systems, and they acted out of self-interest.

The songwriter, then, had to engage individuals with beliefs, symbols, and ideas that met their personal needs while at the same time carving out a vision of a community that would meet the needs of everyone. This meant bridging and uniting a number of worldviews, including, as Bernard Bailyn notes, rationalism, a reliance on classical learning and history, Puritanism, opposition theories, and English common law (1967, 34), all of which would be drawn upon to define America's special place in the world.

This was rather a large order. Most balladeers—although a few were well educated for their day—were little more than average citizens. Nevertheless, many managed to draw together these disparate strands in the verses of a broadside, bringing together the mythemes of God's role in the country's destiny, the sacrifice of the forefathers, the land, and the principles upon which all were based: liberty, opportunity, and equality. In doing so, they helped people deal with the frightening idea that they were engaged in changing their world.

The broadside ballad forms an important component of the artistic response to the Revolution in the eighteenth century. "Broadside balladry," as I use it here, is the practice of taking an existing melody —song, hymn, anthem, or traditional folk tune—and setting new words to it. The practice of writing broadsides is quite old. In England, broadside balladry had proved itself in the preceding two centuries to be an excellent vehicle for tapping into—and assessing—public opinion about everything from criminals to taxes to Papists. Moreover, the success of John Gay's *The Beggar's Opera* (1728) did much to advance the viability of the form as a weapon for satire and protest in both England and America.

Traditionally, the broadside—sometimes called the black letter ballad—had a relatively short life span. It was written, printed (usually in very crude fashion) on a single sheet, distributed, sung, and then, in all likelihood, tossed.

In America, it dominated the musical scene during the Revolutionary War years. Songs were conceived, typeset, and distributed quickly to take advantage of the moment, then discarded. We are fortunate that so many managed to survive. The broadside ballad, along with the speeches of Patrick Henry and the writings of Thomas Paine and Jefferson among others, was instrumental in carving out a mythic vision that could at once assimilate and obviate the many differences that existed among the colonists. And the writers of the songs were clearly aware of the efficacy of the form. Joel Barlow, who bacame a chaplain in the Revolutionary army, wrote in 1775:

> I do not know whether I shall do more for the cause in the capacity of Chaplain than I would in that of a poet; I have great faith in the influence of songs; and I shall continue, while fulfilling the duties of my appointment, to write one now and then, and to encourage the taste for them which I find in the camp. One good song is worth a dozen addresses or proclamations. (Quoted in Ewen 1977, 13)

This sentiment must have been shared by many because the ranks of those who supplied lyrics for broadsides includes some quite respectable names, Dr. Joseph Warren, Thomas Paine, Peter St. John (a schoolteacher) among them.

What makes the broadsides of the Revolutionary War period so successful is the delightful combination of the new vigorous "American" sentiments and patriotism of the lyrics wedded to, for the most part, traditional English ballad tunes. Consequently, the audience always had in the melody some familiar element to aid in performance and memory. The new ideas presented in the lyrics—and in some cases not so easily digested—had a better chance of reaching the audience because they were couched in a singable, rollicking, or inspiring tune.

But there was an extra delight. By using some traditional tune —often of a British patriotic nature—the writers could enjoy the ironic pleasure of standing the sentiment of the song on its head. As the singer and audience sang the new song, the old lyrics would resonate in the back of their minds. What a treat to take a tune extolling, say, the exploits of brave British soldiers and turn it into an anthem extolling the American minutemen; it was the musical equivalent of turning the enemy's weapons against themselves.

The practice is still going on. As recently as the 1988 elections, Democrats turned a sentimental Indiana song into a joke at Indianan

Dan Quayle's expense: "I Spent the War in Indiana." On a grimmer note, in the 1960s, antiwar protestors achieved a similar end by wearing army shirts and jackets with the peace sign emblazoned on them. The song then becomes even more memorable because of the ironic and satiric twists that resulted by judging the import of the new lyric against the sentiments of the old one.*

The role the broadside ballad would play in the Revolution was portended earlier in the century with the publication of "A Song Made upon the Foregoing Occasion" (1734) and sung to the tune of "Now, Now You Tories All Shall Stoop." The foregoing occasion referred to here was a local election in New York where the Popular Party, consisting of local artisans and merchants, defeated a well-entrenched candidate. This particular song is interesting because it is one of the first broadsides to enunciate a crucial mytheme: that of liberty. In one stanza the authors write:

> Come on brave boys, let us be brave,
>   For Liberty and law,
> Boldly despite the haughty knave
>   The would keep us in awe. (Quoted in Silber, 1973, 26–29)

Note that liberty and law are yoked in the cause here. Thus, the idea of civil law, as well as the idea of natural law, was important in shaping the myth.

Liberty (or freedom) is the mytheme that predominates—along with the mytheme of God's providential role—in the music of the Revolution. The mytheme of liberty did not play a major role in the music of the Puritans, but it was a recurring motif in their other writings, according to Daniel Boorstin (1958, 30). As a result, it speaks to tradition and reaffirms an important ideological premise for the revolutionary generation. Freedom is, in fact, *the* issue that crystallizes and synthesizes the belief, values, and aspirations of the American people. Patrick Henry, the orator par excellence of the Revolution, knew well what he was doing when he said, "Give me Liberty, or Give me Death." This focused the conflict clearly, made it an either/or proposition, and gave it cosmic proportions. James

---

Mad Magazine often publishes lampoon lyrics to established tunes. Irving Berlin once sued the magazine for satirizing "Easter Parade," and *Mad* won.

Oliver Robertson writes:

> And not until the Revolution was the idea of independence for the individuals in a society made the goal of a whole nation. While freedom, or as they would have said, "liberty," may well have been already part of the lives of most eighteenth-century colonists, independence, equality, and a political life based upon the sovereignty of the people were not. (1980, 71)

Liberty is a highly symbolic word. It has as many different meanings as there are people who use it. But for our purposes, it speaks both to the need to preserve the efficacy of individualism and to the need to preserve that individualism through some form of government. It was by no means a Hobbesian vision; it was instead animated as much by Old Testament myths as by contemporary philosophy.

Liberty's place in the myth of America became manifest early in the growing Revolutionary struggle. And also early on it was linked with the other mythemes that constitute our American myth. A song written in 1765 by Peter St. John produced, according to Irwin Silber, "what may well be considered the opening anthem of the revolution. . . ." (1973, 36). The song, to the tune of the "British Grenadiers," was written as a response to taxation, and it makes the point early on that the British have seemingly enlisted the aid of Satan in their plot to subdue North America; this sentiment not only captures the fear felt by many of a full-fledged conspiracy against the colonies but also prepares the listener for the cosmic and "divine" implications of their struggle for liberty. First, there is mention of "Britain's fading glory."

For now, however, we must look at the final stanzas where the songwriter draws together most of the dominant mythemes and, with great effectiveness, reconciles the colonists' secular faith in liberty with their religious faith in God's providential role.

> Our fathers were distressed, while in their native land,
> By tyrants were oppressed, as we do understand;
> For freedom and religion, they were resolved to stray,
> And trace the desert regions of North America.
>
> We are their bold descendants, for liberty we'll fight,
> The claim to independence we challenge as our right;
> 'Tis what kind heaven gave us, who can take it away—
> O, Heaven sure will save us in North America.

The mytheme of the pilgrim's sacrifice sets up beautifully the historical/Biblical imperative for the establishment of liberty in the New World. The "desert" theme is already important in these songs as an allusion to Moses' wanderings and Christ's temptations; in both cases there was a regeneration (communally and individually), and this song implies that Americans will similarly be regenerated as "Heaven will save us in North America." And if there is any doubt that this is the promised land, that is dispelled in an earlier verse where the songwriter points out that a "wealthy people" sojourn in the land; he then reinforces the mytheme by alluding to the Biblical concept of the promised land:

Their land with milk and honey continually doth flow,
The want of food or money they seldom ever know:
They heap up golden treasure, they have no debts to pay,
They spend their time in pleasure in North America.

The wandering in the "desert" of America by our forebears then was but a prelude to the "claim to independence," a claim which cannot be denied because it is bestowed by heaven itself. Hence, the songwriters have been able to transform a largely secular idea —liberty—into a religious imperative, transcendentally linked with our mission in the world.

In a mere three years the Revolutionary fervor would intensify. One particularly effective ballad was "Liberty Song" (1768) sung to the same tune as the later "Heart of Oak" and with words by John Dickinson, the author of *Letters from a Farmer in Pennsylvania to the Inhabitants of the British Colonies* (1767–68). The song shows a growing awareness of the power and influence of the mythemes as he utilizes them in much the same way as did Peter St. John. Three of the mythemes predominate: the Pilgrim's sacrifice, the theme of liberty, and God's role. The song in fact begins with this rousing invitation:

Come join hand in hand brave Americans all,
And rouse your bold hearts at fair Liberty's call;
No tyrannous acts shall suppress your just claim,
Or stain with dishonor America's name.
  In freedom we're born, and in freedom we'll live,
  Our purses are ready, steady friends, steady,
  Not as slaves, but as freemen, our money we'll give.

Notice that the call to arms is at "fair Liberty's" behest. The personification of liberty—so in keeping with classical tradition—personalizes the concept, and the use of the adjective "fair" suggests that it is a precious virtue that must be preserved. The preservation of that virtue is, as the later verses make clear, a historical necessity because it means validating the past, enlivening the present, and securing the future. The song fulfills the function of myth by collapsing time and making it subject to belief and something greater than mere earthly need.

"Liberty Song" (Sometimes printed under the name "Free America") also continues the tradition of yoking the secular call for liberty with the theme of manifest destiny and the role of God and Providence in guiding the destiny of the nation. This Augustinian notion that history's direction is willed by God was a legacy of our Puritans forebears. It allowed the songwriter, moreover, to place America's role in the world within a larger historico-cosmic framework or paradigm. It remained only for the songwriter to find the appropriate symbols that would enable him to reconcile the rights of the individual and the principles of natural law—which were crucial in the establishment of the Republic—with the principle of the divine scheme of things.

Dickinson's "Liberty Song" achieves this end in what would become a fairly conventional way. Early in the song he alludes to the sacrifice of the Pilgrims:

> Our worthy forefathers—let's give them a cheer—
> To climates unknown did courageously steer;
> Through oceans to deserts, for freedom they came,
> And dying, bequeathed us their freedom and fame.

Then in the next stanza we find the following:

> The Tree their own hands had to Liberty reared,
> They lived to behold growing strong and revered;
> With transport they cried—"Now our wishes we gain,
> For our children shall gather the fruits of our pain."

Dickinson and his audience would, quite naturally, see themselves as those selfsame children. They are the ones who were foretold in that transcendental vision that sustained and "transported" the Pilgrims. Of particular interest here is the symbol of "the Tree." Kent Bowman writes of the symbolism of the tree in the eighteenth century: "A tree is sacred because its growth is symbolic of all life and because it grows according to nature's laws. The tree does not harbor a seditious mob but a group of free men who must assert their natural rights as the tree provides protection from the oppressive midday heat of tyranny" (1989, 4). The tree, as Bowman suggests, would also symbolize natural law; it becomes the physical embodiment, à la Plato, of the ideal form and of the nurturing landscape of the New World. The seeds of liberty were planted by the Pilgrims and now will bear full fruit in independence. The tree would also, to another faction of the audience, suggest the tree in the Garden of Eden, which in turn symbolizes not just the Fall but also the salvific vision in the Cross. These ideas are brought together in codalike fashion in the last two stanzas where Dickinson writes:

> Then join hand in hand brave Americans all,
> By uniting we stand, by dividing we fall;
> In so righteous a cause let us hope to succeed,
> For heaven approves of each generous deed.
> All ages shall speak with amaze and applause,
> Of the courage we'll show in support of our laws.

History then will be the judge, and judge approvingly it will, because of the righteous of the cause. The Will of God will not be denied.

In yet another song from 1768, "Sons of Liberty" (to the tune of "Come, Jolly Bacchus") the same themes emerge. Individual rights are quickly brought to the forefront in the first stanza where the writers note that our motto is "We Dare be Free," and that it is the duty of "each man [to] prove this motto true/And slavery from him sever." It is, in the last two stanzas—as in Dickinson's song —where the themes converge in a transcendent moment.

> See Liberty high poiz'd in Air
> Her Free Born Sons commanding,
> "Come on, my Sons, without a fear,
> Your natural Rights demanding!
> Your Cause, the Gods proclaim is Just
> Can tamely, you, be fettere'd? . . .

> Obey, my brothers, Nature's call
> Your country too demands it!
> Let Liberty ne'er have a Fall!
> 'Tis Freedom that commands it.

The Ax now to the Root is laid.
Will you be Bond or Free?
No time to pause—then "Whose afraid?"
Live or die in Liberty!

Liberty is something of a lightning rod that draws the power of God and nature and brings them to earth. Liberty is the ultimate symbol for the direction God willed history should take and that nature dictates to her children. It speaks to the individual carving out his/her place in the city, territory, woods, and so forth, and to the ideological needs of the nation as a whole. To secure liberty for the whole is to secure it for the individual. The cause, indeed, is "just" and necessary.

The songs that best typify America's God-given role in the world, however, are William Billing's revolutionary war songs, "Chester" and "America." Irwin Silber has written that, "Chester" was virtually "the anthem of the colonial cause. . . . 'Chester' was extremely popular among rebel troops, especially those from New England, who are reported to have sung it constantly throughout the war" (1973, 83). The martial sounding "Chester" states, "We trust in God/New England's God for ever reigns." The assumption is that New England, with God on her side, reigns as well.

Billings also, in what some might describe as typical American fashion, harkens to another secondary mytheme in American culture, that of youth, when he states that "Their Vet'rans flee before our youth." D. H. Lawrence once noted that the myth of America centered largely around her constantly sloughing off the old skin and becoming young again. The notion of "our youth" will emerge in different songs throughout the decades and will in some cases be yoked to a corollary religious mytheme: regeneration.

Billings' "America" is one of the best songs to grapple with the contradictory impulses of the Pilgrim's theocratic ideals and the secular ideals of the founding fathers. The issue, of course, is how does one reconcile the ideals of natural law (equality, reason, a deistic worldview) with the ideals of theocracy (a necessary elitism in the "elect," faith in the higher power and not reason, a theistic worldview). This song, it should be noted here, is the type of inspirational anthem we will see flourish in the nineteenth century, and, with its almost total evocation of all the mythemes, it is one of the first, most complete statements of the myth of America in popular song.

The song is characterized by the vigor of its foursquare harmonies and its strong but slightly angular melody. Because Billings wrote both words and music for most of his songs he was able to achieve, as he does here, a sort of transcendental beauty in his wedding of music and imagery. It begins with a strikingly alliterative apostrophe, "To thee the tuneful anthem soars." The song then proceeds to carve out the dominant mythemes addressed above:

> To thee the tuneful anthem soars
>   to Thee, our Father's God and ours,
> This wilderness we chose our seat,
>   to rights secured by equal laws.
> From persecution's iron claws,
>   we here have sought our calm retreat.
> See how the flocks of Jesus rise,
>   see how the face of Paradise
> Blooms through the thickets of the wild.
> Here liberty erects a throne
> Here plenty puts her treasure down.
>   Peace smiles as heavn'ly cherubs mild.

The mytheme of the land immediately draws us in to the vision. There is a clear evocation of Bradford's and the Pilgrims' encounter with the "wilderness," now transformed by the Pilgrim's sacrifice in fleeing "persecution's iron claw" into a Paradise containing the throne of liberty and equality. The reconciliation of secular ideals with the religious ideal is achieved brilliantly in the image of the throne of liberty being erected in a "Paradise" blooming through the wilderness; it is clear that God's rule and liberty's are one and the same. It is as if to say that God led our steps through the wilderness and transformed it into a New Eden so we could create this more perfect republic. Central to the mytheme of the land, as suggested above, is that God has provided us with a rich bountiful land, a "New Land" and, as the allusion to Paradise suggests, a Promised Land peopled by Jesus' flock, a metonymy for the Good Shepherd and God's chosen race. In this Paradise, we should note as well, treasure (i.e., abundance and, perhaps to a lesser degree, opportunity) will also be found.

In the final verse Billings brings these themes together in a visionary coda where he speaks of liberty and "pure religion" spreading coterminously and wrapping the "globe around":

> Lord, guard Thy Favors; Lord extend
> Where farther Western suns descend;
> Nor Southern Seas the Blessings bound;
> Till Freedom lifts her cheerful Head,
> Till pure Religion onward spread,
> And beaming, wrap the Globe around.

A particularly notable feature of this stanza is Billings's emphasis upon the topological boundaries of the land. This is a mytheme that will be employed by many songwriters from the early nineteenth century up into the twentieth century with Irving Berlin's "God Bless America," Woody Guthrie's "This Land Is Your Land," and some country songs in the 1980s. Billings's song is one of the few from this period actually to glory in the mere topography of the land; he, like others, is using the land to show the bountiful gift God has willed us. The song clearly anticipates the great spread of manifest destiny in the nineteenth century, and it shows graphically the genesis of that mytheme.

Other songs of the revolution spoke of the myth of America. In keeping with their roots as broadsides, they have more of a secular ring reflective of the values of the Enlightenment. Nevertheless, they are of a piece with Billings's more transcendental vision, because they attempt to conflate ideas of God's vision and man's vision as embodied in natural law. Dr. Joseph Warren's "The New Massachusetts Liberty Song" (c. 1770 and set to the tune of the "British Grenadier"), for instance, alludes to Greece and Rome and sends a warning in the first stanza to beware of how those great powers fell:

> That Seat of Science Athens, and Earth's great Mistress Rome,
> Where now are all their Glories, we scarce can find their Tomb:
> Then guard your Rights, Americans! nor stoop to lawless Sway,
> Oppose, oppose, oppose, oppose,—my brave AMERICA.

This, of course, is part of the pattern in American literature and art of looking back at the Old World and setting America apart as the New World. The implication is that as great as those decadent empires were, they will be superseded by this New World. Bernard Bailyn notes, "By the early 70s a few colonists were even comparing the king with classic tyrants like Nero or the Stuarts and calling

the monarchy a curse visited upon the people because of their sins"
(1977, 266).

The "New Massachusetts Liberty Song" also effectively employs
the mytheme of the Pilgrims' sacrifice. Like the Billings songs, there
is an allusion to the Pilgrim's "desart" in the third stanza:

> We led fair FREEDOM hither, when lo the Desart smil'd,
> A Paradise of Pleasure, was open'd in the Wild;
> Your Harvest bold Americans! no Power shall snatch away,
> Assert yourselves, yourselves, yourselves, my brave AMERICA.

As in Billings's "America," the wilderness has been transformed into
a paradise, and with that follows the triumph of America. The choice
of the term "desart" here is also very interesting. For the listener
this image would draw together significant Biblical images and
touchstones from their own experience. They could see themselves,
like Moses, wandering through the "desart" in search of the promised land, and they could also see themselves as Christ, who wandered in the desert and fought the temptations of Satan. The Bible
recounts how God the Father guided their journey and aided them
in their struggles and renewed both at journey's end. And so he does
here in the New World. And for God's chosen people there must
be a larger role to play in the world, just as there was for the Israelites
and for Christ. Not only shall the country enjoy "The Harvest" but
it shall go on to play a role in the world:

> Some future Day shall crown us, the Masters of the Main,
> And giving Laws and Freedom, to subject France and Spain;
> When all the Isles o'er Ocean spread, shall tremble and obey,
> Their Lords, their Lords, their Lords, their Lords
> of brave AMERICA.

Although the hand of God does not appear to be shaping the destiny
of the country in this song, the message is nonetheless as clear as
in Billings's hymn: Out of our strife and divisions will emerge a
paradise where the secular ideals of liberty and freedom will bloom
and ultimately spread throughout the world, under the guiding hand
of God.

In the late 1770s songwriters finally had the name "United States"
to employ in their songs, and employ it well they did. "On Independence" (sung to the tune of "The Jam on Gerry's Rocks") written
by Jonathan Mitchell Sewall, a grandnephew of Samuel Sewall,

makes an interesting statement in its first stanza: "Come all you brave soldiers, both valiant and free,/It's for Independence, we all now agree." This seems to suggest that divisions had been smoothed over and a unified purpose could now be universally espoused. However, looking at the rest of the song one finds a reinforcement of the mythemes employed in previous songs. For instance, in the fifth stanza Sewall writes:

> May heaven's blessings descend on our United States,
> And grant that the union may never abate;
> May love, peace, and harmony ever be found,
> For to go hand in hand America round.

Finally, the British had to suspect that at some time or other their own national anthem, "God Save the King," would be the subtext and/or melodic inspiration for an American broadside. Their suspicions would be realized in 1779 with "God Save the Thirteen States." The song works extremely well, since in the opening stanza, it uses Britain's anthem to refer to the British as tyrants. It also states that the colonies will resist oppression "Till time's no more." The song confirms the belief that America is part of an ineluctable historical pageant, where freedom will establish its special domain:

> This Liberty, when driv'n
> From Europe's states, is giv'n
> A safe retreat and hav'n
> On our free shore.

Just as the songwriter has appropriated the melody of the song, so have we as a nation appropriated that gift which many songwriters and authors said England should have maintained and preserved for its colonists: liberty. In the last stanza we find once again an evocation of the mytheme of God's providential role:

> Oh, Lord! Thy gifts in store,
> We pray on Congress pour,
> To guide our States,
> May union bless our land,
> While we with heart and hand,
> Our mutual rights defend,
> God save our States.

Although the objective is more clearly articulated because they now have the names (i.e., Congress, United States, etc.) the sentiments are the same as those of 1734—the year the "Foregoing Occasion" was published, the first of the American broadside ballads. The destiny of the land is the destiny of the individual as they defend their "mutual rights" and God's hand is still there guiding his people in that quest.

The myth, as presented in these songs, is meant to assuage the fears many had as the country went its own way in the world. England, in her tyrannical "conspiracy" to subvert the rights and freedoms of her people, had abdicated its role as beneficent world leader. Worse was the fact that she had placed herself in direct opposition to the will of God in attempting to thwart the growth of liberty's tree and the destiny promised in the Pilgrim's trials and regeneration on New England's shores. Bradford described how he and his companions looked back on the vast ocean and then were forced to turn their eyes to God as the only means of survival in this new world. The songwriters of the Revolutionary War era, similarly, forced Americans to look back on a vast ocean—this one an ocean of differing ideologies and principles—and then helped them turn their eyes toward God. The songwriters saw the theocratic vision wedded to the strength of natural law in the form of Liberty and Freedom. As the citizens of the new republic turned their backs on the Old World and took up arms against it, the myth sustained them in the belief that to take up arms was a necessity ordained by God and nature and law. And they saw that, with God's help, there would be more than mere survival; they would, like their Pilgrim/Puritan forebears, experience a sense of transcendence and glory as they took their solitary place in becoming a leader in the world.

CHAPTER III   **"From Every**
                Mountainside"
                From the Revolution
                to the Outbreak
                of the Civil War

With the end of the Revolutionary War in 1783, the number of songs dealing with the myth of America decreased considerably. Times of crisis, as we shall see, occasion more reflection on the state of the country and its dominating ideologies. However, there were to be a few incidents that would send the broadside balladeer and the aspiring composer scampering for paper and pen to create a song that could be used in the cause—whatever that cause might be. Interestingly enough, these crises actually did more to give "final" shape to the myth and establish the parameters it would carry into the twentieth century than the efforts of the Revolutionary generations of writers.

We are, in a sense, looking at two distinct periods here: first, the three decades immediately following the end of the Revolutionary War; second, the five decades before the Civil War and commencing with the end of the War of 1812. The songs written immediately following the Revolution largely perpetuate the myth as created during the Revolution. An example of this belief in America's destiny to be at once expansive and free of control from any outside source can be seen in Jezeniah Sumner's "Ode on Science" (1798):

> Fair freedom, her attendant, waits,
> To bless the portals of her gates,
> To crown the young and rising States

With laurels of immortal day.
The British yoke, the Gallic chain,
Was urg'd upon her sons in vain;
All haughty tyrants we disdain,
And shout long live America.

Similarly, we shall see in upcoming chapters that the other songs in this time period perform the mythic functions of reconciling troubling contradictions and conflicts as well as providing Americans with a sense of transcendence by continuing to map a way in the world that was guided by the hand of Providence.

The songs written in the decades before the Civil War perpetuate the same mythemes and intensify America's exclusionary role in the world, but additionally bring new emphasis to the aspect of the land itself as a rich and vital part of the myth. The geography of the land under the divine imperative of Providence, becomes almost a metonymy or synedoche for the whole by suggesting, on the one hand, that our boundaries are inviolate and secure, and, on the other, that our new frontiers and freedom are boundless. The songs written during these two periods reveal a people breaking out and away from the memories of the Old World but trying desperately to anchor themselves and their quest in the principles of their Pilgrim and Revolutionary War forebears.

I

The first flurry of songs dealing with the myth of America occur during the 1790s, with 1798 being the year of greatest activity. The country had won its independence, but now it needed to establish itself as a self-contained entity "among the Powers of the Earth." Naturally, there were differing opinions on how the country would achieve this. The drafters of the Constitution brought varying ideological perspectives to their deliberations on what the country's charter should contain. The tensions of the war years created a climate where, as in ancient Athens, involvement in—or, minimally, knowledge of—politics was part of a citizen's responsibility and duty. Taking a lead from the cultural scene in London, the theater was an important force in the political life of the average citizen, and musical theater in particular. Not surprisingly, in the four years preceding the flurry of "America" songs in 1798, Americans were treated to *The Patriot; or Liberty Asserted (1794)* by James Hewitt and *The Patriot; or, Liberty Obtained* (1796) by Benjamin Carr. Both employed music to politico-satirical advantage.

Elsewhere out among the "ordinary folk" there were those who maintained loyalist ties, those who thought the highest good existed in the pursuit of individual freedom and self-interest, and those who, as part of the Second Great Awakening, needed to reaffirm the spirit of the "Holy Charter" established by the founding fathers. And in the Great Awakening was an attempt by people to reconcile the secular thrust of the Constitution with their own abiding faith in Holy Writ. For some, the images in Jezeniah Sumner's "Ode on Science" (1798) would probably have suggested too much the influence of secularism in American life. In the song he states that like the sun spreading its rays from east to west,

> So science spreads her lucid ray
> O'er lands that long in darkness lay;
> She visits fair Columbia,
> And sets her sons among the stars.

It is, for Sumner, not God who "sets her sons among the stars" but science personified. The Second Great Awakening, then, was for some a reaction to a troubling cultural drift, leading people away from a faith in eternal verities to a narrow-minded preoccupation with temporal realities of politics and business. And if we, as a nation, turned away from those eternal verities—so the argument ran —we would in one stroke repudiate both the reasons that impelled people to settle here and our providentially guided destiny. Consequently as Gordon Wood notes, "The various religious groups espoused a common creed of identity with the nation that worked to unify the culture more than any legal establishment ever could have" (1977, 408). These antinomian currents were reconciled and then forged into a cohesive vision in the songs of the 1780s and 1790s that carried over into the troubling early decades of the nineteenth century.

A tune that anticipates most of the songs to be written during this time period is Timothy Dwight's "Columbia" (1789). The song was written about the same time that Joel Barlow was beginning his epic of the American experience *The Vision of Columbus* (1787), which was later revised and published as *The Columbiad* (1807). Dwight's song perfectly draws together the strands of secular and religious thought current in the culture, and it anticipates the new approach to the theme of the land which will characterize the songs of this time period. In the first stanza we find the secular themes enunciated:

> Columbia, Columbia, to glory arise
> The queen of the world and the child of the skies
> Thy genius commands thee; with rapture behold
> While ages on ages thy splendors unfold.
> Thy reign is the last and the noblest of time.
> Most fruitful thy soil, most inviting thy clime
> Let the crimes of the earth ne'er encrimson thy name
> Be freedom and science and virtue and fame.

The sense of the country's destiny is captured effectively in the lines about how through the ages our splendor will unfold and in the line where he states that it is our mission to "be" freedom, science, virtue, and fame, four words which summarize the ideological and valuative subtext of the myth.

There is also evidence of how myth can masterfully evoke and reconcile ostensibly conflicting ideologies with his line about, "Thy reign is the last and noblest of time." If you are a believer in enlightenment values, this line validates the role of reason, science, law, progress, as embodied in the Declaration and the Constitution, in the creation of the nation; and if you are one of those feeling the spirit of the Lord moving in your life as the Great Awakening begins to gather energy, the lines suggest an apocalyptic vision and a sense of being in the community of a chosen people who are now, by merit of being Americans, situated perfectly in anticipation of the last days.

Finally, the allusion to the land is one of the first that acknowledges the land as something of value for itself and not something which needs to be transformed (i.e., from a "desert") or as merely symbol for natural law or higher power. It quite clearly seems to be a rebuff to those European theorists, such as the Comte de Buffon, who in his *Natural History* (forty-four volumes published between 1749 and 1804) perceived that the irregular topography of our land, the extremities of climate, not to mention the forests and swamps, had a deleterious effect upon people.

In the next stanza the same values are reaffirmed and drawn together in a coda celebrating our manifest destiny.

Thus as down a lone valley with cedars o'erspread
From war's dread confusion I pensively strayed
The gloom from the face of fair Heaven retired
The winds ceased to murmur, the thunders expired.
Perfumes as of Eden flowed sweetly along,
And a voice as of angels enchantingly sang
Columbia, Columbia, to glory arise
The queen of the world and the child of the skies.

The envelope structure of the song, where the first two lines of the first stanza serve also as the last two lines—and, hence, the cadence —for the second stanza, nicely focus all the images and draw the listener toward creating the secular vision of us as the "queen" of the (material) world and as the progeny and manifestation of God's design for humanity. There is the image of the lonesome valley— with an attendant allusion to the cedars of Lebanon (a favorite image from the psalms)—which will figure in a great gospel song later on, and images of Eden and angels, all suggesting the Biblical imperative whereby we will live and prosper. We see that Dwight, for all his obeisance to the growing secular values existent in the culture, is still driven in his evocation of the myth by those themes that have animated the passions and beliefs in the preceding century. And so it will be in the flurry of songs written in the late 1790s.

In that period, it must have seemed to the average citizen that the very world was teetering on the bring of disaster. A crippling economic depression, fears of a war with France, the Second Great Awakening—with its implicit suggestion of the country's moral and religious bankruptcy—and the institution of the Alien and Sedition Acts all suggested that the country had lost (if it had ever had) its special mission—divine or otherwise. Where was power concentrated? How would it be used? Which party best could ensure private and public freedoms? When the troops were called out in 1798, were they there to safeguard our shores from French invasion or to keep order on the homefront? Troubling questions. Questions that led one writer to observe in 1800 that America appeared to be "tottering to its foundations."

You wouldn't really know it, however, by looking at the songs of the period. Beginning with a tune entitled "Song for the 4th of July"

(1796) the songs communicate an image of a country firmly in control of its historical mission. The "Song for the 4th of July," which uses the "Anacreontic Song," the melody of our national anthem, boldly asserts:

> In climes where fair FREEDOM, secure from her foes,
> Sees millions who bow at her shrine with devotion.
> Where vet'ran patriots in laurel'd repose,
> Lament to see arrogance crimson the ocean:
>   Where order pervades
>   The mountains and glades,
> Where COLUMBIA reclines in her own native shades,
> Hark! millions of Freemen with joy hail the day
> Which rescu'd their Country from Tyranny's sway.

If one characterized this as a classic or even stereotypical enlightenment image of the country, there probably wouldn't be much disagreement. The topography conforms to classical ideals of order, patriots wear the laurels, and freedom—in her archetypal feminine personification—is deified. The writer, by locating the genesis of the mythemes in the date of the signing of the Declaration, astutely brings together past and present and future to communicate a feeling of cohesion and unity. It is a reminder to all Americans that our path was set once, and we persevered, and now, with threats from the outside and inside imminent, we need to recall that galvanic moment and re-create ourselves.

Other songs responded to these threats in an even more comprehensive fashion. Two songs which do this and which also serve as transitions to the fully realized myth in songs such as "My Country, Tis of Thee" are Thomas Paine's "Adams and Liberty. The Boston Patriotic Song" (1798), which was set to the "Anacreontic Song," and Joseph Hopkinson's "Hail! Columbia" (1798). The first stanza of the Paine song opens with the classic evocation of the Pilgrims/patriots mytheme and includes a not too heavily veiled allusion to the Bible:

> Ye sons of Columbia, who bravely fought,
>   For those rights, which unsustain'd from your Sires had
>   descended,
> May you long taste the blessings your valour has brought,
>   And your sons reap the soil, which fathers defended
>   Mid the reign of mild peace,

> May your nation increase,
>   With the glory of Rome, and the wisdom of Greece;
> And ne'er may the sons of Columbia be slaves,
>   While the earth bears a plant, or the sea rolls its waves.

As in previous songs, the necessity for establishing a sense of historical continuity in the myth is evident. Past, present, and future are
simultaneously observed in the myth. History figures in other stanzas of the song as well. The fifth stanza claims boldly that "Rome's
haughty victors" should beware of "collision" because even if they
bring all the "vassals of Europe in arms,/We're a WORLD BY OUR-
SELVES, and disdain a division!" There is a decidedly judgmental tone
in the use of "vassels," which implies that we enjoy freedom and
individual ownership of land and are not subject to old feudal inequi-
ties. But more important is the statement "WORLD BY OURSELVES,"
which implies that we will not look back but will stand solitary
and alone but unified in purpose. Again, this reinforces the paradoxical nature of our destiny to be at once expansive and exclusionary.

The mytheme of the land also plays an important role in the song.
We are, however still far removed from the fully realized image of
the land we will see in the songs of the nineteenth century and
early twentieth. It is also interesting, having seen the rather forward-
looking allusions to the land in Dwight's "Columbia," that the
image of the land in this song is seen more in the light of reason,
progress, and science. The first stanza fleetingly mentions the land
as a place to reap the harvest made possible by the Pilgrims' sacrifice.
The second stanza reinforces the more pragmatic and mercantilistic
aspects of the topography when it states, "In a clime, whose rich
vales feed the marts of the world," which also suggests our growing
global reach and our destiny to play a role in the world beyond our
shores. In these cases the allusions seems to reflect more
Crevecoeur's vision of the land as private property and as a vehicle
for self-determination and its ancillary value, opportunity. The land,
however, has yet another role to play during these times of crisis.
Recalling that the song was written partially in response to the
threat of war with France, we find Paine in the sixth stanza yoking
the bounty of the land with the necessity to defend freedom:

> Our mountains are crown'd with imperial *Oak*,
>   Whose *roots*, like our Liberties, ages have nourish'd;
> But long ere our nation submits to the yoke,

> Not a *tree* shall be left on the field where it
> flourish'd.
> Should *invasion* impend,
> Every *grove* would defend
> From the *hill-tops* they shaded, our *shores* to defend.

This image of the trees recalls the old Tree of Liberty imagery from the songs of the Revolutionary War era while adding an interesting militaristic twist. First of all, it is significant that the oaks have been placed on the mountains for henceforth the mountain will be a crucial image in the mytheme of the land. Second, the mighty oak here suggests that the very bounty of the land is our strength, because it, symbolizes that our quest for liberty is founded in the virtue of natural law and in addition—in what some might see as classical American fashion—it practically and actually functions as the defense of those liberties.

Hopkinson's "Hail! Columbia" begins by referring to the sacrifices of the patriots and elides their identity with that of the promised land and God's providential role in our history: "Hail, Columbia! happy land! Hail, ye heroes, heav'n born band!" The songwriters make reference to the blood shed during the Revolutionary War and that our independence was achieved at a cost. We will see this theme repeated in the songs of the Civil War and World War I. And then in the final lines, Hopkinson masterfully yokes religious and secular imagery in recounting our quest for freedom and liberty:

> Let Independence be your boast,
> Ever mindful of what it cost,
> Ever grateful for the prize,
> Let its altar reach the skies.

The suggestion—one that will also crop up in Civil War and World War I songs—is that the sacrifice for the secular ideals of the enlightenment ultimately will result in a regeneration of the spirit (perpetual gratitude for the prize and transcendental experience—the exaltation of independence on the altar).

In the chorus of the song itself, the songwriter anticipates one of the popular themes of the nineteenth century: brotherhood.

> Firm, united let us be,
> Rallying around our liberty.

> As a band of brothers join'd,
> Peace and safety we shall find.

This clearly anticipates the feeling of brotherhood that will pervade much of Romantic literature and thought. It also addresses the growing concern among Americans about disunity. The rise of the self-made man, the growing sectarianism in religion, the great proliferation of business corporations and of voluntary organizations were for some Americans not necessarily a sign of a healthy Republic but merely expressions of a fragmented and diffused society. Hopkinson, however, is able to transcend those growing differences by focusing our energies on the enemy ("rude foe with impious hand") who is about to attack the heart's blood of the society: liberty and our rights. To attack these, he states, is to attack our "sacred history": "Immortal patriots! rise once more,/Defend your rights, defend your shore." Is this a call for resurrection or regeneration? Does it make a difference? This attack is, moreover, a threat to our destiny as willed by God: "Let no rude foe with impious hand,/Invade the shrine where sacred lies,/Of toil and blood the well-earned prize." Thus Hopkinson would have us see that it is important for us to join as brothers, to forget petty differences and our own petty self-interest, and be reminded that there are higher stakes here; to partake in the struggle is to share as brothers in the maintenance of the divine mandate. To jeopardize that mandate is to undermine the very freedom—the "rights"—that allows for those individual differences; only through brotherhood will the efficacy of individual "rights" and, consequently our ability to have differences, remain sacrosant.

It is not hard to understand, then, how "Hail! Columbia," to quote David Ewen, "For a quarter of a century after [its premiere] . . . was America's national anthem. It was heard on every American ship at the lowering of the colors at sunset. For still another half century it shared its stature as a national anthem with 'The Star-Spangled Banner.' During the Civil War, 'Hail! Columbia' was the anthem sung and played most often in the North" (1977, 18–19).

Next, we have James Hewitt's "New Yankee Doodle" (1798), which contains ideas that will be echoed in future songs dealing with war. Its images and evocation of the mythemes are focused around the threat from the outside. The first stanza states: "Columbians all the present hour as Brothers should Unite us,/Union at home's the only way to make each Nation right us." The sacrifice of the patriots is used to strengthen our resolve to defend the principles for which they fought (and also make us feel guilty if we fail):

> Great Washington, who led us on,
> And Liberty effected,
> Shall see we'll die or else be free—
> We will not be subjected.

This will become a common device for songwriters when using the myth of America during wartime. They will remind the listener that their heritage must be maintained and that the sacrifices (i.e., of Valley Forge, Bunker Hill, Gettysburg, the Battle of the Bulge, etc.) were made in the name of freedom, and the present generation must be up to the task of preserving that heritage. The song ends with an interesting twist on the destiny mytheme as it states that our renewal will have a capitalistic twist as "Commerce, free from fetters prove/Mankind are all relations"; this will then lead to the transfiguration of that most durable symbol of the broadside ballad: "Then Yankee Doodle, be divine/Yankee Doodle Dandy." We have come full circle with the secular symbol of our revolution taking his place in the starry firmament.

Finally, we have another song whose sentiments would be echoed in successive eras up into the days of *Sing Out!* in the 1950s: "Jefferson and Liberty" (1800). Jefferson would soon be added to the list of patriots evoked when dealing with the myth. (This particular song found popularity among the folk-protest movement in the twentieth century, because it deemphasized the role of God and exalted the secular values inherent in the myth, in addition to reaffirming the continual struggle to be waged to break the bonds of oppression and fulfill the destiny of freedom for each person.) The mythemes that are featured most prominently are those of liberty, of course, and the land. The song reminds us that we are a home for "strangers from a thousand shores" who because of tyranny are forced to roam. Here they find "abundant stores,/A nobler and happier home." Here also opportunity is greater, for

> Here Art shall lift her laurel'd head,
> Wealth, Industry and Peace divine;
> And where dark, pathless forests spread,
> Rich fields and lofty cities shine.

One notices that "secular" values are exalted and become the means whereby the individual achieves that sense of transcendence. The promise that one will "never bend the knee" to a tyrant nor be subject to some lord who will "wring from industry the food" is paramount and made possible not by God but by Jefferson, whose election has dispelled the gloom of night and "reign of terror." The last lines are particularly notable as they anticipate the sentiments expressed by Katherine Lee Bates in her "America the Beautiful" as they unite the images of nascent capitalism (the cities) and the abundant richness of the land.

II

Looking ahead to the quintessential expressions of the myth in the twentieth century, such as Irving Berlin's "God Bless America" (1939) and more recent songs like Lee Greenwood's "God Bless the U.S.A.," we find their roots firmly planted in the songs of the nineteenth century. The music of the post-Revolutionary War period is, in a sense, only a preface for the establishment of the complete myth in the nineteenth. Three songs, "The Star-Spangled Banner" (1814), "My Country! 'Tis of Thee" (1832), and "America the Beautiful" (1895) most consistently and fully articulate the mythemes identified at the outset here.

In the early nineteenth century songwriters did little to alter the myth of America in popular song. But, after all, why should they? This century, perhaps as much as the former, needed the basic myth inviolate. The nineteenth century witnessed major transformations in the lives of Americans. The economic base made a slow but inexorable shift from agrarian to industrial, the ideals of Jefferson and the enlightened Republicans of the eighteenth century gave way to the rough-and-tumble democracy of Jacksonian Democrats, and the middle class emerged as a moral and political power. The country, moreover, seemed to know no geographical bounds as pioneers pushed ever farther westward. Finally, the period witnessed the rise of the rugged, self-reliant individual, embodying, Emerson's notion of the "infinitude of the private man."

Americans saw in all these developments great opportunities; everyone could have a voice, everyone could have a share of the land, everyone could have a share of the power and the wealth. Indeed, the century would be animated by an energy as dynamic as that which fueled the culture of Revolutionary America. People were optimistic, expansive in their thinking, aware of the promise of the Declaration and the Constitution and ready to realize the potential promised in those magic words, "liberty and freedom." And all of these developments would be overseen by the providential hand of God in the theme of manifest destiny. Manifest destiny, which had been hinted at in the popular songs of the eighteenth century, would in the nineteenth become a credo of self-determination. But what would such growth and expansiveness mean to the ideal of the Republic and the collective identity of the American? David Brian Davis has written of the period:

> But for many thoughtful Americans . . . there was a danger that these expansive energies [devoted to self-betterment and self-determination] would erode all respect for order, balance, and communal purpose; that the competitive spirit would lead to an atomized society ruled by the principle, "Every man for himself and the devil take to the hindmost"; that the American people would become enslaved to money, success, and material gratification; and that the centrifugal focus of expansion would cause the nation to fly apart (1977, 426).

To keep the nation from flying apart, Americans found affirmation and consolation in a number of myths, and most notably in the myth of America. Some of the most eloquent and complete statements of the myth were contained in the popular songs of the nineteenth century.

Surprisingly, however, not nearly as many songs dealing with the myth were written in the eighty-year period preceding the Civil War as were written during the twenty years of revolutionary activity in the eighteenth century. There were enough crisis to occasion hundreds of such songs, but what seems to emerge here is a portrait of a country which, in contrast to the Revolutionary War era, no longer needed to define itself. The crises of the nineteenth century did not center on establishing a cultural identity, but, instead, on maintaining its established identity and enlarging its scope. Thus, some of the songs written during this era reflect that cultural label, "The Era of Good Feelings." The songs, according to Sarah Brodsky Lawrence, "Reflecting the balmy political climate [from 1817 to

1840] . . . tended to be more social than political: lilting waltzes replaced martial tunes, and odes of praise were chanted instead of derogatory political ditties" (223). Interestingly enough, however, two of the dominant songs—and two that have survived longest into the twentieth century—have a martial air and were occasioned by military events "The Star-Spangled Banner" and "Columbia, the Gem of the Ocean."

Most of the dominant mythemes enunciated in the songs of the eighteenth century would play an important part in songs dealing with the myth in the nineteenth. The perpetuation of them bears witness to the pervasiveness of our belief in the myth. Americans saw the need to hold on to their faith in our providential role in the world.

Some minor variations on earlier themes occur in the songs of this new century, but three of these songs should be viewed as a sort of musico-mythical apotheosis, surviving as they did into the twentieth century. "The Star-Spangled Banner," "My Country! Tis of Thee," and "Columbia, the Gem of the Ocean" contain refinements and amendments to the mythemes which would affect and determine the content of songs up to our own days.

Looking at songs of the nineteenth century proper, our starting point is, appropriately enough, "The Star-Spangled Banner" (1814). "The Star-Spangled Banner" is typical of the songs written during the War of 1812 in that it makes specific references to an actual battle and event; in fact, its original title was "The Defense of Fort McHenry." Most of the songs written during this war—unlike the majority of songs written during the Revolutionary War and World Wars I, II—generally deal with specific events such as "Constitution and Guerriere" (celebrating a famed sea battle) or "Decatur's Victory" or "A Happy New Year to Commodore Rodgers." The national anthem does this, but it also does more—one reason, perhaps, that shortly after its initial publication, it assumed the new title "The Star Spangled Banner." It is universal in its appeal, it tells an exciting story, and it proved so durable throughout the nineteenth century that eventually (1931) it became our national anthem.

The lyric achieves its universal quality by having as its focus the flag itself, which was not only a common symbol for most Americans but one which would have meaning to people of any culture. The image of the flag, illuminated by the "Rockets' red glare, the Bombs bursting in air," still waving proudly over the bombarded fort symbolized our need for independence and isolationism. The invasion by the British of Maryland brought into question how inviolate our shores were and how safe our homes. "The Star Spangled Banner," moreover, waves "O'er the land of the free, and the home of the brave," an evocation of the mytheme of freedom simultaneously yoked with another image and crucial symbol in American culture; home. By combining the image of home with those of bravery and patriotism, Key suggests that we are all patriots because America houses only the brave. Without directly using the mytheme of the patriot's sacrifice, Key is able to evoke it nonetheless in these final lines, the only lines, by the way, which are repeated in every stanza adding even more to their import.

The little-sung last stanza moves the song out of the solely militaristic by reaffirming the mytheme of God's role in the destiny of the nation:

> O! thus be it ever when freemen shall stand,
>   Between their lov'd home, and the war's desolation,
> Blest with vic'try and peace, may the Heav'n rescued land,
>   Praise the Power that hath made and preserved us a
>   nation!
> Then conquer we must, when our cause it is just,
> And this be our motto—"In God is our Trust;"
>   And the Star-Spangled Banner, etc.

Two major mythemes that will reverberate throughout the decades are enunciated in this stanza. First, Key picks up on the theme of home he established in the first stanza and adds a slightly sentimental dimension to the notion by placing it in the context of war. He also suggests that to protect one's home is also to "preserve" the nation. The other idea, that "our cause it is just," is a theme that will remain with us up to the present-day, despite satiric attacks during the 1960s, such as Bob Dylan's, "With God on our Side." "The Star-Spangled Banner" also evokes the mytheme of the promised land ("heav'n rescued land") and the mytheme of the role of Providence, and thereby reconciles the more troubling issue of God's role in war. The song suggests that in times of crisis and uncertainty, as war rages about, the God who led the pilgrims, who "made and preserved" this new promised land and who established our inalienable rights (the just cause), will not fail in the regeneration of the nation.

This is exactly the message Americans needed during this time when the war was seen not only as a test of our mettle in dealing with invasion from abroad but also as a test of our internal mettle. The myth as expressed in this song confirms the transcendental hope that the destiny of this country is greater than the current war and that this conflict is only part of that great American Puritan tradition of trial and tribulation, purification and regeneration.

The view of the new world represented in "The Star-Spangled Banner" is one perspective. The other is represented in the gentler, more hymnlike tunes such as "My Country! Tis of Thee" (1832)—now most often titled simply "America"—and, to a lesser extent, those of the Hutchinson family. These songs are not radically different from previous tunes in their treatment of the mythemes with the possible exception of the image of the land. This is clearly more in keeping with attitudes toward nature that flourished in the nineteenth century. Previously, the image of the land in the songs was vague. Most allusions were drawn from the Biblical image of the "desart." In short, the country was seen either as a backdrop for the ritual of trial, temptation, and regeneration or, in light of the eighteenth century's more rationalistic worldview, as a metaphor for the workings of natural law. The Liberty Tree was not a tree necessarily of good and evil, but, instead, a reminder of how the rights of man flowed naturally from the virtue inherent in the natural birthright of every person. Not so in the nineteenth century.

One of the most striking features of the songs of the nineteenth century is how the land has become an object with a significance apart from any religious or moral associations—although these qualities are not entirely absent from the songs either, just as they are not absent from the canvases of Cole, Durand, and Kensett. Carl Bode writes: "Clearly, the American public had rediscovered nature, for the most popular kind of canvas by far was the landscape. But it was nature of a particularly significant kind: nature in its kinder aspects, tame, gentle, and no longer a primeval frontier foe" (1959, 66). Consequently, we find songwriters drawing more attention to the details of the landscape and also using the landscape to suggest the growth and bounty of the land. Painters and songwriters of the early nineteenth century alike concerned themselves with the panoramic aspects of the American scene, with its sweep and scope and symbolic importance.

In the late eighteenth century, one could see the growing popularity of theories of the sublime in nature not only in Edmund Burke and the occasional poems of Thomas Gray and James Thomson, but also in an occasional popular tune. A song which clearly anticipates the changes in the mytheme of the land and speaks to the sense of transcendence people were feeling in the wake of the Revolutionary War is the spiritual "The Promised Land" (1787). The first lines state: "O the transporting rapturous scene that rises to my sight." Then in the next lines the songwriter describes the bountiful land in imagery that anticipates the great songs of America in the nineteenth century; there is, for instance, a "sunset field . . . rayed in living green." Then the songwriter draws together two interesting images as he states: "There generous truths that never fail on trees immortal grow:/There rocks and hills and brooks and vales where milk and honey flow." The line about "generous truths" is ambiguous enough to suggest the truths of the Bible as well as those of the new American Constitution. But what is most stunning here is the portrayal of these truths hanging, like the rich fruit of Eden, from trees. The daunting thicket of trees that Bradford and his companions encountered is slowly and inexorably giving way to a richer, more bountiful specter: a land of "milk and honey." The primary difference in the two perspectives on nature is that in the colonial vision, man with God's help cleared the thicket to make a paradise, an altar for freedom; in the nineteenth century, nature is already an altar for freedom and in its wild state symbolizes the rich bounty of paradise.

The American song par excellence of the nineteenth century, however, is "My Country! 'Tis of Thee" (1832) with words by Samuel Francis Smith. Of course, the grand irony of this tune is that it is set to "God Save the King," which is also the British national anthem. However, unlike his Revolutionary forebears, Smith had no ironic intent in mind when he drafted his lyrics; he merely liked the tune and decided it needed American words. Moreover, it was not written as a response to an immediate crisis as most of our previously discussed songs had been. There were some troubling currents and increasing tensions abroad in the early 1830s, created by growing problems with the Bank of the United States, which Andrew Jackson denounced as a promoter of privileged monopoly. But the country had not yet fallen into the panic of 1837, and Texas troubles still lay in the future. Smith simply wrote the words to please himself.

The song, with its hymnlike qualities, its strong harmonies, and stately tune, which almost perfectly complements the nobility of its sentiments, strongly reaffirms the fundamental premises of the myth while, at the same time, enlarging its scope through its depiction of the land. In keeping with the traditions established previously, America is apostrophized as the land of liberty in the lines, "My country 'tis of thee,/Sweet land of liberty/Of thee I sing." ("Of thee I sing" will appear some one hundred years later in a George and Ira Gershwin song, but with entirely different intent.) The song also alludes to the mytheme of the patriot's sacrifice and gives it, in the process, a personal touch by using the first person pronoun: "Land where my Fathers died." This device, moreover, draws the singer/listener more intimately into the song while reminding him/ her of our shared destiny. (It is a technique that Woody Guthrie used in his "This Land Is Your Land" and Irving Berlin in his "God Bless America" over 100 years later.) The allusion to the mytheme of the founders is carried on in the line immediately following, which sings of America as the land of the Pilgrim's pride. And the first stanza ends with the songwriter drawing together images of the landscape itself and democratic ideals: "From every mountainside,/Let freedom ring." The church-of-nature imagery and symbolism begun in Revolutionary times is carried over here, but nature, in keeping with nineteenth-century values, is a more positive force.

The changing role of nature in the myth of America is most evident in the second stanza of "My Country! 'Tis of Thee." This, in fact, is the first song that truly brings together all the mythemes in a unified whole, and thus it stands as one of the most complete statements of the myth of America. In the second stanza Smith writes:

> My native country thee—
> Land of the noble free—
>   Thy name I love:
> I love thy rocks and rills,
> Thy woods and templed hills;
> My heart with rapture thrills
>   Like that above.

As in past songs, our encounter with the natural is a springboard for a realization of the transcendental, but in previous songs nature was transformed into a paradise by God for the new Americans. In this song the land itself inspires feelings of heavenly rapture, and this rapture brings us closer to God's appointed role in the country's destiny. What is particularly notable here is the amount of detail Smith provides. This is something we have not encountered before. He carefully selects images from the topography of the land that will carry some symbolic import. His use of rocks, water, woods, and—in perhaps the most powerful and influential image—the "templed hills" suggest the bounty and expansiveness of the continent. That these images can excite a contemplation of the sublime enables this song to share similarities with the work of the Hudson River school of artists.

The mytheme of the land also plays a crucial role in the third stanza. Smith immediately asks the singer/listener to draw a connection between nature and freedom: "Let music swell the breeze,/ And ring from all the trees,/Sweet freedom's song." It is as though the land has been given a role in perpetuating the sacred ideal of freedom. He next suggests that freedom, like some divine presence, courses through every aspect of creation and unites us:

> Let mortal tongues awake,
> Let all that breathe partake,
> Let rocks their silence break,
>   The sound prolong.

The images of resurrection and renewal are powerful here. For Smith, freedom becomes something of the common person's "oversoul," a force that courses throughout the land and that the land and its people celebrate by their mere existence. It inspires a mystic contemplation and draws us together in a mystical hymn of oneness. The landscape in "My Country! 'Tis of Thee," by its mere presence, sings a song of freedom, and to contemplate it is to be reminded that we must, like nature, "The sound prolong."

In the final stanza, Smith unites the mythemes of manifest destiny, freedom, and the land in a transcendental coda. Where freedom had, in previous stanzas, functioned as the power to draw together inanimate nature and the "noble free," in the final stanza it becomes the vehicle whereby the ideals of the Revolution and the ideals of the theocratic society are confirmed and reconciled:

> Long may our land be bright
> With freedom's holy light;

Protect us by Thy might,
Great God our King.

The land, in this case, suggests more than topography. It brings together all the images suggested earlier: rock, rills, woods, noble free, mortal tongues, and so on, in short, the people and the landscape. But this land will enjoy a favorable status only if we safeguard freedom. Freedom has been the mytheme that previous songwriters used to highlight our special place in the world; it is the thing that makes us unique and that binds us together. Consequently, freedom here is imbued with a numinosity by merit of its being described as a holy light. The proximity of "holy light" to God's role further strengthens how we have reconciled the secular and the divine in this country. For this God whom we rely upon is still the God of the Old Testament: the Power who led His people to the Promised Land, gave them the gifts of freedom and independence, and who now protects us by His might.

The song "Columbia, The Gem of the Ocean" (1843) by Thomas a Beckett has a more pronounced militaristic tone than "My Country! 'Tis of Thee." Written at a time when Americans began to think deeply about expansion across the continent, when the term "manifest destiny" was first coined, it seems almost a throwback to Revolutionary times in its glorification of the sacrifice of the patriots. There is one stanza however, in which the songwriter talks of how war "threatened the land to deform," but "The ark then of freedom's foundation,/Columbia rode safe thro' the storm." The term "ark" here has a dual meaning: a clear allusion to Noah's ark, plus a more subtle allusion to the ark of the covenant, the bond between Moses and the chosen people. Either way, it expresses the mytheme of the chosen people, whose destiny is guided by the hand of Providence. One sees in it, as well, the anticipation of what would become a declared ideology of manifest destiny.

No examinations of songs dealing with the myth of America during this era would be complete without at least a passing nod to the Hutchinson Family. The Hutchinsons were a singing troupe from the farming country of Milford in southeastern New Hampshire, consisting of brothers John, Asa, Judson (with brother Jesse as manager) and a sister, Abigail. Known as the Tribe of Jesse, the Hutchinson Family, as Caroline Moseley notes, "hymned reassuringly traditional values of home, family, and farm; and, they sang of the past and the future, thereby lessening the threat of the present" (1989, 63). Unlike some of the other contemporary performers, such as Edwin Christy and Dan Emmett, they also sang about social problems and issues, chief of which were abolition and women's suffrage. They were, first and foremost, entertainers who were able to establish a warm relationship with their audiences by playing to those audiences' values. Consequently, even though an audience might be slightly shocked by an emancipation song like "Get Off the Track," the singers knew that their sweet harmonies and their honest commitment to the cause would strike a responsive chord.

The Hutchinson Family played to their audiences' emotions and basic beliefs. Their "Uncle Sam's Farm" was totally unlike the stately anthems of a previous age. Their musical style blended the traditions of church music and what can almost be called a folk style. There is a lilting grace to their tunes, not unlike that one finds in the "Ethiopian melodies" and dance tunes of Stephen Foster. The opening stanza of "Uncle Sam's Farm" seems to owe more to Crevecoeur's ideals than to Bradford's:

> Of all the mighty nations in the East or in the West
> This glorious Yankee nation is the greatest and the best.
> We have room for all creation and our banner is unfurled.
> Come along . . .
> Our lands they are broad enough,
> Don't be alarmed,
> Uncle Sam is rich enough to give us all a farm.

Obviously the image of Uncle Sam here is not of a government welfare program. "Uncle Sam" serves as a metonymy of the bountiful natural wealth of the country. Subsequent stanzas then flesh out the role and relationship between the land and the people. The second stanza, for instance, offers physical details to show how large the country is, while the third stanza identifies a product and industry with each region and states in the closing that our motto is "Go Ahead." The song definitely draws on the Romantics' fascination with nature, and it ever so subtly sets up a shift in the perception of the country: the greatness of the country has less to do with God, perhaps, and more with the nature of the land itself. This a sentiment that "My Country! 'Tis of Thee" seemed to be suggesting in its first three stanzas, but which, as we have seen, merely serves as a preface for a reaffirmation of the notions of manifest destiny. However, the Hutchinsons' song, by emphasizing nature and the bounty of the land, might strike one as a forerunner of Woody Guthrie's populist sentiments in his 1939 song "This Land Is Your Land," which makes no references at all to God, but only to His people. Similarly, "Uncle Sam's Farm" makes more reference to growing secular ideals of work, private property, and the land itself.

In their music, the Hutchinsons, like Woody Guthrie, Chuck Berry, and Bruce Springsteen, almost transcend the myth of the country as a whole. It is as if they knew that the myth was inadequate to deal with the diversity of the populace. They were, moreover, concerned with the state of the disenfranchised, as in their songs about abolition and women's rights. As a result, their songs have a breadth that one does not find in many composers of the early nineteenth century. The myth serves as something of a subtext in their work—much as it does in songs about war. In their most popular tune, "The Old Granite State" (1843), for instance, they cleverly link their state (New Hampshire) with the quest for equal rights and the myth of America. An early stanza states:

> Liberty is our motto,
> Liberty is our motto,
> Equal liberty is our motto,
>   In the "Old Granite State."

Note that the emphasis is shifted slightly from the mytheme of freedom to equality, which functions as equally important in the myth. It is a shift, but only one of degree. Then later they tie their state to the goals of the country as a whole:

> Now three cheers altogether,
> Shout Columbia's people ever,
> Yankee hearts none can sever,
>   In the "Old Sister States."

And then they reaffirm the mythemes of the patriot's sacrifice and the role of God in our history:

> Like our sires before us,
> We will swell the chorus,
> Till the Heavens o'er us,
>   Shall rebound the loud hussa.

This is very reminiscent of the image in "My Country! 'Tis of Thee" where the song of freedom swells the breeze and resounds throughout all of creation. One sees here as well the suggestion of the transcendental function of the myth as the Hutchinsons imply that by joining in the chorus (natural for a group of performers) one partakes in the spirit that animated their forebears and gives glory to that Being who watches over our destiny.

Other composers and performers as well as the Hutchinsons raised their voices in defense of their oppressed brethren. A recent study of abolition and antislavery songs by Vicki Eaklor (1988) reveals an immense number of lyrics written to support the cause. They are usually similar in purpose and intent and in their treatment of the myth of America, so I will only be looking at a few representative examples.

In general, the abolitionists reaffirm the basic myth of America. Their major argument with it was in the execution of its promise, in the country being true to its mission. T. W. Higginson's line about "The land our fathers left to us/Is foul with hateful sin" pretty much sums up the dilemma for the nineteenth-century American, who was faced with the prospect that the covenant made between God and Pilgrims and fought for in the Revolution (and subsequently preserved in the Constitution) might be tainted. The most important connection the abolitionists made was between Liberty and God. Here they largely inherited the approach taken by the songwriters of the Revolutionary War era. Vicki Eaklor notes: "The bond that united [liberty and God] . . . had been transformed gradually from a specific and well-defined Protestant covenant into a contract whose central tenet, the preservation of God-given liberty among his chosen people, made it paradoxically simpler yet more diffuse" (16). The mandate for the abolitionist songwriter to translate into musical terms was that our special mission was to bring the fruits of democracy to all peoples; the abolitionists pointed out that this needed to start at home with the enslaved blacks. To fail in extending them the blessings of liberty, opportunity, and equality was a failure of the national mission. As Higginson's "National Anti-Slavery Hymn" states:

> What good, though growing wealth and strength
> Shall stretch from shore to shore,
> If this the fatal poison taint
> Be only spread the more?

No outward show, nor fancied strength,
From thy stern justice saves,
There is no liberty for them
Who make their brethren slaves!

If this sounds slightly contemporary, do not be surprised. The same theme pervades treatments of the myth by minority songwriters from the 1930s to the 1990s. Let us see how the songwriters reconciled the promise of America with the realities of slavery.

One of the most popular means of dealing with the issue of slavery and the national mission was to use parody, and there was no more favorite song to parody than the recently popular "My Country! 'Tis of Thee." The use of this tune, of course, dramatically pointed up the failure of the democratic mission. In 1839 *The Liberator* published a parody, which contained this first stanza:

My country! 'tis of thee
Strong hold of Slavery—
Of thee I sing:
Land, where my fathers died;
Where men *man's* rights *deride;*
From every mountain-side,
Thy deeds shall ring.

The remainder of the stanzas utilize much of the original song as a contrast with the wrongs being done in the name of slavery; the author states that she loves the hills and dales but hates "thy negro sales," and later says that "wailing" should swell the breeze, "And ring from all the trees/The *black* man's wrong."

Another parody, this one from 1854 by Joshua Simpson, entitled "Song of the 'Aliened American,'" features this opening stanza:

My country, 'tis of thee,
Dark land of Slavery,
In thee we groan.
Long have our chains been worn—
Long has our grief been borne—
Our flesh has long been torn—
E'en from our bones.

One of the more interesting features of the antislavery songs is how completely they echo the entire myth. "Convention" (1836) by M. W. Chapman declares that as long as we are "Bound with the bondsman" we may not "utter the patriot's prayer"; it then goes on to ask people to throng from "your mountain's green" and from your "hill-tops white" to take a stand for freedom. Similarly, John Greenleaf Whittier's "Original Hymn," which appeared in *The Liberator* in 1838, begins by evoking the mytheme of the patriots:

> Oh, Thou, whose presence went before
> Our fathers in their weary way,
> As with Thy chosen moved of yore
> The fire by night—the cloud by day!

And then he immediately moves into the role of God:

> When from each temple of the free
> A nation's song ascends to Heaven,
> Most Holy Father!—unto Thee
> May not our humble prayer be given?

The suggestion that God may be removing his blessings from the nation is an effective technique, but he is quick to point out in the next stanza that he knows that all God's children, "though hue and form/Are varied in Thine own good will," have been fashioned in His image. In the next two stanzas he recalls the blessings of the land ("hill and plain/Around us wave their fruits once more") and that we possess peace and hope and love.

All of this is but a preface to heighten the tragedy of slavery, for those who "And bound in SLAVERY's fetters still" can not thrill to the joy of these blessings. From this point on he shows how much more blessed we will be as earth and people in concert praise the abolition of slavery:

> Behold the cane-fields smile,
> In living green arrayed;
> They wave their flags, and sing meanwhile
> "Our laborers are paid."
> Praise ye the Lord, Hallelujah.

The use of the "living green" suggests that the country will be regenerated once slavery is abolished. This theme is quite common. In William Lloyd Garrison's "Independence Day" (1841), the author states in his last stanza that once oppression has been effaced and the tyrant's rod broken by the moral powers, "Then a glorious jubilee we'll keep/On Independence Day." In other words, we really cannot celebrate our independence until we have reclaimed the moral vision embodied in our special divine mission.

The abolitionists, then, did not carve out any new ground in dealing with the myth, but they were among the first to hint at problems that would haunt twentieth-century songwriters. They are among the first to highlight the anomalous relationship between reality and the myth; they chose not to question the myth, but only to ask that the country renew its promise to live the myth and be true to its special mission. In fact, they effectively used the myth to demonstrate that the failure to secure the blessings of democracy for one individual—regardless of "hue or form"—is to jeopardize the blessings of freedom and opportunity for the entire national community.

We see, in the songs preceding the Civil War some minor changes taking place in the myth. We have not reached a juncture, as we will in the 1960s, where the fundamental assumptions of the myth are seriously questioned. The major change comes in presenting the mytheme of the land. The nineteenth-century songwriters although they appreciate the national landscape in new ways, see nothing anomalous with the image depicted in the songs of previous generations. Instead, in these songs the landscape performs an expanded cosmological function. In place of the "desart," which symbolized struggle and ultimate renewal, the nineteenth-century songwriter attempts to show that the land is a metaphor for God's bounty and the gift of freedom. In essence, there is a sense that the country has become a New Israel. Michael K. Stone (1976) notes that the hymn "The God of the Fathers," found in an 1845 hymnal, suggests that the "nation is no longer just Israel incarnate, but an improvement on the original":

> Like Israel's hosts to exile driven,
>   Across the flood the pilgrims fled;
> Their hands bore up the ark of Heaven,
>   And heaven their trusting footsteps led,
> Till on these savage shores they trod,
> And won the wilderness for God.
>
> Then, where their weary ark found rest,
>   Another Zion proudly grew;
> In more than Judah's glory dressed,

With light that Israel never knew.
From sea to sea her empire spread,
Her temple Heaven, Christ her head (136).

One almost immediately recognizes familiar images: the ark, the wilderness, light. In addition one recognizes new images, which will influence later versions of the myth, most notably the phrase "sea to sea" which echoes the images of the expansive idea of manifest destiny. The mytheme of the land in the songs of this period represents boundless boundaries: breadth, grandeur, glory, bounty, differences, and unity.

In the early nineteenth century, then, the "final" version of the myth of America was established. The first real test of this myth would come in midcentury as the country discovered that it did, indeed, have profound disagreements, which could only be reconciled in a savage war. Thus myth *does* transcend history; for if Americans had found a common ground in their acceptance of the values perpetuated in these images and themes, they differed on what they meant.

CHAPTER IV   **"Who Shall Rule**
This American Nation?"
The Civil War Era

Who shall rule And so wrote Henry Clay Work in 1866.
this American Nation? The lyrics show plainly that this is a
Say, boys, say! blast at the defeated South, but ironi-
Who shall rule cally the title might have been chosen
this American Nation? by a rabid confederate as well. The
Say, boys, say! South believed as firmly as the North
Shall the men that it should rule this American na-
who trampled on the tion, that Southerners were as much
banner? heir to the spirit of manifest destiny as
They who would now any Yankee. They had, after all, sup-
their country betray? ported a number of "filibustering" ex-
They who murder peditions into Cuba and Central Amer-
the innocent freedmen? ica in the hopes of finding territory
Say, boys, say!* congenial to their peculiar institution:
slavery. Their failed efforts forced them
back on their own resources and those of the continent proper and
inspired the fierce struggle over slavery in the newly admitted states.
Opposition to their peculiar institution was strong from the North,

*Unless otherwise cited, songs in this chapter are from either Richard
Crawford, ed., *The Civil War Songbook* (New York: Dover, 1977) or Irwin
Silber, ed., *Songs of the Civil War* (New York: Columbia University Press,
1960).

and as Eileen Southern notes, as early as 1857 the famed Dred Scot decision made the armed clash inevitable (1983, 225). Both sides, indeed, had seen the coming of the Lord, but only one could rule the American nation.

Music was important in Civil War years. The war produced a staggering output of songs from both sides. Vera Brodsky Lawrence estimates that "more than two thousand [songs] were reported published during the first year alone" (1975, 341). The songs, moreover, dealt with every aspect of the conflict from "The First Gun Is Fired" to "The Soldier Coming Home." Songs such as "John Brown's Body" or "The Battle Hymn of the Republic," "The Battle Cry of Freedom," and "Dixie" were the songs that sustained soldiers on long marches. Robert E. Lee is reported to have said, "I don't believe we can have any army without music" (Bowman 1987, 91). The songs weren't merely vicarious venting of emotions. They had, on occasion, palpable and electrifying significance. It is reported that, during a period of particularly low morale among the Union troops in 1863, a glee club sang "The Battle Cry of Freedom" for the men. According to David Ewen, "One unidentified soldier remarked that the song 'ran through the camp like wildfire. The effect was little short of miraculous. It put as much spirit and cheer into the camp as a splendid victory. Day and night you could hear it by every campfire in every tent'" (1977, 77). This may be apocryphal, but even if it is, the fact that legends such as this would survive attests to the power of music during the war years. Songs such as "Tenting Tonight" and "All Quiet Along the Potomac," on the other hand, allowed Americans to give vent to the fears and sadness that accompany any armed conflict. It is not surprising then to encounter quotes like that of the Southern major who remarked, "'Gentlemen, if we had had your songs, we'd have licked you out of your boots'" (Ewin, 1977, 72).

There is something else that becomes apparent as we examine the songs of the era. By focusing on the myth of America as it was sung by both sides, we can better appreciate the truly tragic nature of the war. Both sides held to the basic myth as it had been perpetuated since Revolutionary War times. They evoked the same mythemes to support their cause and stake their claims to justice and liberty. The differences between the two sides are only subtly revealed in some of the songs. The myth, therefore, was essential to their songs, because so many contradictions and conflicts needed to be addressed in the war. The chief contradiction was, of course, the fact that fellow countrymen were spilling one another's blood, giving the lie to a belief in America as one nation under God.

The South's claim to the myth centered ironically around the agrarian base of their culture and the "peculiar institution" of slavery. An Alabamian wrote in 1858: "'Ours is an agricultural people, and God grant that we may continue so. It is the freest, happiest, most independent, and with us, the most powerful condition on earth'" (McPherson 1988, 99). They believed that this agrarian culture could not be sustained without slaves and, moreover, that the slave wanted it that way, too. Southerners, if asked why they fought, would respond as Jefferson Davis did: that they were fighting for the same "'sacred right of self-government'" that our revolutionary forebears had fought for (McPherson 1988, 311).

As one looks at the quote of that Alabamian and Davis one must be struck by certain terms—"independent," "happiest and freest," "self-government"—words which we have encountered in previous songs dealing with the myth. The paradox in the songs of the South is that their "freedom" was predicated on their ability to keep another people in bondage. They enjoyed the fruits of the Declaration, the Constitution, and the sacrifice that had been made by their forebears, and they had the right, like any American, to do what they pleased. Northerners could do as they pleased. Therefore, should not Southerners be treated *equally* and be allowed to live the life they thought best? In short, prior to the outbreak of hostilities, Southerners truly felt that the North was intent upon excluding them from the blessings of life, liberty, and the pursuit of happiness. In the spirit of their forefathers they would not submit to any tyrant. Consequently, in the songs of the Confederacy not much is made of the actual differences that separate them from the North. Instead, the songwriters refer to the Union as tyrants and vandals—sometimes the "vandals" is capitalized, suggesting the invading hordes who overran ancient Rome.

Well, the Northerners were vandals. What were the Confederates? The word that appears most often is "traitor." Metonymy and personification figure a lot in the songs of the Union. Henry Clay Work's stirring "Marching Through Georgia" (1865) states, "Treason fled before us, for resistance was in vain." While J. G. Clark's "The Children of the Battle Field" (1864) contains the following passage:

Upon the field of Gettysburg
The summer was high,
When Freedom met her haughty foe,
Beneath a northern sky.

There would be no mistaking the personification of freedom with the forces of the Union. These passages, furthermore, underscore the conflict as it is presented in most of the songs. We will see that Northern songwriters differ little from their Southern counterparts in presentation of the essentials of the myth.

But as they fought, the North used "Dixie's Land" against the south and the south used "Yankee Doodle" against the North, each side supplying its own lyrics to the enemy's tune in actions reminiscent of the balladeers of the Revolutionary War using English tunes against them. Such was the case with "Maryland, My Maryland!" (1861) and "The Battle Cry of Freedom" (1862). Each side tried to show that the other side was the outsider, attacking the fundamental mission of the country. Each side portrayed itself as the defender. It is, in a sense, the myth that each side was defending.

Both sides needed the myth to reconcile troubling contradictions and conflicts raised by the nature of the war itself. Both sides needed, to preserve a sense of national community while at the same time sustaining the notion of individual rights (or sectional, regional, or state's rights). As a result, we have a number of songs which seem to deal with all the mythemes, much like "America" or "My Country, 'Tis of Thee." But there is also a considerable body of songs that may evoke only one or two of the individual mythemes. One song, for instance, will focus on the patriot's mytheme and perhaps that of manifest destiny, while another will deal with the mytheme of the land and the freedom mytheme. The myth then comes together almost mosaiclike and cumulatively from different songs. This is, a pattern we shall observe in future songs dealing with war, and so my approach here—and in the songs of World War I and World War II for that matter—will be to look at how each side treated the individual mythemes, rather than the myth in toto.

The obvious starting point is the role of God in the conflict and the mytheme of manifest destiny. As one might expect, both sides claimed God was on their side. George F. Root, that most prolific of Northern Civil War songwriters, claimed in his "Just Before the

Battle, Mother" (1861), "Now may God protect us, Mother/As He ever does the right." Similarly, the "Southern Song of Freedom" states: "The God of our fathers looks down/And blesses the cause of the just"—a line that also evokes the mytheme of the patriot's sacrifice. Thus both sides claimed God's protection and guidance and, by extension, the right to engage in war. The songs, in fact, portray war as a moral necessity. The song that makes this most obvious is "The Battle Hymn of the Republic." It seems to have little or no relevance to the myth of America, but in the context of the Civil War, its presentation of the conflict as second coming is a powerful image. The Union army, could readily see themselves as the soldiers of Christ: As Christ trampled out the vintage, so would they; they were his regents on earth. The lyrics state, "Let the hero born of woman crush the serpent with his heel." This is a reference to the salvific vision of Christianity, but it also had a more immediate meaning for Union forces. Kent Bowman writes, "The second intended meaning in this line is the thought that secession, like slavery is evil. Equating the Union cause with Christ's mission" (1977, 98). Thus, the troubling issue of engaging in mortal conflict with one's fellow countrymen is made palatable and given the urgency of a moral mission.

The Unionists also saw themselves, like their forebears, fulfilling the Mosaic tradition of leading a chosen people to a better world. Bernard Covert's "Can I Go, Dearest Mother" (1862) contains the following lines: "He who led His chosen people, in their efforts to be free/From the tyranny of Egypt, will be merciful to me." The idea that the Americans are a chosen people was still a compelling notion in the 1860s, and although one does not find as many references to spreading democracy as in previous tunes, there are occasional suggestions that the world must be watching as we secure liberty and freedom for all; as Henry Clay Work's "Marching Through Georgia" states in the opening stanza: "Bring the good old bugle, boys! we'll sing another song—/Sing it with a spirit that will start the world along."

The Confederacy made equal claim to God's role in the destiny of their nation. In fact, they produced a couple of songs that compellingly declare that they, and not the North, are the true inheritors of our manifest destiny. Albert Pike's variation on "Dixie's Land" (1861) begins by accusing the North of "faith betrayed and pledges broken/Wrongs inflicted, insults spoken," and then goes on to encourage Southerners to

> Swear upon your country's altar
> Never to submit or falter! . . .
> Till the spoilers are defeated,
> Till the Lord's work is completed.

The reader might find the use of the sprightly melody of "Dixie" for the heavy-handed sentiments of Pike's lyrics a bit disconcerting. However, as we think back on the songs of the Revolutionary War and look forward to those of World War I and World II, it is important to note that sense of urgency created by getting songs out to the public during wartime often militates against aesthetic considerations and, sometimes, good taste. There are not many William Billings amongst popular songwriters and, interestingly enough, many of our greatest popular composers do not have significant war songs to their credit. The war song always runs the risk that its sentiments may not be compatible with current musical styles. Consequently, during World War I one finds some rather nasty denunciations of the "huns" couched in ragtime inspired melodies and rhythms. In some of those cases the intent is humorous, in others it is not, but it comes off as such. On the other hand, some of the songs written during World War II completely eschew the aesthetic standards of the day and harken back to the sounds of the previous war because the harmonic language characteristic of the 1940s would make the sentiments of the songs—sentiments which would be applied to past wars—seem, perhaps, too sophisticated and, therefore, too detached or cool. Whatever the case, as one listens to the songs of our past wars today one cannot help but experience, to borrow a phrase from T. S. Eliot, a certain dissociation of sensibility.

Confederates saw themselves as trampling out the vintage where the grapes of wrath were stored. And they saw themselves living out the promise of the Declaration of Independence as is evident in these lines:

> Halt not till our Federation
> Secures among the earth's powers its station!
> Then at peace, and crowned with glory,
> Hear your children tell the story!

This is similar to many of the songs of the Revolutionary War era, where the songwriters declared that the war was the Lord's work and that it was necessary to secure these blessings into the future. Finally, one Southern songwriter went to the Old Testament to find some figure who symbolized their cause. A. E. Blackmar's "Southron's Chaunt of Defiance" (1861) uses the David and Goliath tale to frame the nature of their struggle:

But the battle to the strong
  Is not given,
While the Judge of right and wrong
  Sits in heaven
And the God of David still
Guides the pebble with His will,
There are giants yet to kill,
  Wrongs unshriven!

The image of there being "giants *yet* to kill" (emphasis mine) nicely suggests that the Southerner's cause is one with historical—as well as moral—precedent and that it is a struggle that is destined to be and must continue. This idea of the ongoing struggle, in a sense, also then reinforces the notion of manifest destiny.

One might have noticed in the above songs an interesting piece of imagery: the altar. The image of the altar is used in conjunction with the mythemes of God's role and manifest destiny and is one of the ways in which the songwriters from both sides reinforce the transcendental function of the myth. The image had been used previously in "Hail Columbia" (1798) and is used in similar fashion here to suggest the common person's role in the nation's great mission. Julia Ward Howe used it in her "Battle Hymn," where she wrote, "They have builded Him an altar in the evening dews and damps." But others employed it even more effectively to suggest the metaphysical dimensions of the struggle. "Can I Go, Dearest Mother," for instance, has the young narrator saying, "Or should this, my bleeding country, need a victim such as me,/I am nothing more than others who perished to be free,/On her bosom let me slumber; on her altar let me die." Similarly, Southern songwriter Will S. Hays mixes the powerful secular symbols of mother and home with the religious image of heaven in his classic "The Drummer Boy of Shiloh" (1863):

"Oh, Mother," said the dying boy,
  "Look down from heaven on me,
Receive me to thy fond embrace—
  Oh take me home to thee."

And in a later stanza he pictures the boy's Confederate comrades standing beside his grave: "The flag his winding—sheet—God's Book/The key unto his grave." In short, the sacrifice for the country will assure him his place in heaven. The idea of sacrifice is a powerful one because it shows the individual playing a key role in the destiny of the nation. The notion of manifest destiny then becomes less an abstract blueprint, where the entire community plays some ineffable role in spreading the fruits of democracy, and more an expression of the individual's role in the history of his/her country. As one sings these songs, one may indeed feel that he/she is walking in the footsteps of the Lord.

In the myth, the vision of who should rule this American nation is built upon the struggle and sacrifices of our patriotic forebears. Both sides in the Civil War claimed that their "forefathers" began the struggle which they are now carrying on. "The New York Volunteer" (1862), for instance, states:

'Twas in the days of seventy-six,
When Freemen young and old,
All fought for Independence then,
Each hero brave and bold.

While his Southern counterpart declares in "God Save the South" (c. 1861):

Rebels before
Our fathers of yore;
  Rebel's the righteous name
Washington bore.

One Northern writer, John Hogarth Lozier, drew heavily on imagery and symbols from previous songs associated with the myth in his "The Old Union Wagon" (1863), which was inspired by the Emancipation Proclamation. In the second stanza he writes: "The makers of our wagon were men of solid wit,/They made it out of 'Charter Oak' that would not rot or split." The allusion here is to the Liberty Tree, which we encountered quite often in songs of the Revolution. He then goes on to link the charter they drafted with the war they fought: "Our wagon bed is strong enough for any revolution,/In fact, 'tis the 'hull' of the old Constitution" (quoted in Lawrence 1975, 390). One could, of course, read Constitution in two ways: It could be the actual document or it could be the famous fighting ship. He goes on to show how the nation "admired" the Union wagon and how it "was the glory of the world," which is his way of stating that the first claim to the true goals of the Revolution and the Constitution must fall to the North.

In conjunction with the image of the Pilgrim settlers and the patriots of '76 a new symbol is added: the flag. The remainder of the verse to "The New York Volunteer" states:

'Twas then the noble Stars and Stripes
In Triumph did appear,
And defended by brave patriots,
The Yankee Volunteers

In the songs of the Civil War, the flag—and actually the flag of the South as well—becomes symbolic of the patriot's sacrifice. The Northern songwriters enjoy painting the portrait of the Southerner desecrating the flag. For instance, "The Hero of Fort Sumter" (1861) by Anna Bache and C. Munzinger states: "When factional hand debased the flag/Our fathers raised so high" (quoted in Heaps 1960, 16). While a Northern parody of "Dixie" declares:

Away down South where grows the cotton,
Seventy-six seems quite forgotten;
  Far away, far away, far away Dixie land.
And men with rebel shout and thunder
Tear our good old flag asunder" (50)

In another tune, "Rally Round the Flag Boys"—don't confuse with "Battle Cry of Freedom," which uses the same line as a chorus— Northern songwriters James T. Field and William B. Bradbury state: "Their flag is but a rag, Ours is the true one."

Of course, the South wouldn't agree with that. Irwin Silber notes, "A favorite theme of the inspiration and propaganda songs of the Confederacy was the glory of the South and the new nation" (1960, 49). In short, Southerners saw what they were doing as a reenactment of the struggle of 1776. James Pierpoint, the composer of "Jingle Bells," wrote in 1861: "Go forth in the pathway our forefathers trod,/ We too fight for Freedom, our Captain is God,/Their blood in our veins, with their honors we vie." And they too used the symbol of the flag to rally support and focus their ideas. The most famous "flag song" is probably "Bonnie Blue Flag" (1861) written by Harry MacCarthy and set to the tune of "The Irish Jaunting Car" of the 1850s. The songwriter uses the conspiracy theme to establish the reason why they fight—a device employed by songwriters during the Revolutionary War and the early nineteenth century when the country was threatened by war with both France and England.

> As long as the Union was faithful to her trust,
> Like friends and like brothers kind we were and just;
> But now, when Northern treachery attempts our right to mar,
> We hoist on high, the bonnie blue flag that bears a single star.

"The Bonnie Blue Flag" is also notable as the one song that clearly identifies a cause for the conflict: "We are a band of brothers, and native to the soil,/Fighting for the property we gained by honest toil." This imagery draws on some basic values that Americans had grown to cherish: property and hard work. Once these principles are established, the songwriter then provides what could loosely be termed an epic catalog of the states who are involved in the "revolution" to show the scope of support. He then adds in the last verse: "Then here's to our Confederacy—strong we are and brave,/Like patriots of old, we'll fight our heritage to save."

The sentiments are very similar to those of the Northern writers, which is probably why this particular song inspired a Northern version. It draws immediately on the symbol of the flag: "To protect our country's glorious flag,/That glitters with many a star." The songwriter goes on to say:

> False to their vows, and to the flag
>   That once protected them,
> They sought the union to dissolve,
>   Earth's noblest brightest gem.

The oblique reference to manifest destiny in the last line provides the perfect lead-in for the first lines of the last stanza:

> We're in the right and will prevail,
>   The Stars and Stripes must fly,
> The "bonnie blue flag" be hauled down,
>   And every traitor die.

Thus to tear down the Stars and Stripes is to sully the symbol, as one song put it, which speaks "loud to all hearts/Of a freedom won . . . [and] Bought with precious blood."

In retrospect, each side saw themselves as continuing the mission of their forebears in establishing freedom and the rights of the individual. The issues are not clearly defined. Songwriters instead employ the symbol of the flag to galvanize emotions, focus mythic memories, suggest simple truths, and finally differentiate ideological positions. The flag then was an important symbol. It signified, as e. e. cummings said of World War I, what it was everyone was fighting for: the self-same things their forefathers had fought for, virtues that would make Columbia the Gem of the Ocean—freedom and liberty. That both sides could go into battle with the images of Washington and other Revolutionary War heroes before them and slaughter one another in the spirit of 1776 is only one measure of the tragic dimensions of this war.

Let us next look at the freedom, opportunity, and equality mytheme. "The First Gun Is Fired" (1861), written by George F. Root shortly after the fall of Fort Sumter, uses the mytheme of the patriot's sacrifice to bring these ideals into focus. Root encourages the "freeborn sons of the north" to avenge the wrong, and then he asks in the second stanza:

> Shall the glorious Union our fathers made,
>> By ruthless hands be sundered,
> And we of freedom's sacred rights
>> By trait'rous foes be plundered?

In general, Northerners saw themselves carrying on the tradition of the Pilgrim forebears of beating a path for freedom through the wilderness. Henry Clay Work's "Marching Through Georgia"—although it speaks specifically of bringing literal freedom to the slaves —goes on to evoke a more abstract kind of freedom: "So we made a thoroughfare for Freedom and her train"; this sentiment and imagery will be echoed thirty years later in Katherine Lee Bates' "America the Beautiful." Songwriters were also quick to point out that the secular ideals underlying the Declaration and the Constitution were first drafted in the divine plan of the Almighty. This theme is picked up by Charles C. Sawyer and Henry Tucker in their sentimental hit, "Weeping, Sad and Lonely, or When This Cruel War is

Over" (1862) where the mother of the soldier asks that "Angels cheer" her son's way and then encourages him:

Nobly strike for God and liberty,
  Let all nations see
How we love our starry banner,
  Emblem of the free.

When one strikes a blow for liberty, one simultaneously strikes a blow for God. The song contains other allusions as well; the symbol of the flag; the mytheme of manifest destiny, implicit in the allusion to God's role; the implied boast that all nations were watching. The last might imply that other countries are poised to invade and drive a wedge into the Union, but the line also suggests that America is now a world power and, the hope of the world, because of its divine mission to spread liberty and freedom.

Finally, occasional Northern songs seemed to deal head-on with the issues that aggravated the conflict. George F. Root's great "The Battle of Cry of Freedom" (1862) states in the third stanza: "And altho' he may be poor he shall never be slave." But one notices here that Root does not focus on race as the issue, but instead wraps the conflict in the cloak of economic disparity. The majority of songs, that enjoyed widespread appeal seldom dealt with the issue of slavery. The Union songwriter seems to have echoed Lincoln's sentiments, when he declared in his first inaugural address, March 4, 1861, "I have no purpose, directly or indirectly, to interfere with the institution of slavery in the States where it exists." There were some, however, who felt music could be used to "interfere" in the issue.

Antislavery songs continued to play a role during the war years. These songs did clearly outline the ideological conflicts inherent in the war but did not deal with the war itself. As we saw in the previous chapter, these songs, because they attack the ideological foundations of the country, truly dealt with the whole myth of America and bring into relief how fundamental the myth was to the conflict then raging. In "The Patriot's Banner. A Parody" (1858) by "S.G.C.," set to the tune of the "Star Spangled Banner," we find that the banner waves "O'er the land no more free—'tis the land of the slave!" The songwriters claim in the first stanza that the sacrifice of the previous generation is seriously called into question because of the existence of slavery. Later the songwriter says that those who fought for "their nation's just rights" are "gone from the earth but their children remain/To witness the shame, and to see the foul stain/On the star spangled banner..." And in the final stanza, they call upon God, who, they pray, will lift His "own banner against each dark foe" and once again allow the star spangled banner to "glow" (quoted in Eaklor 1988, 221). There were countless other songs like this, sung during the war years. Taken in tandem with a growing body of Emancipation songs, they provided Union forces with a rationale for fighting that was grounded in religious belief, historical necessity, social conscience, and belief in reform.

The Southern perspective on the ideological origins of the conflict differs little from the Northern one—with, of course, the exception of the antislavery songs. One of the first tunes written to celebrate the southern secession, "The Palmetto State Song" (c. 1861) begins with imagery that could have been lifted from a Revolutionary War song:

> All hail to the dawn of this glor'ous morning,
> The genius of liberty lights from the skies,
> Points to the Palmetto, our banner adorning,
> And bids us at once from our slumbers to rise!

In short, liberty is the issue, and making a claim similar to the Northern combatants, they state that "Like freemen [will] stand, or... perish in glory." Southerners portrayed themselves in song as being treated unequally, claiming they were denied their rights and being "ground beneath the tyrant's heal/For [their] demands of justice...." ("The Southern Soldier," Silber, 1960, 217–18). "The South" (1862) by "C," a clumsy parody of Burns's "Scots wha Hal," underscores the irony inherent in the stated claims of the South to go to war:

> Now's the day, and now's the hour;
> See the front of battle lower;
> See approach fanatic Lincoln's power,
>   Chains and Slavery.

They felt they "must strike for FREEDOM" and "Lay those Vandal hordes low," and they believed they would persevere because "Liberty's in every blow."

Thus, in songs, the issues that separated North and South become pretty murky. The stated reasons for going to war degenerate ultimately into name calling—one group is vandals, the other traitors —and in the end all that is left is the resolve to, as "The Southern Soldier" states, "die for my home and land . . . Upon my country's altar." Thus, both sides reaffirm the mytheme of freedom, liberty, opportunity, and equality. It is in the issue of equality and the ironies inherent in the Southern claim that we come nearest to observing a genuine cause for war.

"Who shall rule this American nation" was the central question of the war, and part of that question is the issue of "nation." In previous generations the idea of "nation" was largely defined by ideology. But beginning in the nineteenth century the mytheme of the land played an ever-increasing role in that definition. During the war, "nation" presented problems for the songwriter. The land now was clearly divided, one's sense of place distorted. One could no longer identify the standard boundaries (ocean to ocean, southern gulfs to northern woods); similarly, as the boundaries disappear, so does the meaning inherent in them: the nation's bounty. Consequently, war songs seldom evoke the vast bounteous land.

War songs are different from standard songs dealing with the myth of America, especially those written after the War of 1812. These war songs no longer raise the question of what is America? Instead they evoke the image of the land to suggest unity and community. And, because war songs often have narrators (soldiers, mothers, sweethearts, children), there is a different perspective on the idea of homeland. In fact, what becomes more important is not the land itself but the home. In times of war the symbols most often used to suggest the land were home and mother. Let us first look at the image of land as symbol of unity.

Songwriters of the North and South both try to convey a sense of the unified effort in the sweep of the country. William Cullen Bryant's and L. O. Emerson's stirring "We Are Coming Father Abra'am" (1862) anticipates Woody Guthrie in identifying the boundaries and then associating the breadth of those boundaries with dedication to the cause: "From Mississippi's winding stream and New England's shore;/We leave our plows and workshops our wives and children dear." Similarly, the "Southern Song of Freedom" states:

> They gather from morass and mountain,
>   They gather from prairie and mart,
> To drink, at young Liberty's fountain,
>   The nectar that kindles the heart.

The last lines nicely tie in the regeneration or rebirth theme, and this song also employs images from the land to help the singer/listener associate a sense of place with the noble cause.

> All hail to the land of the pine!
> The home of the noble and free;
> A palmetto wreath we'll entwine
> Round the altar of young liberty.

The ever-present palmetto emblemizes South Carolina, the state where secession was first declared, and by extension the entire Confederate cause. The imagery, moreover, like that of the songs of the North, reinforces the close union of sacred and secular in the establishment of Southern liberty and rights. Considering the affection Southerners had for the soil, it is surprising that the mytheme of the land does not play a stronger role in their songs. One of the few Southern songs in which it does is "The Southern Cross," and even then it uses the mytheme, chiefly as a jumping-off point for a comment about the North:

> How peaceful and blest was American soil
> 'Til betrayed by the guile of the Puritan demon,
> Which lurks under Virtue, and springs from its coil,
> To fasten its fangs in the life blood of Freemen.

The inversion of the Edenic myth is effective in reinforcing the Confederacy's belief that they had been betrayed by serpents parading in saints' clothing

In the images of home and mother that dominate the songs of the Civil War, we see the soldier not fighting for abstract principles but for those symbols closest to his daily life, principally mothers. To nineteenth-century audiences the image of Mother alone was enough to evoke home, family, native soil, and all. Nina Auerbach notes of Victorian images of women and home, "Mid-century feminist policy worked toward greater equity for women within existing institutions of education, marriage, and law, but the fundamental equivalence of woman and home was scarcely questioned" (1982, 43). Quite a few examples of "mother" songs have been cited thus far. Here's another, "The Conscript's Mother" by Henry Bedlow, typical of both Union and Confederate songs. In the first stanza the mother declares that she is saddened that her son is going to war but that she will let him "behold not my grief but my pride." She asks if her "womanish fears" should interfere "When the flag of his country is scorned and defied?" That question is answered in the following stanza:

> He's my all, he's my treasure! But take him dear land,
> And add him, a jewel to Liberty's crown.
> One hero the more to your patriot's band,
> The widows last mite to the nation's renown.
> (Quoted in Heaps 1960, 94)

The bounty of the land is no longer its rich topography but the willingness of the mother to sacrifice her "treasure," her son. But there is the assurance that, in making this sacrifice, she will achieve a sense of transcendence. The young man, so painfully sacrificed, becomes a part of history and "the nation's renown."

The mother song functions as something of a parable for what a nation hopes to achieve through war: the country (mother) may have to sacrifice the bountiful present (our youth) in order to perpetuate those ideals, that we have fought for in the past, and once again to restore the bounty of the land for future generations.

What did the slaves and ex-slaves sing? As one might suspect, the Civil War did not produce a large body of music from African-Americans dealing with the myth of America. The songs of the slaves, which have come down to us through oral tradition or through recorded versions from the time, are predominantly spirituals. Higginson (1962, 187–213) devotes a whole chapter to the rousing or plaintive songs of his men. Black soldiers would also sing songs by white composers; "John Browns' Body," according to Eileen Southern, was an especial favorite (1983, 231).

The worldview that dominates the music of the African-American during these years is conditioned by two general factors: first, religion and the Bible; second, their African culture and its song patterns. The idea of a better world, for the slave does not often seem to be that of a reconstructed America but, instead, heaven (or, in a few rare cases, passage back to Africa). Like the Pilgrims, they saw their condition as similar to that of Moses leading his people out of bondage; unlike the Pilgrims, what they wanted was not the New Canaan but forty acres and a mule. Tragically, they found neither.

They liked to see their plight in Biblical terms. In one song cited by Miles Mark Fisher, a black soldier sang that he and his comrades had successfully crossed over the river (i.e., the conflict itself) but that, "O, Pharaoh's army drowned," a not too thinly veiled allusion to the Confederate forces (1968, 153). In another stanza the singer states they will cross the River Jordan, a common motif in spirituals. Not surprisingly, nowhere does one find references to the principles of the Declaration and Constitution or to the sacrifice of the patriots. But when taught "white" songs, like William Bradbury's "Marching Along," they sang those lustily too. We have seen with what fervor ex-slaves sang "My Country! 'Tis of Thee."

The true voice of African-American was represented, chiefly in the spiritual ("Go Down Moses," "Many Thousands Go," and innumerable others), but in what is more relevant to the national mythology, a fictional kind of ex-slave was given life by dialect songs, such as Henry Clay Work's phenomenally successful "Kingdom's Coming" (1862), which shows the African-American triumphant over buffoonlike Southern overseers. The humor in the songs—largely communicated through mangled English and satirical jabs at Southerners—tends to mitigate what could be a true celebration of the "Year of Jubilo." Occasionally, however, one will find a nondialect song, like the "Colored Volunteer" (c. 1862), which presents a serious portrait of blacks engaged in the war; this particular song, not surprisingly, differs little from those numbers dealing with the condition of white soldiers:

> Give us the flag, all free without one slave,
> And we will defend it as our fathers did so brave.
> Onward! boys, onward! it's the year of Jubilee,
> God bless America, the land of liberty.

Most interestingly—and perhaps fittingly—this may be the most complete statement of the myth in all of the songs of the Civil War. The dominant mythemes are all present, and the lyrics nicely remind the singer/listener that slavery is a central problem in achieving and perpetuating the dream of freedom for which the patriots fought so valiantly. That it actually issued from the mouths of a black regiment is, of course, highly suspect. Instead, like dialect numbers, it represents a white perspective on the condition of the freedman.

Finally, war—even the "good" war, fought defensively and for moral causes—leaves scars. The Civil War, perhaps more than any other war in our history, left scars that must have seemed unhealable.

It is not surprising then, that a dominant theme in songs of the Civil War is that of regeneration and God's providential role in the country's future. James Oliver Robertson states:

> The Civil War was the visitation of God's wrath on the land, but the hell and destruction had a useful purpose. Out of it, in the myth, came national growth, expansion, progress, and "reconstruction." . . . War, in the myth, then, was the means of organizing and unifying Americans and their resources to accomplish the great ideals of the nation." (1980, 89)

Thus, in the songs, we find many references to the "year of Jubilee," "redemption," "sacrifice," and allusions to the Second Coming.

"The Faded Coat of Blue" (1865), offers the hope to the living that the sacrifice of a young man's life means that we'll "find you and know you among the good and true,/When a robe of white is giv'n for the faded coat of blue." The major challenge for the song-writer, however, was to reconcile the terrible destruction, the sundering of a nation, with what was gained. Henry Clay Work's "'Tis Finished! or Sing Hallelujah" (1865) states that our "brightest era ever known" has commenced with the overthrow of our enemies, and that the bells have not sung as sweetly,

> Since angels in the advent sang,
> Your message in gladness
> To myriads of waiting souls,
> As onward and world-ward
> The happy, happy echo rolls. (Quoted in Lawrence in 1975, 434)

The suggestion of the manifest destiny mytheme is also strong in this song as it is in "National Jubilee" (1865) by Carlos Wilcox and Konrad Treuer, where they note in the first stanza that all people are free as the "Jubilee hath sounded—/Universal Liberty." And it is carried on in the third stanza:

> Upon the brow of millions
> God hath placed the crown of light,
> And the host of their oppressors
> He hath 'whelmed in endless night.
> We'll shout aloud the triumph
> Through the world, from pole to pole.
> Be the boon for all defended
> As the birth-right of the soul.

The victors, the song suggests, now enjoy the light of wisdom, truth, and liberation while the enemy suffer the same fate as the fallen angels. Moreover the message contained in this event will be sounded throughout the world, since the preservation and protection of our original charter is a boon for people everywhere. One sees then in these songs that the audience is being asked to look beyond, to transcend the carnage and destruction to find an "ultimate" purpose in it all.

Songwriters fell back on archetypal images of rebirth to emphasize the glory of the nation reborn. "The Hero's Grave" by T. H. Howe mixes a number of powerful images drawn from past history, religion, and nature to paint a portrait of a nation renewed.

> Dig his grave where the soft green sod
> By traitors' feet has never trod,
> Where sweet flowers are the smile of God
>   For the patriot pure and true.
> There let a graceful fadeless tree,
> Emblem of hope and liberty,
> Rise, while his epitaph there shall be
>   Sweet flowers red, white, and blue. (Quoted in Heaps 1960, 380)

This must have resonated strongly with postwar audiences. They might possibly identify the allusion to the liberty tree, and they would most assuredly recognize the allusion to the flag. They would also be moved by the metaphor of the flowers as the smile of God (i.e., approving of this young man). The flowers, moreover, suggest the theme of God regenerating His chosen nation.

Southerners also found consolation in the images of nature as we see in "Old Stonewall" by C. D. Dasher and F. Younker:

> The harvest waves over the battlefield, boys,
> And where bullets once pattered like rain
> The peach blooms are drifting like snow in the air
> And the hillocks are springing in grain. (Quoted in Heaps 1960, 379)

There is, of course, more poignancy here, especially in the suggestion of the theme of rebirth, a sentiment which probably did not resonate as strongly among the Confederate ranks as it did among the Northern ones. Using the natural world as a universal referent, the songwriter reframes the April-showers-bring-May-flowers cliché in wartime terms, to show that the rain of bullets will now give way to the flowers of rebirth and healing. Whether a Southerner would see the bullets (like the rain) as restoring *his* "natural" world is questionable. But, again, the myth functions most effectively when it is at odds with history—when it directs our energies and thoughts to something beyond the pain of the present.

The songs reveal that Americans were anxious for healing and some sense of renewal—and perhaps for justification. They also continued to sing the songs of victory and discord. "Marching Through Georgia" would continue to haunt Southerners for decades, and "The Battle Hymn of the Republic" would take its place alongside "America," "Hail Columbia," and "The Star Spangled Banner" in church hymnals and would become a staple for that twentieth-century choral phenomenon, the Mormon Tabernacle Choir.

The myth would continue to play a role in our recollections of the war in future decades. One such song was Phillip Paul Bliss's "Hold the Fort" (1870), which was based on Sherman's wigwagged message to a Federal unit holding a besieged position at Allatoona Pass near Atlanta in 1864: "General Sherman says hold fast. We are coming." As one can see, retrospection enables the songwriter to ground the Union triumph even more firmly in the myth:

> "Hold the Fort, for I am coming,"
>   Jesus signals still
> Wave the answer back to Heaven,
>   "By thy Grace we will."
> See the mighty host advancing,
>   Satan leading on, . . .
> See the glorious banner waving
> Hear the bugles blow,
> In our Leader's name we'll triumph
> Over every foe.

Songs such as "Hold the Fort" demonstrate how doggedly Americans clung to the myth of America, how anxious they were to believe that the war had perpetuated the values of the "founders." But what is perhaps most significant about this song is that it really has less to do with postwar feelings than it does with fears for the future —"the mighty host advancing." Eventually this revival hymn was made into a labor song by the Knights of Labor and the British Transport Workers in the 1890s and entered the *IWW Songbook* in 1914.

Thus, in one sense, it actually contributed to the country's fears of future change.

In the next chapter, we will see that Americans, in the decades before and during the Great War, would experience great changes and would see their beliefs challenged on many fronts. They would continued singing the songs of the Civil War, but they would also write new songs to help them "Hold the Fort."

CHAPTER V

"A Thoroughfare for Freedom Beat"
From the End of the Civil War to the End of the Great War

The United States are destined either to surmount the gorgeous history of feudalism, or else prove the most tremendous failure of time. Not the least doubtful am I on any prospects of their material success.
—Walt Whitman, Democratic Vistas *(1871)*

There died a myriad, And of the best, among them, For an old bitch gone in the teeth, For a botched civilization.
—Ezra Pound, Hugh Selwyn Mauberley *(1925)*

Many profound changes took place in the country in the decades from the end of the Civil War to the end of World War I. The threat from the inside—the dissolution of the Union—was now past, but America found itself dealing with different kinds of threats, mostly economic and social. The country was rocked by a series of recessions and depressions (one of the worst in 1893); there was widespread labor unrest, resulting in violent strikes among textile, steel, and coal workers in 1882, the Haymarket Massacre of 1886, the Homestead Strike of 1892, and the Pullman Strike of 1894. This was, to some degree, a result of a shift in the economic and social base of the country, as we moved inexorably from an agrarian society to an industrial one. Cities boomed, and people left the farms. Composers of the period responded to this migration by yearning for those innocent rural days: "On the Banks of the Wabash" (Paul

Dresser, 1890) or "Down on the Farm" (Irving Berlin, 1914). Workers packed themselves and oftentimes large families into small tenements in factory cities while the Vanderbilts built $5 million summer homes away from the noise, congestion, and frustration of the cities. This sort of economic and cultural disparity led to a reevaluation of the very foundations of the democratic system by the Populists and later the Progressives.

Moreover, the nation was becoming a world power. In 1888, Edward Bellamy's novel *Looking Backward* saw a future world utopia, centered on Boston, by the year 2000. And as, James Oliver Robertson notes, "[Americans] had lived through, and some of them had fought in, John Hay's 'splendid little war,' the Spanish-American War of 1898, and found that a crusade *could* win an empire" (1980, 295).

With America's expansion into international affairs, its beacon light went out to others, and the United States witnessed a staggering increase in immigration especially from Eastern and Southern European countries. From 1865 until 1904 the country routinely averaged anywhere from 150,000 to 800,000 new citizens a year. Then in 1905 alone the number jumped to 1,026,499 and would top 1 million in 1906 and 1907. The immigration totals would exceed 1 million three more times before the outbreak of the Great War. Obviously, this surge of new citizens would have a dramatic impact on Tin Pan Alley. Many immigrants —Irving Berlin being the most famous example—found fame and fortune as either composers or publishers. Similarly, the new immigrants fed the grist mill of the songwriter by providing new stereotypes and themes for their tunes. For some this vast swelling tide of bewildered newcomers was confirmation of our role as democracy's best stronghold, and for others it was something to be viewed with dismay.

During this period, there was upheaval on the domestic front as votes for women became a wider and wider political issue. Moreover, tremendous technological change was taking place in the home. Witold Rybczynski notes that in American buildings, central heating, indoor plumbing, running hot and cold water, electric light, power elevators were all unknown before 1890 but were commonplace by 1920 (1986, 219). Housewives had meantime acquired gas ranges, washing machines, vacuum cleaners, electric irons, electric fans—to add to the even greater boons of the earlier linoleum (1860) and window screens (1885). Add to this, by 1920 Americans had witnessed the development of the major entertainment media of the first half century: movies, the phonograph, and, waiting in the wings, radio.

The music industry would centralize itself in New York and become a monolithic enterprise, shaping and perpetuating most of the major popular myths of the twentieth century. And as America underwent change, there was a growing need for clarification of what it was. Popular songwriters, safely ensconced in their cubicles in, first, Union Square and then later 28th Street in the fabled Tin Pan Alley, proved themselves more than up to the task.

Songwriters who chose to deal with the myth of America found there was a need to reaffirm a sense of unified purpose. The country appeared at times to be steadily unraveling at its very core. People desired to hold on to the values that had shaped the culture prior to the Civil War—values, they believed, that had allowed the North to persevere in that conflict and ultimately "free the slaves." Sen. Albert J. Beveridge noted that, "like it or not, the American people had become trustees 'under God' of world civilization. 'He made us the master organizers of the world to establish system where chaos reigns'" (Quoted in Thomas 1977, 981). Similarly, it was not unusual to hear leading thinkers of the day reiterate the idea that America had surpassed all previous civilizations and was now in control of world destiny. For many, Europe was old, jaded, and corrupt, whereas America was young and offered opportunity to all who sought it, without regard to religion or race. We were, in Israel Zangwills' phrase, "God's Crucible, the great Melting-Pot where all the races of Europe are melting and re-forming! . . . God is making the American." Thoughts like these would animate both Conservatives, Populists, and Progressives alike. Henry May notes, that, "The second article of the dominant American faith was belief in progress. . . . In 1912 . . . the link between moralism and progress seemed not only firm but inevitable" (1959, 20).

That link between moralism and progress would be tested severely however, and very soon at that. In 1913 the world witnessed the riot-riddled debut of Igor Stravinsky's "The Rite of Spring," which seemed to strike deeply troubling chords in music lovers, and the publication of Sigmund Freud's *Introductory Lectures in Psychoanalysis*. These two works raised unpleasant and/or uncomfortable questions about the dark recesses of the human spirit. Some might characterize them as explorations of the destabilizing forces that lie just below the surface drive toward utopia.

The huge influx of immigrants rekindled fear of the alien or outsider threat—a fear that had animated passions in the early 1800s. Many of the newcomers brought radical (or what seemed radical) ideas with them, and these social agitators were seen as dangerous to American ways. Midwesterners and Westerners, engaged in a battle for free coinage of silver, declared with William Jennings Bryan that they would not allow the Eastern industrialists to "press down upon the bleeding brow of labor this crown of thorns [the gold standard]."

These stresses and dichotomous pulls on the hearts and minds of the individual were reflected in the arts. Hosts of dime novelists romanticized the Old West and the now-closed (1890) frontier. Writers like Theodore Dreiser, Upton Sinclair, and Frank Norris would examine the tragic consequences for the individual of the rise of urbanization and "runaway" capitalism. It was an age of reform and muckraking, robber barons and increasingly bitter labor wars, railroad price squeezes on the farmer and scandals in the meat-packing business. A serious writer could explore the ramifications of these things, indeed revel in the ambiguities and ironies they offered the individual. The naturalists would remind us that, in spite of science, reason, and progress we are basically animals at heart, driven by forces beyond our comprehension. The realists painstakingly scrutinized the material condition of the individual and exposed the moral ambiguities and dilemmas that lie beneath conventional behavior. The ordinary turn-of-the-century American looked for solace and a buffer against such critiques in the historical romances of such authors as Mary Johnston and (the American) Winston Churchill, who presented worlds where order and the old verities could flourish inviolate. When knights were mentioned, it was not Knights of Labor, but figures of chivalry such as those in *When Knighthood Was in Flower* (1898).

And they would find solace in the tunes provided them by Tin Pan Alley. During this period American popular music was truly and finally transformed into an "industry." No longer a haphazard collection of publishers scattered throughout the United States, publishers now consolidated their resources—financial and artistic— and refined their methods of distribution. They learned how to create hits. A songwriter, publisher, or performer, through hard work, frugality, luck, and perseverance, could carve out a spot for himself (and in some cases herself) and enjoy incredible material wealth. Thus, a Charles K. Harris, living and writing made-to-order songs in Milwaukee, would realize within a year's time a profit of $25,000 per week—from one song. Songwriters were the embodiment of Horatio Alger's fictional heroes, avatars of the American Dream of Success.

This kind of success was only to be realized, however, if the songwriter could tap into the rich but mercurial vein of popular taste and deal with nearly every aspect of life of the day. On the whole, they were enormously successful at doing this.

Their success was based on some fundamental assumptions about what people wanted and needed. As belief in heritage, cohesion, tradition, and continuity threatened to slip away from the grasp of the average American, the Tin Pan Alley tunesmith pulled it back in again within the sixteen measure chorus of his/her tunes. These first-generation songsmiths and publishers—being themselves only one step off the boat or the farm or the factory—were sensitive to their audience's desires and needs. The stories are legend of composers picking up a scrap of dialogue overheard on the street and incorporating it into a song, two classic examples being Harry Von Tilzer's "Wait Till the Sun Shines, Nellie" and Charles K. Harris's "After the Ball." Charles Hamm notes, "Publishers concluded that the public wanted familiar songs, and new songs in a familiar style. Tin Pan Alley songwriters soon reached a stylistic plateau." (1979, 290).

The same rules applied in lyric writing; the songwriters reaffirmed the cherished myths of the past and used those myths to reconcile the inevitable need for change with the desire for tradition and a sense of continuity. A new invention like the automobile would usually be treated humorously, pointing up the deficiencies of the technology (i.e., it keeps breaking down) while emphasizing that this invention will play an important role in courting rituals. This approach to songwriting, along with the increase in media available to the songwriter, helped make Tin Pan Alley a major cultural force from the 1880s to 1920—and beyond.

Songwriters of this era were presented with numerous occasions when they could evoke the myth of America. Let us begin, however, by looking at how different writers treated the myth in the decades prior to our entry into World War I.

Before the rise of Tin Pan Alley, popular music functioned much as it had prior to and during the Civil War years. There was a grab-bag quality to it, and consequently, one finds voices of dissent.

Labor unrest and universal suffrage were dominant forms of protest in post-Civil-War culture. Not surprisingly, it is within the body of labor-protest songs that we find the first expressions of the myth of America. The labor-protest song attempts to reconcile the role of the individual with the "larger" vision of manifest destiny. We find songs such as John Hutchinson's "The Fatherhood of God and the Brotherhood of Man" (c. 1867). The song does not assail the basic myth—as some of the songs of the 1930s and later the 1960s will do—but instead shows that God's Fatherhood and the laborer's brotherhood are "spreading thro' the land" conterminously. Our manifest destiny, according to the song, is to "rally to the standard/Of equal rights for one and all."* God's role is clear in the movement, for suffrage is a "message that the angels bring" and is "This glorious Christian plan." And if it is achieved we will have a bounteous harvest: "Look! oh look! the field of promise,/White with harvest rich" will make error flee in the wake of a "millennial dawn of light." Thus we have regeneration through the attainment of liberty and equal rights. The vision of the myth is slightly different. Its anomalous aspects are masked by folding them in with the universally accepted mythemes of previous songs dealing with America. One accepts the new version of the myth while believing one is validating the standard version.

The songs of labor also are careful to preserve the essentials of the myth. Workers and Populists often used "Marching Through Georgia" and "The Battle Hymn of the Republic" as the melodic base for their ideas, reminders of the Civil War, and they generally reaffirm the dominant mythemes. For instance, "The Workingman's Army" (1884) begins by noting that the presidential candidate on

*The lyrics for this song are from the New World recording *The Hand That Holds the Bread: Progress and Protest in the Gilded Age, Songs from the Civil War to the Columbian Exposition.* The Cincinnati University Singers, Earl River, director (NW 267), 1978. Future references to this recording will be cited in the text as *HTHB*.

the Greenback-Labor and Anti-monopoly ticket, Gen. Benjamin Butler, was one of the first to answer Lincoln's call—in other words, he is a patriot. "The People's Rally Cry," to the tune of "Battle Hymn," yokes the land mytheme to that of the theme of freedom, by asking people from "workshop, from city, hill and plain" as well as "North and South, and East and West/To give the slave of wage his freedom."

Where the songs differ from those in past is in the attention given to the theme of the individual. The protester does not accept the idea that, if we are fulfilling a divine imperative in the preservation of the community, we are also securing the rights of the individual. In "A Laborer You See, and I Love Liberty" (c. 1878) by George W. Lloyd, for instance, the narrator declares:

> A laborer you see,
> And I love liberty,
> And I'm bound to have my way,
> For my tax I have to pay.
> (HTHB)

While George F. Root's "The Hand That Holds the Bread" (1874) notes that the "world in expectation waits" for the brothers of the plow to achieve "what was yours by right,/A fair reward for toil,/A free and open field,/An honest share for wife and home/Of what your harvests yield" (HTHB). Notice how the mytheme accommodates a subtle shift in the concept of the nation's destiny and the providential role of God: The individual is seen as being endowed by heaven ("heaven gives the power") because he/she supplies the bounty. The song, however, implicitly affirms the notion of a national community by stating that this mission must be achieved through brotherhood. The songwriter does not call into question the basic assumptions of the myth, but merely recasts them in light of the individual.

There is one final song of the labor-protest movement worth citing because it harkens back to the tradition of parody: "My Country! 'Tis of Thee." Around 1891 H. C. Dodge went to this source once again: "My Country, 'tis of Thee,/Land of Lost Liberty." The lyricist attacks one of the fundamental mythemes, pointing out that there are anomalies in the myth. Liberty is not for all, he states; it is instead a "Land of Millionaires" and the country, "once of noble braves," is one now of "wretched slaves"; too late, he says, "We saw sweet Freedom die" (*HTHB*). The message here is bleak; it forgoes the theme of renewal implicit in the myth and highlights the hypocrisy of closure of the ideologies embodied in the myth.

II

But labor's time had not yet come. In the years between the Civil War and the Great War, conservative voices prevailed. Myth is dynamic, and each generation will probably have a song that expresses its beliefs and worldview more fully than that from a previous generation. Katherine Bates's song seems to accomplish both goals, to embody the best of the previous generation while speaking emotionally and resonantly to her own generation. This may be the most complete and moving expression of the myth in all of American music. Irving Berlin's "God Bless America," the next major expression of the myth, seems only a footnote in light of Bates's paean to our country. Her interpretation is as much a commentary on the nation heading into the twentieth century as it is a summation of nineteenth-century attitudes.

The genesis of the song is quite simple. On a trip to the West, Mrs. Bates climbed Pike's Peak and was struck by the scenery that unfolded before her eyes. She wrote later that she was "impressed by the symbolic beauty of the White City," and had spent several weeks "under the purple range of the Rockies, which looked down with surprise on a summer school" (quoted in Browne 1982, 272). She immediately jotted down the lyric and had it published shortly upon her return. It quickly received attention and a couple of musical settings, the most popular of which was S. A. Ward's "Materna." This is one of the most felicitous marriages of words and existing music in the history of popular music. The music literally fits like a glove. In the first stanza the music moves gently up the scale on "amber waves of grain" to communicate a gently rolling motion, and in the next line the larger intervallic leaps on "purple" and "majesty" nicely complement the sense of awe she must have felt on seeing the Rockies. In the chorus a similar pattern is employed with a gradual stepwise movement upward on "God shed His grace on thee" followed by leaps on crown and brotherhood. Coming as it did in the midst of turbulent clashes between classes and sections of the country—Midwest farmer versus Eastern money interests, labor versus industrial might—Mrs. Bates offered her simple hymn to basic American goodness.

The song begins with a description of the country: "O beautiful for spacious skies,/For amber waves of grain," then follows with the famous lines, "For purple mountain majesties/Above the fruited plain." As symbol, this image signifies a number of meaningful ideas. It reminds one of the art of Bierstadt, Russel, Remington, and others who used the color purple to communicate the grandeur of the West. The myth of the frontier was first fully opening up in the pages of the dime novel and the western romance. Now this song came along to reflect the spirit of renewal that is central to the myth of the west and the significance of purple as symbolic of the royal or the imperial, now shifting the notion of majesty from the human realm (i.e., kings) to the topography of a bounteous land. And finally the chorus: "America, America, God shed His grace on Thee," asks us to associate purple with the Passion of Christ, for God shed His blood for us all, but for America in particular, so that we could be renewed. Thus the purple mountains function as a reminder of that transcendent soteriological vision: that God not only guides the destiny of the nation but that we are the omega point of redemption.

There is something almost Whitmanesque in the songwriter's attempt to contain all of America in the first two lines, and there is something almost Emersonian in the connection Bates draws among the land, God, and finally the brotherhood of all Americans (in the lines "And crown thy good with brotherhood/From sea to shining sea"). In transcendentalist fashion, all elements are linked and animated by the unifying force of Nature's God.

The theme of brotherhood is interesting. One senses here a response to what was a covert and slightly ambiguous threat: With the rise of labor and Populism and poor treatment of blacks and ever-increasing swarms of immigrants and, in general, growing factionalism, Americans were being challenged to address the fundamental notions of democracy and liberty. We have seen some of this in the songs of labor protest, and we see it here in Bates's more general affirmation of brotherhood. It is as though she is saying that the final proof that we are indeed a chosen people, a special land, is when we achieve brotherhood. Throughout the song Bates draws together the strands of transcendental thought and Puritan theocracy quite handily by showing that the land is crucial to the myth and, in fact, only a symbol for the country's virtues and distinctive attributes. Her message, in keeping with the transcendental function of the myth, is that only with the Almighty are we able to achieve that higher, more democratic, state of brotherhood.

One of the most interesting stanzas in the song is the third, because it presents an image not heretofore seen in songs dealing with the myth: materialism, symbolized by her use of the image of gold. Mrs. Bates's use of the image suggests something more than just a reiteration of the nostrum of hard work. She states in the chorus: "May God thy gold refine/Till all success be nobleness/And every gain divine." It is the first time that the actual term "success" has been introduced into a song dealing with the myth—appropriate in this age of the entrepreneur and the Gospel of Success. But she goes on to extol heroes "Who more than self their country loved,/And mercy more than life"—obviously something more uplifting than mere gain. The "refine" image suggests the refiner's fire of the Bible as much as the fiery caldron of an American factory: Just as those heroes lost themselves in the higher goal of patriotism, so should we look beyond mere earthly things and see a metaphor for the transformation of all we do into treasure that pleases God as well.

In the remaining verse Bates deals, first, with the pilgrims beating a "thoroughfare for freedom," and, second, with the heroes who have sacrificed in the past, and finally, with the mytheme of manifest destiny:

> O beautiful for patriot dream
> That sees beyond the years
> Thine alabaster cities gleam
> Undimm'd by human tears.

This is perhaps the most powerful image of manifest destiny in any of the songs dealing with the myth. It extends a transcendental vision into the urbanized world of the late nineteenth century. The song, although drawing on the mythemes of the agrarian ideal, clearly anticipates the twentieth century by suggesting that the tremendous urbanization of the country was but part of the founding father's vision. It is John Winthrop's "shining citie on the hill"—perhaps not the New Jerusalem, but a city nonetheless of destiny.

As noted earlier, "America the Beautiful" was published on the eve of the Spanish-American War, and, considering its great popularity, one might presume that it would be the inspiration for a flurry of tunes dealing with that conflict. The war did produce a few sentimental songs like, "Break the News to Mother" by Charles K. Harris, but it was too short (four months) to inspire as many effusions. One of the biggest numbers, "There'll Be a Hot Time in the Old Town Tonight," seems like one of those happy accidents in popular music history, but its connection to the war was tenuous at best. The subtext is that we would be victorious, and that alone was enough to make it a wartime favorite.

The songs written specifically to highlight the conflict confirmed the drive for empire. Paul Dresser, brother of Theodore Dreiser, penned two hits which in classic Tin Pan Alley fashion combine sentiment with the drive to empire: "Our Country May She Always Be Right (But Our Country, Right or Wrong)" (1898) and "Your God Comes First, Your Country Next, Then Mother Dear" (1898). Dresser's "Our Country" makes no mention of God's role, but there is an oblique allusion to manifest destiny: "March toward the sea,/And hurl defiance at our foes,/Whoever they may be." The mytheme of the patriot's sacrifice is evident in the chorus when he states that "our fathers" fought for America. In the second chorus he anticipates what will be a major trend in World War I songs by using images of home, mother, and the flag. By this time the flag has come to signify the reasons we fought in the first place: for freedom, equality, and opportunity. Dresser's song is classic Tin Pan Alley, utilizing highly evocative and symbolic formulas as a sort of shorthand to communicate its point quickly and effectively. Dresser knows these images and symbols work because they have in the past.

Next, we need to make mention of two major figures in American popular music who are also intimately associated with notions of patriotism and the country during this time period: John Philip Sousa (1854–1932) and George M. Cohan (1878–1942). Oddly enough, neither really supplied a song or body of songs that deal directly with the myth. Both, however, are composers whose work seems to embody American ideals and whose personalities are emblematic of America during this time period.

Sousa's reputation, then as now, rests on his mastery of the march form. He produced a body of marches, most notably "The Stars and Stripes Forever" (1896), that for generations of listeners have come to embody the spirit of America.

George M. Cohan provided lyrics for his tunes and the image of him is that of the archetypal American patriot. He did much to promote this image in his lifetime, beginning with a lie about his birth date; he was actually born on July 3 but chose throughout his lifetime, like his character Little Johnny Jones, to declare to the world that he was "born on the 4th of July." He also endeared himself to turn-of-the-century audiences (but not with critics) with his famous flag dance, in which he draped an American flag around himself and did one of his characteristic energetic dances. Cohan wrote plays with titles such as *George Washington Jr.* (1906) and *The Yankee Prince* (1908) and songs like "(I'm A) Yankee Doodle Dandy" (1905), "You're A Grand Old Flag" (1906), "Under Any Old Flag at All" (1907), "Any Old Place the Old Flag Flies" (1911), "My Flag" (1915), and "Over There" (1917). In "Yankee Doodle Dandy," he declares himself the nephew of Uncle Sam, born on the 4th of July, but in "You're A Grand Old Flag" he eschews any reference at all to mythemes. Perhaps this is a reflection of America's growing isolationism.

In short, Cohan's songs are long on patriotism but short on myth. What is important about them, and what will influence songs dealing with the myth in the future, is Cohan's reliance upon established secular symbols, icons, and quotations to suggest the myth —that is, Uncle Sam, the Flag, Dixie, Yankee Tars, the G.A.R., "home of the free and the brave." The burden then for supplying the myth falls to the audience. Considering the popularity of his songs and their continued staying power, one is forced to admit that he judged right. In this regard, in his use of the fragmentary image and the "incomplete message," he may be the archetypal American popular music composer of the twentieth century. We shall see, moreover, as the decades progress, that songwriters more and more rely upon icons and quotations as a sort of musical shorthand to reaffirm, question, and even repudiate the myth of America.

Cohan's success with patriotic themes inspired some other Tin Pan Alley songwriters to try their hand with the same theme: "America I Love You" (1915) by Edgar Leslie and Arch Gottler (the mythemes of the land and the patriot's sacrifice) and "The Good Old U.S.A." (1906) by Jack Dreslane and Theodore Morse (the patriot/Pilgrim mytheme and that of manifest destiny). The Cohan influence in these songs is apparent; they are spirited, and they take the simple tack of highlighting the traditions of patriotism, and they contain no allusions to God's role, an interesting omission.

Before moving on to the songs of the Great War, there is one last song from this time period that deserves special mention. It is James Weldon Johnson and J. Rosamond Johnson's "Lift Every Voice and Sing" (1900), a song which has sometimes been called the Negro National Anthem. A powerful hymn, which has as much of a Wagnerian chorus as a Negro spiritual about it, it is above all a song of hope. The first stanza highlights the mytheme of freedom, liberty, and equality by asking all to sing till the heaven and earth resound with "harmonies of liberty." The second stanza states that, in spite of oppression, African-Americans have arrived at the place where their "fathers" hoped they would be, "Where the white gleam of our bright star is cast." In a sense, this is a variation on the patriot's mytheme, suggesting that the black man has his own "patriots," who made significant sacrifices to bring him (and her) to this point in history. Then, in the final stanza, the blacks call on God to lead them—as He has led them—in the paths of righteousness so they may be "True to our God, true to our native land" (quoted in Southern 1983, 301). Although it is not an evocation of manifest destiny, it still places God centrally in the course of the people's destiny and provides that sense of transcendence so crucial to this myth. The song manages to provide its audience with a sense of its own identity—of having traveled a different path to freedom than white Americans—but at the same time longing, in consort with all Americans, to be part of the community and its destiny—the promised land, where they will enjoy the harmony of liberty.

III

As we have seen in previous chapters, songs dealing with war draw on myth to reinforce cultural ideals and ideology. Hurtling headlong into the chaos and evil of war demands some sort of mechanism for ordering the experience and placing it into an assimilable context. Paul Fussell has shown (1975) that mythmaking enabled the dough-boy to understand the war and record his feelings about it. For a great many British soldiers the mythic frames included Bunyan's *Pilgrim's Progress* and other deeply rooted arcadian myths. For American songwriters there were also mythic frames—in this case the mythemes we have discussed thus far—that they drew on to reaffirm the country's war effort. For the songwriter, however, the mythic references were less literary and drawn more from the mythology of popular song itself and, of course, from long-held cultural myths such as the myth of America. Behind the references to Mother, Daddy's little girl who waited patiently, Kaiser Bill, Heligo, the Hun, "home sweet home," and repaying our debt to Lafayette lies the myth of America serving as a subtext and animating vision for why we fought.

World War I songs, however, are somewhat atypical of songs dealing with the myth. First of all, they seldom have the word "America" in the title, and they seldom deal with the "idea" of America per se as previous songs have done. Second, because they deal with an activity that any civilized nation should by rights abhor, they need to reaffirm positive values and thus draw on different images to reconcile the evils of war with the quest for peace. Similarly, war always means there will be a conqueror, but that would seem to run counter to the mythemes of freedom and egalitarianism.

Since the songs of World War I seem to focus on a particular mytheme, I will first take up some of the general characteristics of the songs themselves, next, deal with the individual mythemes, and, finally, examine how the songs draw on other cultural myths —and popular Tin Pan Alley symbols—to reinforce the myth of America (i.e., the quest for peace, mother, home).

War songs as examples of propaganda have traditionally performed one dominant function: to create a sense (maybe an illusion) of unity and shared purpose. The songs as perpetuators of the myth are able to reinforce this function: to reconcile differences and troubling conflicts within the culture and to provide the listener with a sense of transcendence.

Reviewing the songs of the Great War, one would hardly suspect that there was anything but the most wholehearted acceptance of American involvement. And this is as it should be. The Tin Pan Alley songsmith's job was to communicate that sense of unity. The songs do not tell us that the country was divided on the issue of war, and many people saw the war as a "distant war that had already butchered men by the millions, shredded the social and economic fabric of the Old World, and shaken the very foundation of every belligerent government" (Kennedy 1980, 14). The peace movement was extremely strong during the early years of the war, and in 1916 one of Wilson's major campaign themes was that he was the President, "Who kept us out of war." Tin Pan Alley, in fact, captured some of this spirit in Alfred Bryan and Al Piantadosi's "I Didn't Raise My Boy to Be a Soldier" (1915), which shows on the cover a mother sheltering her son and states in the chorus that if all mothers would say, "I didn't raise my boy to be a soldier," there wouldn't be any war. This was, at the time, a fairly universal sentiment.

The war also stirred other abiding and ideologically divisive currents and conflicts. It was viewed with great cynicism by some. David Kennedy writes that, "To many in the West in 1917, American entry into the war represented what the gold standard had signified to William Jennings Bryan's supporters in the 1896 election: a conspiracy by Eastern plutocrats to fasten suffering on the common people for the benefit of big capital" (1980, 22). On a more personal plane, the war also represented a conflict between "individual freedom and claims of national need" (Kennedy 1980, 44).

There was also another issue, which any country must deal with in time of war: the mythology of war itself. James Oliver Robertson sees three elements constituting the modern myth of war: First, war is the instrument of progress, bringing emotional unity to the country and fulfilling our destiny in the world. Second, war is chaotic, destructive, and evil. Third, war is an aberration, a kink in life's normal thread—best avoided but, if that is not possible, then to be fought with an all-out effort to achieve quick and total victory, so that peace and the blessings of democracy can again be enjoyed.

Songwriters often make the point that we were compelled to join the fray, we had a debt to repay to France, or that, as one team put it, "They want us to settle up that fuss, and they put it up to us." Songwriters, to illustrate the aberrant nature of war and that it is not part of our heritage, populate their tunes with mothers regretfully sending their sons off to war and of little children praying for daddy's return. In short, the element of evil is mitigated by the use of symbols of innocence. Songwriters echo the public sentiments such as "the world must be made safe for democracy" and that this would be "the war to end all wars." In the end, Tin Pan Alley had to affirm the basic principle of the mythology of war: Americans only go to war for good ends.

The music of the war years brings together the dominant trends of turn-of-the-century music. There are a preponderance of sentimental tunes, lively marches in 6/8 and 2/4 time, and some ragtime-inspired ditties; there are dozens of novelty numbers ranging from the immortal stutter classic "K-K-K-Katy" (1918) to "We Don't Want the Bacon (What We Want Is a Piece of the Rhine)" (1918) to "Good Morning Mr. Zip-Zip-Zip" (1918), to "Keep Your Head Down Fritzi Boy" to "If He Can Fight Like He Can Love, Good Night, Germany" (1918) to "Would You Rather Be a Colonel With an Eagle on Your Shoulder (Or a Private With a Chicken on Your Knee)" (1918). The songs form a literal chronicle of the war from "Wake Up, America" in 1916 to "Goodbye Broadway, Hello France" (1917) to battlefield settings ("If I'm Not at the Roll Call (Kiss Mother Good-bye for Me) (1918)" and "You Keep Sending Them Over (And We'll Keep Knocking Them Down)" to songs devoted to returning home ("When the War Is Over, I'll Return to You," and, on a lighter note, "How Ya Gonna Keep Em Down on the Farm," etc.). Songwriters seemed to be particularly taken with France: "Lafayette (We Hear You Calling)," "My Belgian Rose" (1918), "Oh, Frenchy" (1918), "Joan of Arc, They Are Calling You" (1917)).

There is another aspect of the World War I song that I think is important as well. Ian Whitcomb has noted that World War I songs "saw the war not from the high vantage of a General, in grand sweeps, but from the worm's-eye view of the ordinary man" (1974, 63). This corresponds with the idea that war songs deal with the myth of America atypically: They do not approach the myth on a macrocosmic level but instead allow it to emerge in the microcosmic actions of the common person. There is a strong element of personalization in the songs. Soldiers speak directly, mothers and children are dramatic participants. Earlier I discussed how songs from the turn of the century begin to personalize the relationship of individuals to the country. We see this in Paul Dresser's "Your God Comes First, Your Country Next, Then Mother Dear," but the suggestion here is that the three are not separated by much in the hearts of Americans. The music of George M. Cohan is the best example of where the focus is. No longer on "America the Beautiful" but on Little Johnny Jones, an American jockey, the patriot, the bold assertive twentieth-century individual who functions in his music as a metonymy for the country as a whole. The song "America, I Love You" from 1905 by Edgar Leslie and Archie Gottler perpetuates the Cohan ideology:

America, I love you
You're like a sweetheart of mine, . . .
Just like a little baby
Climbing its mother's knee.

On the one hand, by using the symbols of mother, children, and the doughboy, the songwriter is following a basic law of survival: Write songs that people can relate to personally.

Probably the most familiar World War I song to Americans is George M. Cohan's "Over There" (1917). Many consider it one of the greatest war songs of all time. It is, however, an unusual song in the context of the myth of America. Of all the World War I songs, it is perhaps the vaguest in specific imagery concerning the war and the country. This may account for its popularity. Nevertheless, it is important because it was the archetypal war song, one of the first war songs written, and, consequently, allusions to the phrase "over there" are legion in other writers' songs. The song is also important because it introduces themes other songwriters will adopt as the war wears on. First, Cohan begins with a direct call to "Johnny" to get his gun and take in on the run. This is a reference to the common man's role in the war—Whitcomb's "worm's-eye" view—and we should not be surprised that Cohan used the name "Johnny." For Cohan this name was the embodiment of the American Dream and the American spirit. In the verse he goes on to mention the flag and call on us to be "Like true heroes do or die." In the second verse he reinforces the egalitarian ideals of the myth as he asks the soldiers from "the towns and the tanks" to unite so that one's mother will be proud, and so they can remain true to liberty. Finally, he alludes to the notion of manifest destiny when he states that the Yanks are coming and the word should go out to all "to beware" because we won't be back "till it's over over there." In short, America is now in control.

As we have seen in the songs of previous periods, the mytheme of manifest destiny and God's role in directing our history is a crucial one. It offers a moral validation for the myth, and it raises the secular values that comprise the myth to a higher plane; in short, it allows us to make a larger cosmological connection between our earthly ambitions and some divine plan. The song, "A Soldier's Rosary" (1918) by J. E. Dempsey and Joseph Burke, has the narrator tell his mother not to worry because when he serves his country's needs he also serves his Maker. A large number of songs reiterate the "In God We Trust" theme as part of the war effort. In "Send Me Away with a Smile" (1917) the narrator tells his sweetheart that he is fighting for "My Country, home and you," and then in the chorus he admits that we go off to war reluctantly, and that if we have to fight, we will trust "in our Maker." In short, the songwriters make it clear that we indeed do have God on our side, and the prayer of every mother and sweetheart will be that, when the war is over, "God will bring back my soldier boy to me."

Although this mytheme plays an important role in the songs of the Great War, it is expressed a bit differently from previous songs. The songwriter must be careful to couch his sentiments so that the expression of the mytheme does not appear autocratic. What we find, then, is the songwriter linking the mytheme of manifest destiny with the theme of peace. By focusing on the peace theme, the songwriter, for all intents and purposes, was able to state that we are invested with a providential role in world affairs and that role is as peacemakers. If it takes a war to bring a peace, so be it. If indeed our history has been willed by God, then two things are validated: first, that democracy is the chosen form of government, and, second, that it must be spread throughout the world. Here, however, is where the paradox of the peace theme and our involvement in the war enters.

Peace and war are obviously contradictory impulses. The fact that prior to the war Americans were embracing the ideas of the peace movement made our entrance into the war even more difficult. However, in time, peace movement proponents could see the "divine" necessity for war. It forms a sort of twentieth-century correlative for the myth of the fortunate fall. Thus war and peace could be reconciled during the little over a year that we were "over there."

Songwriters were quick to latch on to the peace theme and yoke it to our more deeply rooted belief in manifest destiny. In one of the earliest prowar songs, "Wake Up, America" (1916) by George Graff, Jr., and Jack Glogau, the narrator enunciates the theme of the common man being willing to sacrifice all for sweethearts, wives, mothers, home, and country. In the chorus they then focus on the peace theme by saying they will pray for peace but "peace with honor." They go on to state that we must be prepared so that when "Old Glory is unfurled" the rest of the world will know that we are "ready." In this stanza the writers are giving notice to the world that we stand ready to do our "duty"—and the use of that word is crucial here—to preserve an honorable peace. When America finally entered the war, songwriters Herbert Moore and W. R. Williams in "America Today" (1917) harkened to the same theme, but they added a new twist, noting that, although we're strong for a peace with honor, we're even stronger "for right." The notion that the nation stands for "right" and, as others expressed it, the "just cause" validated our entrance into the war. This noble purpose is given further moral substance, at least in this particular song, by linking it to our past.

The songwriters also emphasize the transcendent nature of the American involvement in the war and the belief that this earthly sacrifice for peace is connected to some higher good and purpose, a purpose, moreover, which courses through history. The idea is not one peculiar to Tin Pan Alley songwriters by any means. It may be stretching the point to say that it was cultural currency in 1918, but there is some evidence that Americans at the turn of the century saw their involvement in wars as part of historical necessity predicated on a divine plan. Justice Oliver Wendell Holmes, Jr., himself a Civil War veteran, told Harvard's graduating class of 1895 that only in war could man pursue, "the divine folly of honor," and that war might be terrible but in time "you see that its message was divine" (Kennedy 1980, 178–79). Similarly, the Tin Pan Alley songwriter found some interesting ways to reconcile the carnage with the canonization of the doughboy. Dempsey and Burke's "A Soldier's Rosary" is perhaps the most stunning example. They create what amounts to a metaphysical conceit when they state that "bullets are his beads," and he prays that they will help end the "misery," that each shot is a "pearl" and each pearl a "prayer." The doughboy is ultimately killed, but the death is linked to the transcendent notion that each bead is a prayer for peace and, as each bullet hits its mark, so peace draws closer to reality.

In "There's a Service Flag Flying at Our House" (1917) by Thomas R. Hoier, Bernie Grossman and Al W. Brown, the songwriters speak first of the pride of mother and father for what their boy has done and go on to say how he may return with "fame and glory," but that if he should fall in the fight, the service flag will be flying at home, and there will be a "new star in Heaven that night." One can see in the allusion to canonization a reminder that the sacrifice is tied to something heavenly, something beyond mere earthly sacrifice. The songwriters are careful to show that the war and the sacrifices that attend the struggle are not for ephemeral or fleeting purposes. Thus songwriters convincingly demonstrate that the common man's efforts to achieve the secular goals of freedom and democracy are part of God's plan for this country. Americans sang songs about the boys who lived down the street and wept for the leave-taking of their mothers, and their dying in "No Man's Land" was not tragedy but apotheosis.

Apotheosis also plays a role in another mytheme: the sacrifice of the patriots. In war songs of the Revolution, the spirit and purpose of the Pilgrims were summoned as a model for behavior in times of stress. In future war songs it would be the sacrifice of the revolutionary War heroes. In each case the function of the mytheme is complex and deeply symbolic. First of all, it serves as a reminder of our history and heritage as pioneers and fighters. Second, it offers continual models for heroic action. Finally, it underscores the necessity for sacrifice in the pursuit of our providential role in the world. These symbolic functions are part of the songs of the Great War. But there is a new function as well.

In war songs the image of our past patriots also serves as an incentive to fight. Songwriters "Kid" Howard Carr, Harry Russell, and Jimmie Havens make this point in the classic "We Don't Want the Bacon (What We Want Is a Piece of the Rhine)" (1918) when they tell us that history has shown that we've "always held our own with any foe." But in the songs of World War I we also find songwriters actually using the patriot's sacrifice as a call to arms. The most popular figure used to draw us into the fray is not even an American but the Frenchman Lafayette. In two songs, "Goodbye Broadway, Hello France" (1917) by C. Francis Reisner, Benny Davis, and Billy Baskette and the very popular "Lafayette (We Hear You Calling)" (1917) by Mary Earl, the songwriters use the expression that we owe "a debt" to France that must be repaid by our involvement in the war. This relieves America of the role of aggressor in the conflict by stressing the historical necessity of our duty. Lafayette is a reminder that America's role extends from the days of our Founding Fathers to the present and into the future. As Lafayette helped establish us as masters of the main, so must we help—as masters of the main —his country stay free from the autocratic threat of the Hun.

Another song that yokes the call to duty with our manifest destiny is "Wake Up, America." In this song the writers ask a series of what are probably intended to be rhetorical questions such as, have we forgotten the battles our fathers fought, and has their blood been wasted, leading up to the ultimate question of whether Columbia is the gem of the Ocean? and Old Glory "the pride of the Free"? The self-reflexive use of myth—in this case the allusion to an earlier song, "Columbia the Gem of the Ocean"—firmly establishes the necessary historical link for the listener. In the second verse the writers ask us to remember Washington at Valley Forge, Jackson, Custer, Farragut, and Perry, not to mention McKinley and Lincoln who "were fighting men" too. It was they who "Made Columbia the gem of the Ocean,/Made Old Glory the pride of the Free." This draws together the mytheme of patriot's sacrifice and that of America's historical role as a world leader.

The mytheme of the patriot's sacrifice serves yet another purpose in these songs: to engage the feelings and animate the aspirations of the common person. The songs provide doughboys—and all Americans, for that matter—with heroic archetypes. "The Dixie Volunteers" (1917) by Edgar Leslie and Harry Ruby, for instance, shows us that the war effort is an egalitarian one by focusing on the soldiers from the Deep South, those "Peaceful sons," who now will shoulder their guns and become fighters like Stonewall Jackson and Robert E. Lee. Songwriters consistently make the point that the doughboys are the new patriots with a direct link to their mythic forebears. By virtue of this connection, they also share in the promise and the pursuit of manifest destiny.

Perhaps the best expression of this mytheme is in "Just Like Washington Crossed the Delaware (General Pershing Will Cross the Rhine)" (1918) by Howard Johnson and George W. Meyer. In the first verse they show the contemporary American's connection with their heroic forebears, and then they remind us that today overseas our doughboys are making history and that the "Yankee spirit" is still alive. In the second verse they reaffirm the tie to the higher purpose in our history;

> As they fought for Independence,
> You and I and our descendants
> Must preserve Democracy,
> In God above we'll trust,

Our sword shall never rust,
We'll tell the world it simply has to be.

In actuality, this is probably the most complete statement of the entire myth in all of the songs of World War I. The only mytheme missing is an allusion to our rich, bountiful land. The worm's-eye view is reinforced and through it the common man achieves that sense of transcendence by sharing in the larger vision of our providential role in world affairs—"it simply has to be."

But what animates the vision? What is it that God would have us spread throughout the world? The stated policy was that we were going to make the world safe for democracy. Songwriters seemed to take a slightly more oblique view of the reasons for our involvement. "We're in the Army Now" (1917) by Tell Taylor, Ole Olsen, and Isham Jones states that from the way things are going they *have* to join the army, which implies something less than enthusiastic acceptance of the war. However, as the song progresses the narrator seems to warm to the idea and states that they will "make things hum." And finally, in the chorus the narrator recognizes that the United States "needs us" because the U-boat war had gone too far; therefore, we will, of course, do "what's right: we'll fight."

It is this last sentiment, the idea of doing what's "right," that is the single most persistent leitmotif in World War I songs dealing with why the United States is involved. Among the other songs that use almost exactly the same words are "The Battle Song of Liberty" (1918) by Jack Yellen with music adapted by George L. Cobb from F. E. Bigelow's "Our Director" (we're on our way to do what we know is right), "Keep the Trench Fires Going for the Boys out There" (1918) by Edward Moran and Harry Von Tilzer (we're not afraid "to take a chance" because the cause is right); "Bring Back My Daddy to Me" (1917) by William Tracey, Howard Johnson, and George W. Meyer (homes are yearning for those who will return "With honor, and justice and right?"). But exactly what was "right"?

As I have shown thus far, a kind of religious zeal did creep into the national consciousness about the war. Wilson was able to articulate, to the satisfaction of most people, just, what is was we were fighting for. For instance, progressives were able to embrace the war, according to David Kennedy, partially because of "Wilson's adroitness at figuring the war in terms congenial to the American mind, and particularly appealing to the progressives: a war for democracy, a war to end war, a war to protect liberalism, a war against militarism, a war to redeem barbarous Europe, a crusade" (1980, 51). In that shopping list of causes there is much that could be construed as "right." This notion of "right" suggests a sense of duty, an important theme in the songs. But right also suggests a moral imperative, and that moral imperative is centered around the notion of democracy.

The songs of World War I are the first that actually use the term "democracy" as part of the myth. In previous songs, the idea is suggested through the characteristics songwriters identify as basic to the ideal for which the country stands. The terms one encounters most often are, naturally, liberty and freedom. For example, Bernie Grossman and Alex Marr, in their "Say a Prayer for the Boys out There" (1917), state that the doughboys are the "new patriots" who "fight for liberty," and they write that we are sending our "best" so that the rest may forever be free.

Another example of this mytheme in action, but with an interesting twist, is in the novelty song "Good Morning, Mr. Zip-Zip-Zip" (1918), which states that we come from north, south, east, and west, "To clear the way to freedom" for this land that we love best. Note the similarity in thought between "clear the way to freedom" and Katherine Bates's "thoroughfare for freedom beat" and even, "The New Massachusetts Liberty Song," where freedom opened a way in the desert. Freedom is, indeed, the liberating and expansive force that leads us forward and unifies us, bringing all sections of the country together. Sym Winkel's "When Our Boys Come Marching Home" (1917) notes that we have gone overseas to fight for liberty and at war's end we will return home conquering heroes like Washington and Lee. The allusion to those two great icons of American life and war is an attempt to reconcile national and regional differences by appealing to the pride these two men engender in all Americans. By extension, another American ideal is maintained in these songs: egalitarianism—an egalitarianism made possible only by preserving freedom and democracy throughout the world.

"Democracy," as expressed in these songs, simply means freedom and liberty for everyone. Autocratic governments are antithetical to that philosophy, and when they threaten that ideal, it is only right to join the fray to stop them. These are principles that almost everyone can appreciate. Furthermore, by emphasizing these ideals, the songwriters handle the troubling conflict created by any war of reconciling individual rights with collective need or will. In war one must, the songs suggest, abandon one's individualism to ensure the preservation of that individualism in the future. We have to join Uncle Sammy in the fray to clear our own way to freedom in the future.

The dominant icons in songs of the Great War include "Old Glory" and "Uncle Sam." The songs also feature mother, children and home. Each of these subjects was a popular theme in turn-of-the-century music, so it is natural that songwriters would evoke them in writing about the war. On the one hand, they serve as sentimental devices. The image of a mother saying good-bye to her boy or a son asking a buddy to tell mother good-bye was sure to strike a responsive chord in the listener. The theme of the severed bond between son and mother has always been one that could be expected to move an audience. Mother was an important cultural symbol in turn-of-the-century music, as in "I Want A Girl (Just Like the Girl That Married Dear Old Dad") and Theodore Morse's incomparable "M-O-T-H-E-R (A Word That Means the World To Me)" (1915) ("'M' is for the million things she gave me"). Mother represented home, fidelity, love, caring, and a moral goodness matched only by the angels. Moreover, her presence in the songs corresponded with the worm's-eye view of the common man, and was a symbol that everyone could relate to, from the Boston Brahmin to the immigrant just off the boat. Thus, when she was asked to give up her boy, it was seen as the ultimate sacrifice. The image of mother plus the icons of child and home, give us the basic units of society, the frame that supports the whole idea of America.

It is not surprising that there should be some new and different images and symbols in the songs of World War I. They make no mention of one of our most important mythemes: the land. Instead focus is concentrated on the human element, concerned with the role people play in preserving the idea of the country. These people and things serve an important iconic function in the songs by suggesting we look beyond the person/object and glimpse some greater truth. They not only serve as symbols for certain American ideals related to the myth, but they also enable the songwriter to reconcile the myth of war with the myth of America.

In referring to Arcadian myths and the pastoral ideal as portrayed in English literature of the Great War, Paul Fussell has written: "Recourse to the pastoral is an English mode of both fully gauging the calamities of the Great War and imaginatively protecting oneself against them" (1975, 235). For Americans, the same could be said of mothers and children. In "If I'm Not at the Roll Call (Kiss Mother Goodbye For Me)" (1918) by George Boyden, we find the doughboy near death (the calamity of war), but he has no fear because he is sending a message to Mother. Where does his strength come from? It is a combination of love and faith. He tells his buddy in the trench to tell his mother that he knows she loves him and prays for him; he asks that the "angels attend her," and, finally, that his brave "comrade" befriend her and kiss her good-bye for him. The lyric enables the listener to hold off the calamity of war by evoking the religious elements of prayer and the attendant angels. This is a reiteration of the notion that God is watching over us, and ultimately it is into His hands that we commend the dying and those who are left to grieve. The song also suggests that the spirit of Mother's constant prayers is carried over in the fidelity of the buddy. This quasi-mystical connection between the mother's prayer and the buddy's fidelity (i.e., the camaraderie of the fighting men) is another means of holding off the calamity of the war. In a sense, Mother has come to embody the spirit of Columbia: She is an inspiration, a symbol of fidelity, strength in the face of death, and the handmaiden of the angels. And as the Statue of Liberty holds aloft the flame of freedom, Mother, according to L. Wolfe Gilbert and Anatole Friedland in "While You're Away" (1918), will keep the lovelight shining to light her doughboy's way at night.

Children similarly are used as a sentimental device, and, like Mother, they allow the songwriter to reconcile the evil of war with the moral necessity of it. Children are the embodiment of innocence, representing purity and openness, a hope for the future, and a reason to fight. And, like Mother, they also symbolize total and unqualified love. In "Just A Baby's Prayer at Twilight" (1918) by Sam Lewis, Joe Young, and M. K. Jerome, the writers state that Mother's precious child is "Dad's forget-me-not." Children are always connected with the divine in some way. In most songs, including great ones such as "Hello Central, Give Me No Man's Land" (1918), the child inevitably says a prayer for her Daddy over there (yes, most often the children are little girls). The song "Just A Baby's Letter (Found in No Man's Land)" (1918) by Bernie Grossman and Ray Lawrence strongly suggests the transcendental overtones of the child's love for Daddy as they describe "baby's letter" being "Filled with crosses" (kisses) at the end. The child's faith and her own innocent sacrifice, symbo-lized in the crosses, are powerful notions here. "Little girls," more-over, symbolize the role of the doughboy as protector of basic Ameri-can values: domestic virtues, symbolized by Mother, and innocence and purity as symbolized by the child. The icons of mother and child suggest that our cause is indeed sacred (God's presence is a unifying element in the two icons), because we are fighting to pre-serve virtue; they reconcile the paradox that one must sometimes embrace the evil of war if innocence and good are to persevere and if the country is to survive.

Finally, we encounter the icon of the home. The preservation of home is, for all intents and purposes, the preservation of democracy. Furthermore, songwriters self-reflexively draw on the mythology of popular song itself in employing this theme by alluding to the nineteenth-century classic "Home Sweet Home." That song obliquely drew a connection with our earthly home ("seems to hal-low [make us holy] us there") and the home that we would find after death. Similarly, the songs of the Great War often attempt a similar theme. The purpose here is to mitigate the horror and evil of war by demonstrating that it plays a role in the divine plan and the cos-mos. An interesting early song dealing with this theme is "After the War Is Over (Will There Be Any Home Sweet Home?)" (1917) by E. J. Pourmon and Joseph Woodruff and Harry Andrieu. The chorus states that many a heart will be aching after the war has ceased, but all will be happy in a "place called 'Home Sweet Home'": those whose hearts are aching because they have lost someone, those chil-dren left all alone, and those who have given their lives to preserve that very home; the home, of these last mentioned will be heaven.

Another song, "When the War Is Over I'll Return to You" (1918) by Bide Dudley and Frederic Watson, employs a panoply of iconology in addressing how the world will look after war's end. The narrator states that in the midst of war the Red, White and Blue will be flying "O'er his head" just like a guiding and protecting hand. Mean-while the shells will be flying, but each shell is "Singing 'Home Sweet Home.'" This is reminiscent of "The Soldier's Rosary," where every bullet was a bead in the rosary (i.e., a prayer). Here the shells are but a reminder of what we are fighting for, and that each shell, which potentially brings one closer to death, also brings one closer to a new life after the war. At the war's end the lovers will live in clover—a pastoral image and theme that was a staple of the Tin

Pan Alley lyricist. In short, the world will be returned to its greenness and bountiful richness, a sort of utopia where love will be able to flourish.

This last image of the doughboy returning to a green world of innocence and bounty is perhaps the most striking. The Tin Pan Alley songwriter, like George Fairman in his "It's All Over Now" (1918) paints a portrait of a world where there is joy everywhere, where we are free from cares, and there are no more fears and heart-aches and tears. Indeed, it would seem that the Wilsonian principles and the hopes of those like Walter Lippmann had been realized. The songwriter describes a world regenerated with, according to Fairman, roses blooming in the "lands of the brave and free." "My Belgian Rose" (1918), similarly, uses the central symbol of the rose to reinforce the theme of regeneration. In the verse the rose is wilting and crushed under the tyrant's foot, enunciating the evil of war. But in a subsequent verse the rose will live to "bloom on a happier day" because America is to be her home as well. America's role in the regeneration here is significant. The writers promise that the United States will bring back "your bloom" in a promise of new life as we make an "American Beauty" of her .*

A majority of Americans embraced these tunes and the sentiments they expressed. And this was in sharp contrast to the notions of the serious artist. David Kennedy has written:

> The postwar novelists of protest saw and remembered a different war than that which most of "Pershing's Crusaders" had witnessed. Most of the young men in the AEF had arrived too late and moved too swiftly to be deeply disabused of their adventurous expectations. Between the sensibilities enshrined in the minds of the American Legionnaires and those expressed in the novels of Hemingway, Dos Passos, Cummings and the others, there gaped an immense void of incomprehension. This hole in the fabric of American culture, further separating the intellectuals from the "masses," was one of the lasting legacies of the war (1980, 229–230).

*This theme is strikingly similar to a 1940 song, "Johnny Doughboy Found a Rose in Ireland," a reference to troops stationed in Northern Ireland prior to America's entry into World War II. It too refers to making an American Beauty of "a sweet Irish rose like you," an interesting link between the two wars.

Songwriters from the end of the Civil War up until the end of the teens cleverly mined our cultural mythology to renew the vitality of the myth of America. Thus, by the war's end Americans could still see America as a rich, vital, and bountiful land, which, in taking up arms, fulfilled the role God had chosen for His people in the world. The songs told us that each doughboy fought bravely, just as our forefathers had done, and because they had made this sacrifice, democracy would reign, and everyone would enjoy the benefits of liberty and freedom.

The legacy of the songs of these decades cast a long shadow over the twentieth century. These songs would continue to serve as the touchstone for all future treatments of the myth. In some cases the sentiments of songs such as "America the Beautiful" and "Over There" would be adopted completely and without question to help us through another crisis and remind us of our destiny. In other instances, the same songs will be for some almost tragic reminders of America's unrealized potential; a benchmark that Americans will use in their struggle to reconcile the ideals of the myth with a growing specter of doubt born of failed opportunities.

CHAPTER VI

"Of Thee I Sing, Baby"
The Tin Pan Alley Years,
1920–1950

FULTON: *You've got to preside over the Senate.*
THROTTLEBOTTOM: *And after that I'll be President?*
LYONS: *That's what you will!*
(LYONS and JONES exit. Scrubwoman enters)
THROTTLEBOTTOM: *President! Say! How will that sound?*
President Alexander Bottlethrottom. (Corrects himself) Throttlebottom.
SCRUBWOMAN: *Huh?*
THROTTLEBOTTOM: *(He dances up to her) I'm going to be President!*
SCRUBWOMAN: *I'd rather have this job. It's steady.*
(Exits)
—Of Thee I Sing *(1931)*

From 1919 until 1938, one is hard pressed to find songs that deal with the myth of America in serious fashion. It is not that there wasn't occasion to call upon the myth. Crises aplenty loomed, which could have precipitated serious examinations about the nature of the United States, the Great Depression being the most obvious. Society experienced changes, divisions, contradictions, and disparities, which deeply affected the American citizen. Why, then, was there so little serious mention of this made by mainstream composers?

One of the dominant American themes of the 1920s was the "return to normalcy." When Harding declared that it was normalcy that people wanted, it seemed to have resonated positively throughout the culture. People were satisfied that the world had been made safe for democracy—at least our democracy. Aside from a relatively small band of intellectuals, people threw themselves into living again with little thought of what had just transpired. Some of this was classic American desire to resume an isolationist's role in the world and, hopefully, avoid another war. Some of the desire to get on with life was born of new freedoms—votes for women, bobbed hair, automobiles, "flaming youth," the Jazz Age. Young people especially threw themselves headlong into Life! They raced around in automobiles—and watched the celebration of their hedonism in films such as *Our Dancing Daughters*—caught the fever of professional sports, attended movies regularly (80 million per week attended movies by 1929), drank "bootleg hooch" (and celebrated that in songs like "Button up Your Overcoat" by DeSylva, Brown, and Henderson), listened to radio, misread Freud, and talked a lot about and experimented with sex. Some—the more intellectual—toyed with communism.

Workers also thought the world was new and would offer new opportunities, and they wanted to share in them. But the American businessman had different ideas.

> He wanted to get back to business and enjoy his profits. Labor stood in his way and threatened his profits. He had come out of the war with a militant patriotism; and mingling his idealistic with his selfish motives, after the manner of all men at all times, he developed a fervent belief that 100-per-cent Americanism and the Welfare of God's Own Country and Loyalty to the Teachings of the Founding Fathers implied the right of the business man to kick the union organizer out of his workshop. (Allen 1931,41)

It was the great era of laissez-faire economics, and the businessman could call the shots. The laborer would have to wait for Hard Times to stake a claim to the material world.

The popular arts industries were of a piece with the rest of the culture. The twenties saw the emergence of such talented writers as Ernest Hemingway, F. Scott Fitzgerald, John Dos Passos, and Sherwood Anderson, but the best-seller lists were dominated by authors such as Zane Grey, Rafael Sabatini, Earl Derr Biggers (Charlie Chan mysteries), Agatha Christie, Edna Ferber, and books such as *The Sheik* (1921), *The Covered Wagon* (1922), and *Gentlemen Prefer Blondes* (1925). One serious novelist, Sinclair Lewis, enjoyed great popularity, but his particular vision was a satiric one and, like the satiric songs emanating from Broadway in the late twenties, was consequently embraced a bit more enthusiastically. Suzanne Ellery

Greene has noted of the best-sellers of the twenties: "The decade of the twenties witnessed red flag parades, the Great Red Scare, the Boston police strike, the Harding scandals, the Ku Klux Klan, and the debates between intellectual liberals and conservatives, but little of this excitement is reflected in its most popular literature" (1974, 46). She adds that, "Unlike their more pessimistic contemporaries, most writers of best-sellers did not give in to disillusionment nor did they accept the feeling of lack of mastery of their own lives so strong in the naturalistic writers" (38).

A similar situation existed in the music industry. It too was humming along. Changes were taking place in the structure of the industry which affected the output of songs and the kind of songs that would be written. Like the publishing business, the music business was almost solely concentrated in New York. It directed its product initially to the audiences in that area, assuming that there was uniformity of taste and feeling throughout the remainder of the culture. In the twenties, and to a lesser extent in the thirties, Broadway became increasingly important as the medium for showcasing new songs and disseminating them. Tin Pan Alley—that is, the publishing houses themselves—more and more needed mass media like musical comedy and later radio and movies to plug their wares. Fewer and fewer composers just wrote tunes and hoped that they would be picked up at the five-and-dime. With the increased emphasis on Broadway as the dominant medium, there was, as Charles Hamm has noted, a narrowing of "the expressive range of popular songs. . . . One searches almost in vain for songs touching in any way on the great social and political issues of those years. . . ." (1979, 376–77). Musical comedies, crafted for predominantly middle-class Northeasterners, reflect a preoccupation not with the myth of America but with the myth of success and other lighthearted fare that mirrored the quest for the new material world.

There was also a new breed of composer and lyricist working in the theater and music industries beginning in the early twenties. By 1925 composers such as Charles K. Harris, Harry Von Tilzer, and Jean Schwartz, the Tin Pan Alley giants who had dominated the scene in the prewar years, were seldom heard from. A new generation was in place, consisting of well-trained composers and urbane and witty lyricists. In the preface to his *Lyrics on Several Occasions*, Ira Gershwin says, "Since most of the lyrics in this lodgement were arrived at by fitting words mosaically to music already composed, any resemblance to actual poetry, living or dead, is highly improbable" (1953,xi). Charles K. Harris had cautioned lyricists about using "Many-syllabled words and those containing hard consonants." But the sophisticated new songwriters boldly flouted such advice. By 1940 lines like these of Lorenz Hart were relatively common fare: "Your looks are laughable/Unphotographable." "Too many syllables, Mr. Hart," one can almost hear Mr. Harris chiding. Correspondingly, when songwriters were presented with patriotic subjects, they found they could not easily slip into the old jingoisms. Already in 1916 Cole Porter was displaying characteristics that would make him one of the most popular songwriters and most revered lyricists of the musical theater. He wrote a song entitled "See America First," which in its first version contains the line "All hail salubrious sky." Perhaps he was permitted this because we were not yet in the war. However, he later had to come up with a second version which featured sentiments like getting the strains of Yankee Doodle in one's "noodle" (Porter 1984, 44). Only a war could get such composers to hearken back to the days of George M. Cohan, and even then one does not find many songs by the major writers of the day (i.e., Gershwin, Hart, Hammerstein, Harburg, Dietz, Dorothy Fields, etc). In general, when it came to matters of state and country, the songwriters of the twenties and thirties found themselves more comfortable within the confines of gentle Horatian satire.

I

Virtually no songs from the early and middle 1920s deal with the myth and only a very few from the 1930s. This might strike some as odd in light of cultural ramifications of a social and economic disaster like the Great Depression. It was, after all, a major crisis, and, the majority of songs dealing with the myth have been generated out of crisis. However, the domination of Tin Pan Alley by Broadway and Hollywood ensured that the product reaching listeners would steer a careful course among feelings created by the Depression. Consequently, we find two kinds of song dominant during the 1930s: serious songs dealing with the plight of the individual in the wake of the economic collapse; and satirical numbers where

American institutions come under the good-natured fire of musical comedy. George S. Kaufman is credited with the dictum that satire is what closes on Saturday night, and playwrights, lyricists, and composers must have taken it to heart, for the type of satire they produced is genial and seems more concerned with poking fun at the foibles of our American institutions than with correcting their flaws. It never at any time rails angrily. The anger in the culture is to be found in other songs and, in particular, the songs of the political left and labor (next chapter).

Among the songs that deal seriously with the Depression and that have some relevance to the myth of America are "Brother, Can You Spare a Dime?" (1932) by E. Y. Harburg and Jay Gorney and "Remember My Forgotten Man" (1933) by Al Dubin and Harry Warren. The songs share some interesting similarities. First, both songs depict the disenfranchised individual. Both feature structures that contrast a driving, martial rhythm and melody in one section with a more lyrical section. Both are written in a minor key, which adds an element of poignancy. Both songs also allude to two mythemes: the land and opportunity. And, finally, both songs enunciate a theme that will be common in the Depression and that we will see in the folksong movement during the same period: that of the soldier who has served his country in the preservation of freedom and opportunity but who is now excluded from that same opportunity.

In "Brother, Can You Spare a Dime," Harburg creates an Everyman narrator for his song, a person who has built railroads, skyscrapers, and tilled the fields. This person has contributed to the vast bounty of the land (through his plow) and kept faith with the promise of the land by bearing guns for it in time of war. There is even a veiled allusion to the mytheme of manifest destiny when the narrator tries to understand how, after he has helped build a dream of "peace and glory ahead," he can now be standing in a breadline. And there is a somewhat ironic allusion to the patriot's mytheme in the lines where he describes the half-million "boots" that went slogging through hell "Full of that Yankee Doodle-de-dum." This last line would remind listeners of the old Revolutionary War song, and also of George M. Cohan's "Yankee Doodle Dandy" and his "Over There." The allusion is veiled enough that Harburg wouldn't necessarily bring down the wrath of the man who once "owned Broadway," but the line serves as a mild indictment of the patriotism that swept us into war but seems not to be reciprocal. Harburg has said of his narrator that he isn't bitter, "He's bewildered. Here is a man who had built his faith and hope in this country. . . . Then came the crash. Now he can't accept the fact that the bubble has burst. He still believes. He still has faith. He just doesn't understand what could have happened to make everything go so wrong" (quoted in 1971, Green 69).

Similarly, in "Remember My Forgotten Man," delivered by Joan Blondell in her own inimitable popular *Sprechstimme* style, the narrator seems to be addressing government as she reminds them that her man cultivated the land and carried a "rifle in his hand." The songwriters paint a picture of a man who has contributed to the plenty of the land, fought to defend that land and all it stands for, and is now disenfranchised from it. The narrator also reminds the powers-that-be that, if they forget him, they are forgetting her, because a woman cannot live without a man. There is no cryptic socialist message here, but the audience could walk away from this song with a feeling of solidarity; each of them, like this woman, shared in the tragedy of the forgotten man. The tone of the song, like that of "Brother, Can You Spare A Dime?" is somber and suggests an attitude of despair and disillusionment.

The context of its performance is important to this song. The message one would derive from it if it were played at home or heard in a club would be somewhat different from what audiences experienced watching the film *Gold Diggers of 1933*. In that film, the song is the finale, a huge Busby Berkeley production number, which begins by vividly parading hundreds of "forgotten men" across the stage but ends up on an "up" note as, in typical Berkeley style, the chorus forms the NRA eagle for a classic center weighted shot. The structure of the scene then takes one from despair to hope—an entirely different feeling from what one would have if the tune were heard in isolation.

Both songs leave enough room for people to identify with the narrator. Both songs bring into the treatment of the myth a new dimension, the role of the individual. The idea of God is almost totally absent from all the songs (including those of the folk-protest tradition) in the 1930s, and the sense of community is only marginally suggested in the music of Tin Pan Alley. The individual, however, is given new stature as the personal supplants the communal.

The other type of song that occasionally alluded to the myth of America during the Great Depression was the satiric number. Broadway saw an incredible explosion of satire—much of it in the form of musical comedies—in the 1930s. Among the plays which enjoyed decent runs during these hard times were *Of Thee I Sing* (1931), *Face the Music* (1932), *Take A Chance* (1932), *Red, Hot and Blue* (1936), *Hurray for What* (1937), *I'd Rather Be Right* (1937), and *Leave It to Me* (1938). For the most part, government was the object of the satire, the hard shots being left to playwrights like Clifford Odets (*Waiting for Lefty*), Marc Blitzstein (*The Cradle Will Rock*), and Brecht and Weill (*Johnny Johnson*). So theatergoers could still enjoy their evening out, have their social conscience piqued ever so slightly, and walk out, humming a tune without having had to confront social issues headon. Oddly enough, however, these songwriters played an important role in the steadily growing tradition of cultural criticism.

Considering the backgrounds of the individuals involved in these shows, it is natural they would choose satire. They were, after all, trying to stay within the formal boundaries of the musical comedy formula per se and they did not see themselves as artists and by extension reformers. At best, one could expect their songs to be witty, irreverent (maybe), and skeptical of institutions and established mores. Typical of the slightly irreverent attitude that informs these musicals is the song "Of Thee I Sing" (1931) which uses a line from "My Country! 'Tis of Thee" but works it into a swinging love song, adding the tag "baby." One of the dominant elements of the musical-comedy satires of the 1930s is the air of skepticism that informs the music and situations. Ira Gershwin's "Strike Up the Band" (1927), for instance, states that we fought in 1917 and drove the "tyrant" from the scene. But the chocolate war they are now engaged in is a bigger and better one, "For your patriotic pastime" (Gershwin 1953, 226). He goes on to add that he doesn't know why his country is engaged in the current war, but that's all right, we didn't know last time either. That is a sentiment closer to e.e. cummings (i.e., "My Sweet Old Etcetera") than George M. Cohan.

Another example of the skeptical attitude of the Broadway composer can be seen in Cole Porter's "I Still Love the Red, White and Blue" (1932) from *Gay Divorcee*. At first, it seems to be kind of an old-fashioned paean to democracy, but as the narrator sings to the Bolshevik, she refers to Columbus as a "bimbo." She also refers to our patriotic forebears but updates the list to include—besides Washington, Jefferson, and Lincoln—Pershing, Lindbergh, Morgan,

Mellon, "And Amos and Andy too." Later, the narrator presents a somewhat backhanded endorsement of patriotism when she states that she may be a drag to progress, "But the star-spangled banner is my flag" (Porter 1984, 152). The ever so slight debunking of patriotic fervor doesn't really undercut the myth because, in the end, the narrator pledges her allegiance to the flag.

Lorenz Hart achieves something similar in his "Somebody Ought to Wave a Flag" from the 1932 movie *The Phantom President*, starring none other than George M. Cohan. In the song he mentions the war debt right off the bat, and he makes what was becoming the obligatory reference to the Depression. The key lines, however, come later when he states that there are reds in Russia and whites in Prussia, and the blues are all over the place; his solution: "string" them together "And fly them in the air" (1984, 179). It almost seems like a nonsequitur, it is thrown off so breezily; there is, moreover, a real danger about reading too much into it (i.e., let's conquer Russia and Prussia and maybe that'll help relieve Depression blues). The point seems to be fairly simple: Keep your sense of humor, it can't be too bad if three such threats can be sown up in a flag.

One of the last satires of the decade was another Cole Porter vehicle, *Leave It to Me* (1938), wherein a befuddled Victor Moore, portraying "Stinky" Goodhue, tries to get himself recalled as ambassador to the Soviet Union. Nothing he does can get him removed until he comes up with a plan for world peace. Within a matter of months, however, peace would be no laughing matter. Writing of the year 1938, Stanley Green notes:

> The depressing world situation, as country after country was being forced to give up its sovereignty and its freedom, was accompanied by a corollary belief in the United States as just about the last bastion of liberty left in the world. This renewed faith in America—either expressed or implied—was becoming an increasingly pertinent theme for the creators of musical comedy. It ran all through *I'd Rather Be Right, Pins and Needles*, and *Sing Out the News* (1971,167)

The theme also begins to pop up in individual popular songs for the first time in almost twenty years. In the final analysis, the satiric play and its accompanying songs basically confirm the myth by not attacking the fundamental ideals embodied in it; they merely show that the country's goodness and efficacy can be trivialized by the institutions we have created and have allowed to flourish. America's response to worldwide tensions in the late 1930s was signaled not only in Orson Welles's Halloween broadcast of *The War of the Worlds* but also in a series of four songs written within a two-year period: "God's Country" (1938) by E. Y. Harburg and Harold Arlen; "Ballad for Americans" (1939) by John Latouche and Earl Robinson; "God Bless America" (1939) by Irving Berlin; and "This Land Is Your Land" (1939) by Woody Guthrie. These songs offer some similar views of the myth but they also point up some important differences that will influence later songs dealing with this subject.

"God's Country" is a sort of transitional song, taking us from the witty, satiric thrust of the past decade to the more overtly patriotic tunes of the war years themselves. Featured in the 1939 movie musical *Babes in Arms* with Mickey Rooney and Judy Garland, it received an elaborate and energetic treatment, drawing on the youthful vigor of the leads and Busby Berkeley's considerable skills at moving large forces, to inspire a feeling of patriotism. The first verse employs the mytheme of the land as a unifying factor, with the narrator hailing a neighbor and asking if the person is traveling "East or West on the Lincoln Highway?" It goes on to extol the virtues of the land, citing that we have greener grass, taller timber, bigger mountains, and smaller troubles. In short, we are blessed because it is God's country. The listener is then reminded to be grateful that he/she lives in the United States, because look at what's going on overseas. The writers end the first verse by reminding the listener that we have greater freedom here because every person can be his/her own "dictator." The image is effective in that it creates a sort of ideological dissonance: The audience must reevaluate the "blessing" of freedom by seeing it in light of a term that would be distasteful to an American. It also continues the trend we observed in Harburg's earlier song and "Remember My Forgotten Man"—suggesting the empowerment of the individual within the culture. For one to be a dictator suggests complete control over the destiny of some entity, be it a country, an organization, a business, or one's self. Where the song differs from Harburg's earlier effort is in his suggestion that the empowerment of the individual results from the blessings God has bestowed on His people.

Considering the martial rhythms and serious tone of the song to this point, one is not quite prepared for the almost patterlike quality of the second verse, which contains allusions to Popeye, Mussolini, Gypsy Rose Lee. In short, the whole tone is much more in keeping with the type of song produced in the early and midthirties. Harburg mines popular culture itself to make his point; he notes that we should be grateful because we do not have the "goosestep" and Stalin, but he adds that we do have "Freddie and Gracie Allen," and finally, we should thank God most because we have "Frankie." The colloquial nature of the entire verse comes close to trivializing the seriousness of the fascist threat, but by using the allusions to popular culture, Harburg is able to engage the audience "where they really live."

"Ballad For Americans" was originally titled "The Ballad of Uncle Sam" in the Broadway production *Sing for Your Supper* (1939), and it later achieved wider popularity through, first, a CBS radio broadcast featuring Paul Robeson in the fall of 1939, and then in a fine recording by Robeson in 1940. The work is a cantata by John Latouche and Earl Robinson. Robinson's name will pop up again and then will reappear once more in the next chapter as we survey the songs of the radical left. Only he, Woody Guthrie, and the Weavers share the distinction of having enjoyed popularity within the mainstream and outside it.

The "Ballad for Americans" features choral numbers and antiphonal passages between soloist and chorus. There are snatches of dialogue and recitative, and the entire composition is shaped in narrative fashion. Basically, the composition traces the genesis and evolution of the democracy, beginning with allusions to Washington and Patrick Henry, and eventually announcing one of the dominant themes of the piece: "No one believed it." The point of this is that we should look to our past heroes who did have faith in the idea and, as in the case of Lincoln, "went to his grave" to free the slaves. Where Latouche and Robinson differ from other songwriters, however, is that for them the "idea" of America, the myth, is that the land, the sacrifice of the pilgrim/patriot forebears, and the concepts of freedom, opportunity, and equality are there to nurture, first, diversity and plurality, and, second, the efficacy, of the individual. The divine plan has no place in their saga. It is a story written by people first and last. Throughout Robeson asks the chorus, "You know who I am, don't you?" But the answer is deferred until near the end when he tells them, "I'm everybody who's nobody, and nobody who is everybody." Then he begins an epic catalog stating that he is all nationalities, all religions, all occupations, and so forth.

Toward the end of the composition he does allude to the mytheme of manifest destiny by stating that our greatest songs are still un-sung, but this will only be achieved as all people springing from the plains and mountains keep faith with those who believed, the patriots. And then he asks once more of the chorus, "You know who I am?" and then answers himself saying simply, "America!" Latouche and Robinson (and later Lewis Allan and Robinson) use the individual as the microcosm for the American experience; in this regard they reveal their liberal and leftist sympathies. It should also be noted, however, that by the end of the 1930s more Americans —not just the disaffected liberal intellectual— were embracing concepts like self-reliance and self-sufficiency; Suzanne Ellery Greene notes about the best-sellers of the 1930s: "A number of books, after the effects of the Depression were being felt, make an attempt to define America and to show the good in the American heritage. This is always coupled with praise of self-sufficiency as the element of character that has made America great" (1974, 70). For Latouche and Robinson, the breadth of the land (deep as the valleys and high as the mountains) and the sacrifice of the patriots are but metaphors for the expansiveness of the individual.

The composition then suggests a new version of the myth. The songwriters wisely do not enunciate the anomalous characteristics of the myth—as many of the radicals in later years will do—but instead mask them within the conventions of the established mythemes. They do not deify the individual but they do suggest that a higher meaning is achieved by the communal effort of dispa-rate individuals who have kept faith with our heroic forebears— those self-sufficient individuals who stood firm in their beliefs. By being like them and steadfastly believing in the principles of free-dom, equality, and opportunity, we can sing songs yet unsung. This device is similar to what songwriters do in wartime when they sug-gest that the individuals going off to fight are following in the foot-steps of the patriots, and they are part of the great continuum that ensures the preservation of our ideals. Thus in "Ballad for Ameri-cans," just as our destiny was carved and created by individuals, so will our future be.

In marked contrast to these sentiments is Irving Berlin's "God Bless America." This song has been touted for a number of years as a possible replacement for our current national anthem, and for good reason. It, along with Bates's "America the Beautiful," is probably the single most powerful declaration of the classic myth of America. One of the most effective devices in this song is Berlin's use of the personal pronoun "I." We ask God to bless America because it is the land that "I love," a powerful sentiment. The first-person pronoun immediately draws the listener into the song, so that, no matter who sings it, it becomes a personal utterance.

Clearly, the power of the song is derived largely from Berlin's simple heartfelt rendering of the mythemes. After the above-mentioned opening refrain, he asks the Almighty to show his hand in our destiny. As the melody climbs, it embraces images of the mountains and prairies and the ocean's foam, and then crescendos with "God Bless America." This, however, proves to be only the penultimate moment as, in the last stanza, he directly quotes the title of the great nineteenth-century popular song "Home Sweet Home." Home functions as a metonymy in the song—a familiar object from everyday experience, used to define the idea of the country itself. America then becomes more than merely the land; it is instead private property, a symbol of security, safety, warmth, and independence.

Berlin, like Bates before him, places great emphasis on the physical landscape. For these writers this mytheme is the most compelling, the most concrete image of the munificent bounty that God has bestowed on us. It suggests the immensity of the promise of the country and thus the transcendental nature of our mythic vision. For Berlin, this is the myth of America as imagined by the common man on Memorial Day, 1939, with the world teetering on the edge of war.

Woody Guthrie, however, thought common folk—the hard hit — might view the country a bit differently in 1939. His vision of America is one of the first truly popular ones to have a populist/communist orientation. "This Land Is Your Land" was initially written as a response to Berlin's song—at a time when, as Joe Klein described it, he was "Angry, frustrated, and feeling sorry for himself . . ." (1980, 143). He originally entitled the song "God Blessed America." The opening stanza was not different from the printed one we now have but instead of the line "This land was made for you and me," he had "God blessed America for me." What is interesting about the line is the past tense of the verb. Like a deist, he seems to suggest that the work of the Almighty is done, and now we individuals are the inheritors of the blessing to do with it as we will. But as the revision suggests, he got over his anger and recast the last line to reflect the philosophy that had inspired so many other of his great songs.

The locus of the myth for Guthrie is established in the opening stanza where he writes that the wide expanse of the land from New York to California is "your land" and it is "my land." Guthrie emphasizes in many songs the strong bond between the land and the people. In keeping with the materialistic thrust of communism, the land, in a sense, defines the people, but the image is also tied to the whole mythos of the land in American culture. Private property is perceived to be one of the birthrights inherent in the concepts of freedom and opportunity. Consequently, in this song, he uses the mytheme of the bountiful land to unify his message. The second stanza with its references to endless skies and golden valleys is a celebration of the landscape. In subsequent verses he summons forth images of the "sparkling sands," the "diamond deserts" (which is a telling shift from the Puritan "desart"), "golden valleys," "wheat fields waving," and "dust cloud rolling." (This last image may have some negative connotations, considering the Dust Bowl conditions that riddled the Midwest in the late 1930s.) In short, except that the emphasis is placed on people, the song seems one of a piece with other America songs. That is until you get to stanzas 5 through 7.

In the fifth stanza Guthrie states that he sees a sign that says "No Trespassing," but comments that on the other side is "nothing," and that was the side that was "made for you and me." In the powerful penultimate stanza he declares that not all the people share in the bounty of the land; he describes a scene where hungry people standing by the relief office in the "shadow" of a church steeple. And then he wonders if the land was made for you and me. This is not just a matter of ignoring the providential role of God. By using the image of the steeple, Guthrie brings into question assumptions about God's providential role in our lives, the mytheme of manifest destiny, and the mytheme of opportunity. This question will foreshadow the many questions asked about America in popular songs of the sixties, seventies, and eighties.

Guthrie's final image is once again geared for the common person and geared to the idea that we indeed all do share in the riches of the land, for nobody can stop us or make us turn back as we walk down that "freedom highway." For Guthrie, it is the individual who is at the heart of the dream and, it is suggested, bears the burden of the freedom we cherish. Guthrie's vision derives some of its power from the populist tradition. He has dug back into the ideals of the democratic man pushing onto the frontier. In fact, he has resurrected an ideal that had been lost over the years: the sanctity of the individual in the American experience. Guthrie's response makes sense and is in keeping with the popular sentiments of the day. Suzanne Ellery Greene notes that in best-sellers from 1938 to 1945 authors more and more recognized the plight of the individual and clearly in the books, "the reader's sympathies are to be with the underprivileged." John Steinbeck's *The Grapes of Wrath* (1939) and John Ford's film version of the novel showed people trapped between the implacable and remote forces of the weather on the one hand and big business on the other. Their response was, in Tom's case, to fight back or, in Ma Joad's case, to hold on with dogged determination to the belief that, "We'll go on forever, pa. 'Cause we're the people."

Likewise, for Guthrie, the locus of the myth lies in the basic goodness and integrity of the individual, and the ability of the individual to carve out a meaningful relationship with the land itself. He seems to be saying the land may indeed have been created by God, but it is not sacred because of that; it is sacred because it is ultimately the individual's responsibility. Ownership, moreover, is no more than caretaking, because we collectively share in the freedom promised by the land (not God), and no man can abridge the freedom to share the land. It is this relationship that allows the American to transcend the mundane and the forces that would oppress him and restrict his precious freedom.

The contrast between Guthrie's vision of America and Berlin's is illuminating for what it tells us about the direction of popular music and the new myth of America, which was ever so tentatively taking shape. Both men no doubt felt they were expressing the feelings of the common person, but one is looking back for his inspiration and basing his vision on a myth rooted in the immigrants. These people sought and fought for their freedom, opportunity, and equality, and their vision of the future was fueled by their belief in the theocratic vision. The other's vision is that of the backwoodsman whose greatest resource is his own spirit and who believes that the shaping hand of the country is his own. Berlin's song is the rich pattern of sophisticated Tin Pan Alley harmonies and melodic sureness; it is a material that was brought over by our forefathers (the verse even states that, as storm clouds gather, our voices are raised in solemn prayer) and has been refined through the years. It is drawn from well-established patterns, durable and evocative of the best that our modern well-tooled mills have to offer.

Guthrie's music, on the other hand, never strays far from the Tonic-Subdominant-Dominant chord progressions of folk music; it is verse-refrain storytelling of the most elemental sort. It is a rough cloth, woven on a hand loom, basic and imbued with the integrity of the individual designing it. It is the homespun of America speaking to an old, seemingly forgotten, myth of individualism and anticipating a new populist/socialist myth and vision.*

Woody's song and spirit would reverberate throughout the next four decades. He was an inspiration to Bob Dylan and played an important role in shaping Dylan's vision of America. In the eighties, his song has been reprised by Bruce Springsteen, a songwriter whose own vision of the myth of America is influencing us today.

II

The Good War. So we sum up the popular mythology centering around World War II. And so it seems it was—as wars go. There was a feeling of unity in the country. People's energies were focused again, business was humming, and the Depression was snapped. This is not to say there was not initial revulsion at the idea of another war. James Oliver Robertson notes that, "The Depression also created considerable revulsion against real war" (1980, 331), and we have seen two songs from the 1930s that took satiric jabs at war. Americans had so hastily retreated into isolationism and with such abandon in the 1920s that there must have been those who worried that it would take dynamite to unseat them.

The dynamite arrived in the form of Pearl Harbor. The abhorrence to war felt by many Americans made this "unprovoked attack" all the more heinous. Our myths had reinforced our basic goodness and now, in what must have struck some as a totally irrational act, we

*If a combination of individualism and populism/socialism seems self-contradictory, perhaps it is. Guthrie was an avowed Communist but of his own personal sort. He saw the elevation of the individual through the collective empowerment of all individuals.

were under siege. Well, as the 1940 tune, "He's My Uncle Sam" said, "That spry old chap [Uncle Sam] never picks a scrap, but he's won all he's had."

We have seen thus far that, beginning in the late thirties, Americans were being conditioned to a slight degree for the war. Songwriters had provided tunes which, by drawing on the myth of America, reaffirmed our basic goodness by noting how crucial the preservation of democracy was to us and the world. And so, with the declaration of war immediately following the bombing of Pearl Harbor, the music industry needed to do only a slight retooling for the war effort. As with World War I, most sectors of the music industry—including the emergent fields of folk-protest, country, and rhythm and blues —threw themselves behind the war effort. One could find early in 1942 songbooks such as the *Victory Song Book* published by Robbins Music, which contained all the standards, including songs of the Revolutionary War, songs of the Civil War, and many of the Leo Feist songs from the Great War. Not surprisingly the first song in the book is George M. Cohan's "Over There"; that song, as the film *Yankee Doodle Dandy* attested, was heard quite often in the early days of the war.

Ian Whitcomb has observed that Tin Pan Alley (this taken to include Broadway and Hollywood) was not as dominant an influence in providing war songs as it was in World War I. He believes that, "The Alley was now 'composers' and 'authors,' members of the ASCAP 'country club' and creators of civilized music" (1974, 197), and, he adds, "Instead the war spirit was fostered by musicians on the fringe of the pop—hillbillies who were carrying on the old Alley tradition" (198). We will indeed see in the next chapter how country musicians supported the war effort, but his case against ASCAP composers is a bit overstated. David A. Jasen in his book *Tin Pan Alley* notes that Rodgers (with both Hart and Hammerstein), Porter, Cohan, Hoagy Carmichael, Vernon Duke, and Meredith Willson all produced songs for the war effort (260). The back of a Music Publishers Holding (Remick, Witmark, Harms) song from 1942 reveals around fifty-eight songs devoted exclusively to the war effort. Some of them are older tunes, and probably 80 percent would be consigned to eternal obscurity, but there was considerable activity throughout the entertainment industry concerning the war. Hollywood and radio were extremely strong in their war-oriented musical productions.

Also there was a battery of tunes which, if you just look at the titles, seem to have little to do with the war or America per se but were important parts of America's wartime musical experience. Songs such as "It's Been A Long, Long Time," "I Don't Want to Set the World on Fire," "When the Lights Go on Again," "Don't Sit Under the Apple Tree," "I'll Be Seeing You," and "I Threw a Kiss in the Ocean," all suggested a longing for peace and were as effective as "Tenting on the Old Camp Ground" from the Civil War and "Till We Meet Again" from the Great War. They constitute an unspoken wish on the part of people for the peace that follows the war and that the war will achieve its "proper" end, and they played an important role in helping Americans articulate the mythology of war.

The songs of World War II, like those of World War I, reinforce the megafunctions of myth. As we have seen in Chapter 5, they do this by perceiving war as an aberration of our normal way of life, and they articulate the transcendental hope that greater good is born out of chaos and carnage. The songs of World War II almost form an umbrellalike structure for establishing the myth of America in wartime. We have already observed the top of the umbrella in the four complete statements of the myth ("God's Country," "God Bless America," "Ballad for Americans," and "This Land Is Your Land"). Now we turn to the handle and cane, the songs—as was the case in war's past—which focus on specific mythemes to boost morale and reinforce the sense of a community with a shared purpose.

As in war's past, songwriters need to reconcile the evil of war with the basic good that war was supposed to achieve: the preservation of the democratic way of life both here and abroad. The mytheme that best enables the popular artist to achieve this is our providential role in the world's history. We stand as the beacon of democracy, because God has willed it, and as in the case of this war, we have validated that divine mandate in previous wars. In World War I, we aided the Allies, and they enjoyed the fruits of democracy in the years following the war. James Oliver Robertson notes that the attitude toward America's role in the world was not appreciably different in World War II from that in World War I: "For Wilson, and for the many Americans who took up Wilson's expression of the myth in 1917 [to make the world safe for democracy] and after, there was no contradiction between independence and world leadership, between freedom of action and freedom from entanglement, or between championship of the rights of mankind and a powerful, victorious America dominating the affairs of the world. They were the same" (1980, 327). As a result, it is natural to find allusions to the Almighty in many of the songs. In their "American Prayer" (1942), songwriters Albert Stillman, Lawrence Stock, and Vincent Rose ask God, who "has given us birth," to lend a flaming sword to fight *His* battle on earth. There is an epic quality here; the Almighty, like the Gods of Olympus, is seen moving the participants around to satisfy a personal goal. When the "forces of evil" are overcome, the flag of His kingdom of Heaven will fly high in the breeze, and the boys will return to wives and mothers and our "earth will be like Heaven." It is hard to know how such overly ripe sentiments struck the average listener, but in the context of a church service or song program, the evocation of our manifest destiny and the notion that God was indeed guiding our destiny would have struck some responsive chords.

Other songs are considerably more casual in their allusions to the role of God. The narrator of Harold Adamson's and Jimmy McHugh's "Comin' in on a Wing and a Prayer" (1943) merely states that the whole crew of the crippled plane put their "trust in the Lord." It is a deft elision of religion and wartime technology, emphasizing that when the armaments fail, the strong arm of the Almighty will sustain their effort.

Similarly, Frank Loesser's famous "Praise the Lord and Pass the Ammunition" (1942) casts the chaplain in the role of hero when he is called upon to sustain the fighting man. The song was apparently based on a true story about a sky pilot who on Pearl Harbor day manned a position where a gunner had been killed; after downing a plane he was heard to exclaim, "I just got one of them! Praise the Lord, and pass the ammunition." This story, printed with the sheet music, may be apocryphal, but as I have stated previously, that doesn't make any difference—along with the song it passed into legend. The song itself doesn't say much. It has a kind of folk-song quality to it, with its repeated pattern of dotted quarter and dotted eighth rhythms. The basic message is contained in the final line: "Praise the Lord, and pass the ammunition, and we'll all stay free." So once again, the melding of technology and prayer will sustain the effort to preserve democracy. In fact, these songs suggest that the two are inseparable and that, as long as they are, the chaos and destruction of war will not destroy the ideals of liberty and freedom.

Yoking the mythemes of the patriots with that of manifest destiny is one of the most common and effective war-song strategies. In "Here's To You, MacArthur" (1942) by Nat Burton and Walter Kent (composer of "I'll Be Home For Christmas" and "The White Cliffs of Dover"), the songwriters state the country will sing MacArthur's praises all through history, for it's men like MacArthur that have made us great; they add that he has "the stuff" which is, apparently, a toughness that his dad displayed "in Ninety-Eight." This is an effective use of the mythemes, because it connects MacArthur with our past history and states that his exploits will be heralded in the future as he joins the ranks of the other great heroes in our history. They conclude the song with a promise to fight so "Old Glory" won't fall and to keep on fighting until the "whole darned world" is free.

Any time Old Glory is mentioned, it is a reminder of the sacrifice made to preserve democracy in the war of 1812, and its stars and stripes symbolize not only the states and original colonies but also the purity and sacrifice. In short, the evocation of the flag allows the songwriter a shorthand method of suggesting the mythemes; Cohan said it was the "symbol of the land I love," and songwriters effectively used it as such during World War II.

Other songs that blend these mythemes are the "U.S. Navy version" of Oscar Hammerstein and Sigmund Romberg's "Stouthearted Men," which asks for some stouthearted men who will fight like those in the navy who have fought so bravely in times past, the ones who have "won ev'ry war." For if we have that kind of man, we will never have to worry that "freedom's cause" will die.

Similarly, "You're A Lucky Fellow Mr. Smith" (1941) from the Abbott and Costello, Andrews Sisters film *Buck Privates* reminds the Mr. Smith of the title—who has been complaining about his military duty—that he has "that swell Miss Liberty" (symbol of freedom and opportunity), and he has a distinguished family tree including "Washington, Jefferson, Lincoln and Lee." As we noted in the songs of World War I, the songwriters have added Lee to the pantheon of patriots, to appeal to all regions of the country. Finally, they make a clever allusion to Yankee Doodle by telling Mr. Smith he was born with a feather in his cap and then reaffirm the egalitarian mytheme by reminding him that he doesn't have to be wealthy, but, in fact, he really is wealthy because he enjoys free speech. The final image that the songwriters convey is the image of unity when they remind

Mr. Smith that he should thank his lucky stars—all forty-eight. Here again the songwriters are letting the symbol of the flag do the talking.

Another song that uses the flag to reinforce the myth of America is Mack Gordon and Harry Warren's "Let's Bring New Glory to Old Glory" from the Sonja Henie film *Iceland* (1942). The manifest destiny mytheme is alluded to in the line about showing the world "a parade" and they add that we have the stuff heroes are made of. FDR is connected to the heroes of times past because he stands for *Freedom*, *Democracy*, and *Right*; they conclude by saying that with faith, courage, and the help of God, we'll bring new glory to Old Glory. It basically affirms most of the mythemes minus a reference to the land.

Some of the songs draw particular attention to the themes of liberty, opportunity, and equality. The first two are mentioned most often, but in contrast to songs from World War I and those between the wars, the issue of equality is broached more often. Songs that deal with these themes also take a more "personal" approach to the subject. For instance, one of the most popular songs to come out of the war and to enjoy popularity into the 1950s was "This Is My Country" (1940) by Don Raye and Al Jacobs. Like Berlin's "God Bless America," the song seems a very personal statement. It begins by enunciating the egalitarian mytheme, reminding listeners that it doesn't make any difference where they come from, they will still thrill at the sight of Old Glory. There is another allusion to the flag, this time in the chorus, when they refer to the pledge of allegiance. This is an effective shorthand method for suggesting a cluster of mythemes, most notably our historical heritage ("one nation" and the Republic) and liberty ("with liberty and justice for all"). The songwriters make a second general reference to God in the second verse when they state that we should thank Him for our native land. And then they add that, "My soul is rooted deeply in the soil on which I stand." Although not as powerful as Guthrie's evocation of the land mytheme, it nonetheless establishes the connection between the bounty of the land and the individual's destiny and heritage. In the chorus of the song itself, the writers emphasize the idea of freedom by reminding listeners that America is the land of "my choice." Their final image is a unique one as they reiterate that this is our country "to have and to hold," which elides the myth of America with the institution of marriage and the panoply of values that that suggests: love, devotion, fidelity (till death do us part is a particularly interesting allusion here in light of the imminence of war). We see here, as we have seen in past songs, how the Tin Pan Alley songwriter very effectively draws on other popular myths to reach a wider audience. By using images that are part of the common experience of the individual (home, marriage) and that are rooted in real day-to-day activities, the abstractions integral to notions of patriotism and devotion to country become intelligible.

Another song with a "personal" title came to us in 1941 when Dorothy Donnelly and Sigmund Romberg updated "Your Land and My Land" from their 1927 operetta *My Maryland*. They begin by enunciating the increasingly popular theme of us being "a hundred million strong" and that each and everyone will do whatever needs to be done for "The shining light of liberty," which could allude to the Statue of Liberty or even God's light. They then evoke the egalitarian mytheme that this land of freedom is for both "the great and the small." It is, to be sure, a vague allusion, but it does reflect a growing sensitivity on the part of the mainstream composer to consider those who may feel disenfranchised. In the final measures, they shift from 6/8 time to 2/4 and allude to the pledge of allegiance over a melody line borrowed directly from "The Battle Hymn of the Republic." This musical quotation nicely places the war in the context of other historical battles and reminds one of the sentiments of the original hymn: "Mine eyes have seen the glory of the coming of the Lord." All in all, it is an effective revision.

Two final songs, which lie slightly outside the pale of Tin Pan Alley, are "The House I Live In" (1942) by Lewis Allan and Earl Robinson and "We Are Americans Too" (1941) by the talented team of Andy Razaf, Eubie Blake, and Charles Cooke. "The House I Live In," which enjoyed wide exposure through a recording by Frank Sinatra, is a reaffirmation of the myth of America as first articulated by Robinson and Latouche in "Ballad for Americans." Basically, the song is a catalog of all the elements of the democracy—the house one lives in, the street one lives on, the plot of earth one tills, etc.—that celebrates the diversity of the country. The basic vision of America is contained in the last two lines of the song, where the songwriters state that America for them is "especially the people." In keeping with their leftist sympathies, the songwriters center the myth around the empowerment of the people as a collective entity. There are the standard allusions to the flag and other symbols of democracy, but God does not figure in Allan and Robinson's vision of the country; interestingly enough, however, in one of Sinatra's recorded versions the arranger includes a tag at the end after the last lines which quotes "America the Beautiful" and includes a chorus faintly singing, "God shed His grace on thee." I do not know how this set with Allan and Robinson, but if they had convictions similar to Woody Guthrie, it might have irritated them a little bit.

"We Are Americans Too"* offers the African-American perspective on the war effort. The title is quite revealing: Nearly a hundred years after the Emancipation Proclamation, blacks still feel compelled to convince the dominant culture that they are part of the system. The song itself subscribes to most of the mythemes, citing at one point that from Bunker Hill to the Rhine they have faithfully served the flag; they add as well that, none have "loved Old Glory more than we." They declare themselves as full participants in the myth when they state that they have played their part in the development of the country through hard work (they use the symbol of the plow as Harburg and Dubin had done earlier) and sweat. In short, they have contributed to the bounty of the land. If we can take the allusion to the flag as standing for the principles of freedom and opportunity, we have only to account for the idea of manifest destiny. God, as with the previous song, is conspicuously absent here, but they conclude by noting that all their future and everything they hold dear is here in America. The idea that one's destiny is linked with that of the land, and therefore, it would behoove the individual to work to preserve the future, was becoming more common. It is hard to surmise if the song was a reaction to some of the pacifistic and evenly overtly antiwar songs that emanated from African-American culture at that time. But, like "Lift Every Voice" from the turn of the century, the tone is moderate and well meaning and, cast as it is in the style of the standard Tin Pan Alley thirty-two bar song, one could easily conclude that it might have been written by any songwriter working in the business in 1941.

Finally, as with all the past wars, the prospect of peace is always an issue in the songs of war. This war had as many tunes dealing with loved ones eagerly awaiting the return of husbands, sons, and boyfriends. However, there were fewer tunes that actually dealt with

*Lyrics from Wanda Willson Whitman, ed., *Songs That Changed the World* (New York: Crown Publishing, 1969).

the return home (i.e., no songs like "Homeward Bound" or "How Ya Gonna Keep 'Em Down on the Farm"). One of the primary functions of these after-the-war songs, as we have seen, is to highlight the parenthetical nature of war by emphasizing how life will return to normal or we will be regenerated through the war effort. The most common sentiment expressed is like that in Frances Ash's "I'm Gonna Love That Guy (Like He's Never Been Loved Before)" (1945) when she states that, when the war is over, all their dreams will come true. One classic song, "The White Cliffs of Dover" (1941), anticipates the return of the sylvan world that mythically existed before the war when it states that shepherds will tend their sheep and "The valley will bloom again." Although the images in this song refer specifically to England, the allusions to rebirth and a return to normalcy must have struck a responsive chord in Americans as evidenced by the popularity of recordings of the tune. The evocation of the pastoral, with its strong references to innocence and peace, stands in direct contrast to the reality that many faced as they viewed vivid images of the wasteland of Hiroshima and the ovens of Auschwitz and Treblinka. Would the myth be enough to sustain us were this to happen again?

In spite of the horrors of the atomic bomb and the Holocaust, Americans emerged from the war much as they had from World War I—confident and eager to return to normal lives full of hope in the face of future anxiety. Henry Steele Commager described the situation at midcentury as follows: "In a general way it could be said that the two generations after 1890 witnessed a transition from certainty to uncertainty, from faith to doubt, from security to insecurity, from seeming order to ostentatious disorder. . . ." (1950, 417). Those songs that sustained the troops and those on the home front during the war years would continue to be played and sung on many occasions after the war. "God Bless America," "God's Country," and "This Is My Country" all made their way into the ranks of Tin Pan Alley standards. On appropriate holidays they could be heard on radio and then later on television. The sentiments expressed in them would continue to inspire Americans and be part of the bedrock for their belief that this was indeed the American century.

Many critics objected to the scene in Michael Cimino's *The Deer Hunter* where the characters sing "God Bless America" at Nick's funeral and after their lives had been incontrovertibly altered—and not for the better—by the war in Vietnam. But there is something quite honest about that scene, because the people depicted in that film went into Vietnam with convictions that were shaped by the mythology of World War II. Cimino shows them, at that point where their faith in the country is on the verge of being shattered, falling back on the myth to sustain them and help them make sense of the tragedy. As we shall see, forty-five years after the end of the World War II, the traditional myth is still a vital part of our culture, even for those who would repudiate its ideals.

The end of the war did not signal a total cultural capitulation to the old verities and beliefs. The spirit of irreverence and skepticism was still alive. In fact, in 1946, the first year following the war, Ira Gershwin collaborated with Arthur Schwartz on a tune entitled "The Land of Opportunitee" from the musical *Park Avenue*, which talks about immigrants coming to the United States because they heard the streets were paved with gold. They, of course, find out this isn't so, but they are undeterred because "The pioneer spirits still carry on." The songwriters go on to show how one can find gold if one plays the stock market or go to the race track. Or one could become a contestant on a radio quiz show, where, if one is able to recognize which country has the red, white, and blue flag, they might throw in the "sponsor's daughter" as a gift. There is hardly an allusion to the myth in this song—except for the one to the flag, and that's an oblique one at best— but instead it portrays the epitome of the American experience to be one of rampant consumerism. In short, it seems that mainstream songwriters picked up right where they left off around 1938 and held the mirror of satire up to expose the foibles of the booming material world emerging after the war.

And there would be other critiques of the system to emerge in the postwar years, but they would come less and less from Tin Pan Alley, Broadway, and Hollywood. They would come from people whose musical experience lies outside the pale of Tin Pan Alley. Like the Scrubwoman in *Of Thee I Sing*, they wanted work, steady work if possible. They were people who saw the new material world as real.

CHAPTER VII

"This Land Is Your Land"
The Folk-Protest
Movement and
Other Voices,
1920–1960

"They's an army of us without no harness." He bowed his head and ran his extended hand slowly up his forehead and into his hair. "All along I seen it," he said. "Ever' place we stopped I seen it. Folks hungry for side-meat, an' when they get it, they ain't fed. An' when they'd get so hungry they couldn't stan' it no more, why they'd ast me to pray for 'em, an' sometimes I done it." He clasped his hands around drawn-up knees and pulled his legs in. "I use ta thank that'd cut 'er," he said. "Use ta rip off a prayer an' all

"There's mean things happenin' in this land" the song went, and for a number of Americans in the period from 1920 to the late 1950s this pretty much summed up the American experience. While the songwriters on Tin Pan Alley, Broadway, and Hollywood chose wit and satire to deal with national issues, other voices, reflecting a different worldview and tone, addressed the same issues in a spirit of dead seriousness. African-Americans, laborers, disenfranchised farmers from the Midwest, communists, intellectuals, and to a lesser degree rural Southerners lifted their voices in a new musical spirit and sound to share with one another and the world a vision of life that was alien to the experience of Tin Pan Alley. Although these voices hardly posed a threat to the music industry, their legacy is enormous. By the late 1950s they

the troubles'd stick to
that prayer like flies on
flypaper, an' the prayer'd
go a-sailin' off, a-takin'
them troubles along. But
it don't work no more."
—*John Steinbeck,*
The Grapes of Wrath

were challenging the hegemony of Tin Pan Alley, and in their approach to the idea of America, they laid the foundations for some current interpretations of the myth.

In this chapter we will see how African-Americans, radicals and leftists, and country musicians all called upon the myth to help their communities through these crisis-ridden years. Their new version of the myth is not a radical shift in perspective, but it is highlighted by significant differences. What occurs in this time period—primarily in the music of the folk-protest movement and to a lesser extent in that of African-Americans—is a paradigm shift. There is a move from viewing the United States as a country with a divine mission to one with a human mission.

Our destiny is not to be read as some divine plan revealed in the blessings of the Almighty on the land, but as the ability of individuals to establish a bond of solidarity with other workers and create a meaningful relationship with the land through work. In the music of these subcultures, the ideas of liberty, equality, and opportunity are tied to the concept of work; through work one comes to share in the bounty of the land. God's work is done, and now it is time for people to do theirs.

The introduction of this version of the myth into the musical life of Americans happened subtly over the thirty-year period under consideration here. The way it happened is a good example of what Prof. William Brown terms anomaly-masking. Anomaly-masking occurs when a new ideology—or, in this case, a new mytheme—is introduced that is anomalous to the established ideology. In order to gain acceptance for the new idea, the songwriter must mask the difference so that it does not threaten the basic foundations of the audience's beliefs. Once this is done, the audience can more readily accept the new myth (or paradigm). The songs of the period under consideration here not only broach new ideas but also open the way for what we will observe in the 1960s, where songwriters can freely engage in what Brown terms anomaly-featuring—highlighting the differences in the ideology—and the audience is willing to accept the differences as the new reality. In the years from 1920 to 1960 songwriters paved the way for the radical revision of the myth that figured so prominently in the music of Bob Dylan, Phil Ochs, Paul Simon, Sly Stone, and others.

But in our 1920–1950 period, let us begin with the music of African-Americans.

I

To say that African-Americans made great strides in the music industry in the years between the wars is perhaps to overstate the case, but their lot improved some from what it was prior to the Great War. More media was available for "their" music. Great artists such as Louis Armstrong, Bessie Smith, Billie Holiday, Coleman Hawkins, Duke Ellington were heard by wider audiences, because of the proliferation of recordings and the invention of radio. Sales of Bessie Smith's records helped keep Columbia afloat during the lean years of the 1930s. Record companies and eventually radio also discovered that a burgeoning market for black music was growing in other regions—other than the Northeast—specifically the South.

But whereas these jazz artists were trying to establish themselves within the larger community of Tin Pan Alley, the Delta blues artists and the urban blues artists of the twenties, thirties, and forties sought to speak almost exclusively to a smaller and more immediately sympathetic audience of their peers. Consequently, in their music we do not find the same approach to problems that we encountered in the more widely disseminated music. The blues artist's audience placed less value on *how* something was said and more on *what* was said. Wit and irony and verbal facility—although hardly alien to blues lyrics—were not the chief end of Robert Johnson, Lonnie Johnson, Big Bill Broonzy, and Leadbelly. Instead, their audiences wanted something personal, something carved out of the experience of hard living and hard loving, which formed a deep bond in the black community.

It is not too surprising that the myth of America plays no major role in the lyrics of blues and rhythm and blues. This is not to say that protest is absent from the lyrics about the system; one could probably demonstrate that all blues lyrics are a protest about the American experience. But what is missing is an emphasis on the abstractions and ideologies that form the foundation of the myth.

In my own personal survey of some 2,500 lyrics I did not encounter a single song that dealt with all the mythemes in the myth of America and only a handful that dealt with even one of the mythemes. Protest centers around work and the lack thereof and with immediate dealings with bosses and law enforcement. Typical of the sentiments in an African-American protest song would be the lines about blacks not being able to get "justice in Atlanta town" or the idea that "there ain't no heaven on the county road."* The allusion to heaven in the second example owes more to the gospel tradition than to our ideas of manifest destiny. I suppose what one could say is that the argument in African-American music is with the institutions and not necessarily the ideological abstractions that inform the institutions.

Why is there so little actual criticism (or praise for that matter) of America in the blues lyric? Jeff Todd Titon offers some reasons in his *Early Downhome Blues*. The form of the blues is very fixed, not only musically, but also lyrically. A second reason offered by Titon is that a protester could conceivably be tracked down and punished for his/her ideas (1977, 190–193). Or perhaps such abstractions as "purple mountains" and "Pilgrim feet" are so remote from his experience as to have no meaning for or against. His disenfranchisement with the American experience is much more immediate.

The only mytheme that figures prominently in African-American music between 1920 and 1950 is the freedom-opportunity-equality mytheme. Some of the rhythm and blues numbers in the 1940s and 1950s tackled other issues, but not in the same way that the folk-protest songs by white performers did. In general, the African-American's exclusion from the American experience centers largely around the material preferments that attend the myth. Symbols of what it is to be an American are those icons we associate with social status, almost exclusively the province of white Americans. America is the rich man's America, a point made abundantly clear in Leadbelly's "Red Cross Store" written around the time of the Great War and published in 1936. In the song he states that he doesn't really have anything to fight for and declares that he isn't going to go down to the "Red Cross Sto'" because he isn't going to play in "no rich man's show" (Lomax 1967, 354). There are, in short, two

*From Lawrence Gellerts' recording *Negro Songs of Protest* (Rounder Records 4004).

America's: one for whites and one for blacks. African-Americans locate themselves outside the mainstream, alienated from the myths that animate the visions of white middle-class citizens. As Lonnie Johnson's "Hard Times Ain't Gone No Where" (1937) declares, it's not just the Depression that has created this sense of otherness because, "they didn't have no money when times was good." This image of the alienated American will continue to influence songwriters and will explode into the mainstream with a vengeance in the 1960s.

In a few songs of the twenties, some writers held out hope that America would be a harbor for freedom for blacks as it had been for others. Lonnie Johnson's "Life Saver Blues" (1927), in fact, uses the image of the boat on storm-tossed seas as a central symbol for oppression and freedom. In the opening stanzas, the captain of the boat tells the passengers to grab their life jackets, because they are sinking. Once in lifeboats they spot "Uncle Sam's ship coming: painted in red white and blue." That boat takes them to New York City, which signals a new beginning. Similarly, Maggie Jones's "North Bound Blues" (1925) speaks of going north where she "can be free" of Jim Crow laws and—naturally for a blues lyric—be with her man. In short, in the twenties, the north still held out the promise of the American Dream. But the quest for America still centers on finding economic opportunity and not on sharing in a divinely mandated quest for freedom and opportunity.

With the Great Depression, a harsher tone enters the repertoire of the bluesmen and women. Mary Ellison notes, "Blues mourned the loss of a dream: the failure of the American system to allow the acquisition of land by any means and on almost any scale" (1989, 54). The quest for opportunity forced the blues writer to fall back on another myth: Mobility equals opportunity. So we have Will Weldon's "W.P.A. Blues" (1936), which details how he lost his house and must keep moving because he can't pay, and we have Robert Hicks, in his "We Sure Got Hard Times Now" (1930), talking about how hard times not only contribute to decreased employment opportunities, but to more drinking and more traveling to find work. The land is not evoked, but references to cities such as St. Louis, Memphis, and Santa Fe capture the sense of dislocation felt by many Americans (Taft 1983, 108). Similarly, Skip James's "Hard Time Killin' Floor Blues" (1931) speaks of people who drift from "door to door" and "Can't find no heaven" (123). As with the earlier reference to one of Gellert's *Negro Songs of Protest*, this line seems to owe more to the tradition of the spiritual than to a take-off on the mytheme of the providential role of the country. However, thinking of the common associations in African-American music with heaven and the promised land, a listener could draw a negative inference about God's blessing on His land. Finally, in a real reversal of the sentiments expressed in two songs mentioned earlier, we have Joshua White's "Welfare Blues" (1934), which states that welfare isn't helping him any, so he'll just go back down South. Carl Martin's "Let's Have a New Deal" (1935) paints an even more desperate scenario as he asks for a New Deal, "Because I've got to make a living: if I have to rob and steal."

Throughout most of these songs one finds a strong level of discontent but never a wholesale damnation of the system. The songs are very personal, confessional at times, and reflect an almost stoic approach to Hard Times in the United States. However, in the 1940s and 1950s, the gloves go off, so to speak, for some of these musicians. Breaking away from some of the conventions of classic blues, certain songwriters begin taking a more critical look at the system and use the media available to them to express their view. One of the most interesting aspects of Robert Palmer's *Deep Blues* (1982) is seeing how many blues artists were featured on radio during the thirties and forties, especially in northern cities such as Chicago. African-Americans found an increasing base of support among radicals (white and black), who also took up their cause in song (Earl Robinson is a case in point). Thus the approaches to problems are a bit bolder and wider in their sweep than we have observed in the blues of the preceding two decades.

We have seen in one song that African-Americans had ambivalent feelings about war. Because they saw themselves as outsiders, war is perceived as something started by whites to defend white values; but there is also the tacit knowledge that in turning their backs on the cause, they face uncertainty and, perhaps, a different and worse kind of domination. Therefore, songs written by African-Americans often support the war efforts. Son House's "American Defense" (1942) notes that the "Red, White and Blue" represents us and that we ought to do everything we can to defend it. He includes an obligatory slap at the enemy reminiscent of those seen in country music when he remarks that, at the war's end, there won't be enough Japanese left "to shoot a little game of craps." Similarly, Mary Ellison writes that J. B. Lenoir of "Eisenhower Blues" fame saw it "as an unpleasant but God-given mission to fight in Korea" (1989, 136); this would seem to be an endorsement of sentiments similar to those expressed by the Tin Pan Alley songwriters of the past.*

When World War II was over, however, and the hopes that African-Americans would have a new order steadily dissipated, a more critical tone entered the repertoire. One of the most striking blues numbers from the 1940s is Big Bill Broonzy's "Black, Brown and White Blues" (sometimes called the "Git Back Blues") from 1946, which in a series of striking images points up the incredible disparity between white opportunity and black opportunity. He talks of going to the unemployment office and, like everyone else, choosing a number but not having it called. Then he gets a job, but he gets fifty cents while the white man working next to him gets a dollar. In the fifth stanza he introduces a theme that was common among the songs of the labor and folk-protest movement: He states he "helped build" the country, fought for it, and helped "this vic'try" with his spade and hoe, and now he wants to know what we're going to do "about Jim Crow?" The demand is more militant, and he echoes Woody Guthrie's sentiments about the role of the individual in carving out the destiny of the country by working the land. Broonzy engages in a bit of anomaly-masking here, suggesting that the country's destiny is predicated on individual effort and assurance of equal rights, not some divine plan. He played his role in the manifest destiny by working the land which, in turn, helped bring victory. Thus the mythemes of freedom, the land, and manifest destiny are all suggested, but they are seen not as blessings pursuant to God's plan, but as fruits of individual effort. The African-American artist stresses almost exclusively the theme of equal opportunity, and with Broonzy's song we observe songwriters looking more at the total myth to bring this theme into focus.

Next, we have the calypso song, "Walk in Peace" (1946) by Sir Lancelot (Hille, 1948). This song is unusual because it is one of the

---

*It is possible that Korea may have had a fraction more meaning to African-Americans than earlier wars, because it was during that conflict that President Truman ordered segregated black regiments broken up and the soldiers integrated into other units in the army. This may have been seen as a small first step toward the long-postponed fulfillment of the American dream for African-Americans.

first to highlight the true anomalies in the myth. We can't hope, as the second verse states, to teach Hungarians democracy if at home we "practice racial bigotry." And he clearly questions the notion of manifest destiny when he writes that the "know-how" of being free isn't just a monopoly of the Yankees. Later in the song he states that we can't condemn Russia for tyranny if black men do not "walk with noble dignity" in the United States; this is a reiteration of an old socialist theme that Russia, unlike America, did not have a history of racial bigotry and oppression. Finally, he reminds the listener that if we hope to be "A shining example of democracy" we have to practice what we preach. Obviously, a song like this would only strike a responsive chord among a small audience. Since it came so soon after the war, its sentiments would have grated on the sensibilities of the average American, flush with the glow of victory. To point up the hypocrisy of the basic mythemes would become more common in the 1950s and 1960s, especially in the pages of publications such as *Sing Out* and *Broadside*, but in 1946 Sir Lancelot was in virgin territory with his ideas.

Over the next twenty years from the end of World War II and through the heroic days of the civil rights movements in the 1950s and early 1960s, African-Americans would increasingly take stronger stands on the issues until, in the age of rock, they clearly and forcefully articulated their skepticism about the myth of America. They would measure their progress against the promises of the myth and then use the myth to show white America how it had, by failing them, fallen short of those promises. Taylor Branch records a striking incident that occurred in January of 1956 when the house of Dr. Martin Luther King, Jr. was firebombed. As soon as the King family was found to be safe, a crowd congregated outside his home. Branch writes, "Shouts of anger and recognition competed with sirens and the background noise of earnest Negro women singing, 'My Country! 'Tis of Thee' " (1988, 165). This is a dramatic and ironic reversal of that episode in which freedmen sang the song as their rite of passage into free society on Emancipation Day. In time, moreover, songwriters would begin to highlight the ironies that the myth possessed for African-Americans. Leadbelly, for instance, evokes the myth when he declares in his "Bourgeois Blues" (1959), that he doesn't care to be "mistreated by no bourgeoisie" in this "home of the brave, land of the free." With "The Star Spangled Banner" and other songs expressing the myth serving as a backdrop, a new generation of black and white musicians would, as Paul Simon said, "All come to look for America."

II

Woody Guthrie once said, "Let me be known as the man who told you something you already know." That simple and self-effacing philosophy masks one of the major revolutions to occur in popular music in America. As Woody Guthrie, Pete Seeger, and others sang their simple songs during the dark days of the Depression, probably even they had no notion of what their efforts would yield over a thirty-year time period. In fact had you told someone in 1939, "Someday you'll hear this music all the time," it probably would have met with derisive laughter. But within thirty years, not only would the popular music world be adopting the ideology of this generation of folk-protest artists but their musical gestures as well.

The crisis created by the Great Depression was first and foremost one of economics, but attending that, were sociological and ideological crises. Even Tin Pan Alley couldn't turn altogether away from the human dimension of the tragedy. But there were others who were hit harder by the catastrophe, others who did not frequent the theater or get to the movies except maybe once a month (if at all), who were lucky if they owned a record player or a radio. They, like African-Americans, found themselves alienated from the dream and felt they had become outsiders in their own country. By 1932 the ranks of these outsiders had swelled. Woody Guthrie was among them. He and fellow minstrels saw underlying the 1930s crises—and, in fact, after the war into the 1950s—a need not only to improve people's material lot but to redefine the idea of America. There were mean things happenin' in the land.

The musicians who formed the core of the folk-protest movement believed that music could help rid the country of some of those mean things. Drawn from the ranks of labor, the American Communist Party, socialist groups, progressives, liberals, and intellectuals, these musicians held on to one basic belief: Music could make a difference. Alan Lomax, in his introduction to *The People's Song Book*, stated that as he watched these "folk" songs grow since the mid-1930s, "Slowly I began to realize that here was an emerging tradition that represented a new kind of human being, a new folk community composed of progressives and anti-fascists and union members. These folk, heritors of the democratic tradition of folklore, were creating for themselves a folk-culture of high moral and political content" (Hille 1948, 3). One is struck by the passion of the statement and the suggestion that the music would be part of transcendental experience. This feeling is also captured in these words by Irving Howe about joining the Communist Party: "To yield oneself to the movement . . . was to take on a new identity. Never before, and surely never since, have I lived at so high, so intense a pitch, or been so absorbed in ideas beyond the smallness of self. . . . The movement gave me something I would never find again and have since come to regard with deep suspicion . . . it gave my life a 'complete meaning,' a 'whole purpose'" (quoted in Lieberman 1989, 15). The musicians who produced songs to support the labor movement, the homeless, and all the others hard hit by the Depression were part of this passion, part of this quest for something "beyond the smallness of self."

Ever since the days of the Knights of Labor and through the trials and tribulations of the International Workers of the World (IWW), music had been viewed as a key component in mobilizing the working person and bringing about social change. The same was true in the 1920s and especially the 1930s. One of the early advocates of using music to mobilize the workers, Charles Seeger, wrote: "We felt urgency in those days. . . . The social system is going to hell here. Music *might* be able to do something about it" (Lieberman, 29). However, efforts of Seeger and others in the Composers Collective were not as successful as they would have liked. Consequently, around the mid-1930s a shift occurred; musicians turned from the revolutionary chorus rooted in classical and art song forms to music drawn from "folk" culture. This was part of an effort by the Communist Party and labor movement to establish a real "people's music."

The musicians used "traditional" instruments such as the guitar, the banjo, and the mandolin, and borrowed tunes from established folk tunes (which could include anything from "Aura Lee" to a Stephen Foster melody or "The Battle Hymn of the Republic"). The first requirement of the music was that it be simple and be drawn from the experience of the working person. Classical and popular forms were thought to be too bourgeois—a shortsighted view, as they were to find out when they had difficulty "selling" the folk style (rural and Southern) to urban workers. Back in the teens one of the Joe Hill's more inspired methods for the IWW cause had been to use currently popular tunes, songs that the worker would have heard in an urban setting. However, by the 1930s the music industry was dominated by the American Society of Composers, Authors, and Publishers (ASCAP), and so folk-protest writers, if they borrowed a tune from the Hit Parade, would open themselves up to possible litigation. Instead, they selected tunes in the public domain, or current folk tunes, or wrote their own.

Helped along by some major strikes in the early thirties (notably the Gastonia-Loray and Harlan County conflicts) and New Deal programs like the National Labor Relations Act (1935), the Wagner Act (1935), and the WPA (1935), there was a glimmer of hope among workers and a more fertile seedbed to sow the seeds of discontent in song. Eventually things coalesced for the movement, and during a period from 1939 to 1942 folk music experienced a renaissance and a growing appeal even beyond the ranks of labor. As Serge Denisoff notes, "During this time 'folk music' became what one listened to at informal gatherings and social affairs given by radicals" (1971, 68). The major emphasis of the movement was to take the music directly to the people, and to make available to them songbooks so they could sing along; in short, to establish solidarity through a living musical experience.

This is not to say that other media were slighted. Indeed, the folk-protest movement needed recordings and radio, especially during the Depression when people looked to those two media as "cheap" forms of entertainment. Thus, recordings such as Woody Guthrie's *Dust Bowl Ballads* and, later, those of the Almanac Singers and the Weavers were major cogs in keeping the wheels of the movement turning. It was during this time, moveover, that millions of Americans heard the radio broadcast of Earl Robinson's "Ballad For Americans," and tuned into Alan Lomax's "Back Where I Come From" (which featured Woody Guthrie regularly), and purchased the Almanac Singers' "Ballad for John Doe," and heard that same group on a new 1942 radio series entitled "This Is War." It finally seemed that the philosophy of the movement's leaders of what their music should achieve was being proved right. Burl Ives commented after a fund-raiser for the Spanish Civil War, "Why did this particular audience understand me? It occurred to me that people so concerned about other human beings must be men of good will who would understand my simple songs about people" (Denisoff, 1971, 63).

Through the 1930s, the 1940s, and into the 1950s and 1960s people such as Pete Seeger, Lee Hays, Irwin Silber, Earl Robinson, Paul Robeson, Fred Hellerman, and, of course Woody Guthrie maintained their faith in this form of music. They stressed simple melodies and harmonies and accompanying patterns to complement their "simple" message about America and its people. The new music was the perfect complement for a new version of the myth. Nevertheless, the songwriters had their work cut out for them, reconciling some troubling contradictions for workers and Americans as a whole. If God does not play a major role, from what source do we derive our higher sense of purpose? How do we empower individuals and yet maintain a necessary collective strength? If the old world and its ways of doing things must be changed, what happens to our heroes? These were some of the issues that songwriters would have to address as they penned tunes for the masses. And to start they concentrated on what they saw as the central component in the whole American experience: the individual.

The basic task of the folk-protest movement was to get the American citizen to recognize the "sanctity" of the individual. Henry Demarest Lloyd declared at the turn of the century that a "new religion" was looming on the horizon, and at the center would be *"man the redeemer, divinity of democracy—the creative will of the people* which is to be substituted for the old God" (quoted in Wiebe 1967, 64). The songwriters of the folk-protest movement needed to capture this spirit. One encounters in the songs of the IWW, a conscious effort to undermine the mytheme of God's role in the country. For instance, John F. Kendrick's "Christians at War" (1913) paints an entirely different portrait of the American's divine necessity for waging war, by first quoting "Onward, Christian Soldiers!" and then showing the evil inherent in the "duty" that demands one slay one's "Christian neighbor" (*Songs of the Workers*, 12). Similarly, Joe Hill's famous "There Is Power in a Union" makes the point that maybe religion—"blood of the lamb"—isn't sufficient, so one should join the union if they "would have eggs and ham." For Hill, the Wobblies, and to a lesser extent the folk-protest movement of the thirties and forties, joining the union is the real manifest destiny of the nation as "we our share of this earth shall demand" (*Songs of the Workers* 8). But little of this debunking of the Christian mission of the nation carried over into the 1930s. Songwriters would on occasion try to argue that a particular union or group had a divine purpose, as in "Old Sawbucks," but the message is the same as Joe Hill's song: We do not look to the Almighty to guide us in our mission, we must look to ourselves.

As stated above, most songwriters in the 1930s played it a little smarter and did not attack the mytheme of God's role, but at the same time they did not evoke it either. They had to run something of an ideological gauntlet with this issue. On the one hand, they had to face the reality that many of the people whom they were hoping to reach had religion in their backgrounds; in some cases it was at best a casual religious experience (obligatory attendance at some church service); in others, however, it was deeply rooted and probably shaped the individual's view of the world. On the other hand, the musicians themselves, many of whom were better educated than their audiences and had definite communist sympathies, had to be faithful to the realpolitik, which told them that religion (Joe Hill's "pie in the sky") was but an opiate and that the rewards for work had to be found in the here and now. They reconciled this by focusing on the concept of the individual.

The myth of America as implemented by the folk-protest movement was that the individual, especially the worker, was the central component in America's mission to the world. Individuals who had made us great, such as Washington, Frederick Douglass, and especially Lincoln, are portrayed not as dim historical figures working out God's plan on earth but as part of the tradition of the self-reliant individual. The workers had made the country what it was, and they should be the inheritors of its bounty. Not surprisingly two of the most popular figures who emerge in the music of the thirties, forties, and fifties are John Henry and Jesus Christ. "John Henry," as Robbie Lieberman notes, "symbolized the power of the workers whose labor had built America as well as the contributions of black people to enriching American culture" (1989, 101).

Jesus Christ, on the other hand, is the common person of humble origins who preached a philosophy of love and equality (i.e., all are equal in the eyes of the Lord, and he who is least shall be exalted, etc.), and who shed his blood for the sake of others—he was, in short, the martyr par excellence. Christ's divinity is never an issue. His presence in the songs reaffirms the message of the myth that the country's destiny will not be guided by God the Father but by the efforts and sacrifice of the common person. Consequently, Jesus is portrayed, to quote Woody Guthrie's "Jesus Christ," as "A hard working man and brave" who said, "'Give your goods to the poor.'" For this he was laid in His grave, and, Guthrie concludes, if he were walking around New York today preaching what he preached back then, he would also be laid in His grave. He also mentions Jesus in his "Union Feeling" when he says that Jesus told the people, "You got to join my union army." The presence of Jesus in an occasional song is in keeping with the movement as a whole in that they are fundamentally concerned with the human being; the God of the songs of the past was too much the Old Testament figure: divorced from the daily lives of His people but intimately concerned with their destiny. Jesus was concerned about His people, he shared in personhood and was one of them. The figures of John Henry and Jesus are used only occasionally in the songs, but they stand as iconic figures and models for the image of the worker.

John Henry and Jesus give rise to the image of the common person who keeps faith with the promise of the country but whose place in that destiny is brokered away by the collective forces of big business and, at times, government. Joseph Brandon's "A Fool There Was," for instance, paints a portrait of the out-of-work laborer who won't steal or rob and believes what Roosevelt says about this being a grand country "With plenty of everything." However, in the final stanza the subject of the song is found dead of starvation clutching a flag in his hand (Lomax 1967, 361).

Similarly, Woody Guthrie's moving "Pastures of Plenty" states that the migrants have worked the fields all over the land—establishing the point that they are probably closer to the land than the people who own it—and that they will defend that land with their lives if necessary because those "Pastures of Plenty must always be free." In short, one can depend on the faithfulness of the workers, they are the constant in the changing world. As Ma Joad notes in the film version of *The Grapes of Wrath* (1939): "But we keep a comin,' We're the people that live; they can't wipe us out, they can't lick us. We'll go on forever, Pa, 'cause we're the people."

We have seen throughout this study that the corollary to God's role in the formation of this country was our inheritance of a role in world affairs. The destiny of America is inextricably tied to world destiny. Songwriters in the folk-protest movement largely ignore the role of the Almighty in the destiny of the nation, but they have not jettisoned the mytheme of the country's worldwide mission. In most of the songs the destiny of the individual is tied to the union.

It is through the solidarity of the union ("One Big Union") that the individual will achieve some sense of transcendence. Paradoxically, in order for individuals to be assured that their freedom, opportunity, and equality are secure, they must align themselves with workers all over the world. In that solidarity, moreover, is not just shared wealth but shared peace as well. Ralph Chaplin, in his "The Commonwealth of Toil" (set to the tune of "My Darling Nelly Gray"), speaks of having a dream of a world that will be fair because each man can be assured of secure and free life; this will only happen, however, "When the earth is owned by labor . . . in the commonwealth of toil that is to be" (Lomax 1967, 97). One hears echoes of a couple of the mythemes in that passage with the reference to freedom as well as the worker's version of manifest destiny.

Another song, Ethel Comer's "Stand Up! Ye Workers" (1927) (sung to the tune of "Stand Up for Jesus"), asks that we unite for liberty and right, so we can "win the world for labor" by vanquishing every foe (*Songs of the Workers*, 41). Later she asks that people stand up in "every land" and fight for freedom "In ONE BIG UNION grand." The sentiments in both of these songs are so close to those of the songs dealing with the traditional myth in the past that it is almost errie. Were one to substitute Old Glory, God, or United States for more labor-oriented terms, one would have a tune that could have been sung in any era since the Revolutionary War.

The new version of the myth is also similar to the traditional myth in its international perspective. Woody Guthrie, shows how the union is only a microcosm of a new worldwide order in his "Better Go Down and Join the Union," where he begins by noting that Uncle Sam "started him a Union," and then he goes on to catalog all the other unions from the forty-eight states, including Banking Men, Landlords, John L. Lewis, and the Cotton Pickers. Tom Glazer in his "The Whole Wide World Around" (1947) states that the union will "unite us/Forever proud and free." Again, if one substituted the words "God" or "flag" for "Union," one would have a standard version of the myth. This song is one of the most complete statements of the new myth in the whole repertoire of the folk-protest movement. Glazer introduces the mytheme of freedom and equality by stressing universal brotherhood. The fears of all people, be they yellow, white, or brown, he states, will be my fears. And we will all be united in breaking "slavery's chain" and as long as we are united, no tyrant or fascist can defeat us.

In the case of all the above-mentioned songs, the union has taken the place of God as the force that will allow the individual to lose that sense of "the smallness of self." Individuals, through the Union, find themselves part of a larger historical moment. They find themselves empowered individually and collectively through one big union, securing their individual rights by securing those rights for all people. Woody Guthrie's "Seamen Three" speaks of fighting and singing for the Willie McGees and fighting "till the world gets free." It is not dramatically different from the myth of the Revolutionary War; it has just eliminated God from the picture. The sense of destiny is still there. The world is still being created anew. The IWW's version of "The International" states that a "better world's in birth," and Ralph Chaplin's "Solidarity Forever" declares a new world can be born "from the ashes of the old," and this will be possible because of the strength of the union (Greenway 1970, 181). Similarly, Woody Guthrie's "Better World" announces that things will be better "When we'll all be union, and we'll all be free." He goes on to show how war and new atomic technology also play a role in this new world order when he states that we'll "kill Jimcrow and race hate" in the sky and on the sea and that atomic power will be used to build his "new place" from the old ashes. Here is the theme of rebirth in the folk-protest movement's new version of the myth.

Similarly, other mythemes associated with the myth are used. During the Popular Front years (1935—1936), the sacrifice of the patriots and Pilgrims helped the folk-protest movement establish their "Americanism" in light of the negative image and foreign associations with communism. One of the most popular and representative songs was "Abe Lincoln" by Alfred Hayes and Earl Robinson. The song chronicles incidents from Lincoln's life to illustrate his positive qualities of honesty, justice, and concern for African-Americans; key to the song, however, was the chorus itself, which extrapolated excerpts from one of Lincoln's speeches: "This country with its Institutions belongs to the people who inhabit it" and "Whenever they shall grow weary of the existing Government, they can exercise their constitutional right of amending it, or their revolutionary right to dismember or overthrow it." Those quotes might strike the listener as alarming—that is if the listener had forgotten the original sentiments of the Declaration of Independence—but the threatening nature of the words is mitigated by their being placed in the mouth of one of our greatest heroes. Woody Guthrie also summoned the image of Lincoln in his "Union Feeling," when he refers to the slavery problem; he then reminds the listener that no white man is free as long as a "black-skin man's a slave." The mytheme of the patriot is used to remind listeners of their responsibility to uphold the democratic principles of liberty and equality.

The theme of oppression also runs throughout the corpus of the folk-protest movement. "Song of the West Virginia Miners," for instance, describes how the company holds the people in "slavery," while "Down the Street We Hold Our Demonstration" proclaims that "We're fighting for our freedom" (Lomax 1967). Another mytheme highlighted by the folk-protest movement was the theme of opportunity—generally yoked with the principles of freedom and equality—which songwriters communicated most forcefully through imagery associated with work. In fact, it could be said that work was the equivalent of freedom-equality-opportunity. The primary focus of the music both of African-Americans and the radical left was on improving the material lot of their respective communities. Work carries with it important associations within our culture such as ownership of land, providing for family, reward for effort, contribution to the total life of the community, self-esteem, honesty (if you are out of work, you may be forced to steal), and stability (if you are out of work, you may be forced to wander around looking for a job).

We saw in "Brother, Can You Spare A Dime?" and "Remember My Forgotten Man" that work was a central image in portraying the lot of the common person in the 1930s. Writers in the folk-protest movement used the image of work in a similar fashion. Borrowing from the ideas popular among the Wobblies, the songwriters often suggest that opportunity is measured by wealth. The goal, for instance, of the ever-popular "Pie in the Sky" (also called "The Preacher and the Slave") by Joe Hill is for workingmen to unite and fight for freedom until "the world and its wealth we have gained" (Lomax, 1967, 89). Similarly, Woody Guthrie shows the paradoxical nature of opportunity for the working person in his "Do Re Mi." In that song he talks of California being "a garden of Eden", a virtual "paradise," a harshly ironic concept considering that no one will be able to reap the harvest of Eden unless he/she has the "do re mi" (i.e., dough).

Another powerful song is Sara Ogan Gunning's "They Tell Us to Wait" in which, like Leadbelly, she uses "The Star Spangled Banner" as a backdrop to highlight the hypocrisy of the American Dream: "this land of the brave and home of the free [is] full of starvation and misery." In a variation on the patriot's mytheme, she states that it doesn't seem fair that, in one of the oldest families in the United States, whose father was a war veteran, four children and a seventy-eight-year-old grandmother should be starving (1967, 162). There were indeed "mean things happening in the land," and the songwriters took every opportunity to remind the workers and wanderers that they were not alone in their misery. Concurrently, they reinforced the basic goodness of individuals by reminding them that they were entitled to the riches of the land they worked. And in the process they sent out a message: We grew the crops, and now we starve; we grew the cotton, and now have no clothes for our backs, but be cautioned that when you next have a war, and you need us, we may not be there. In short, as long as we (these the least of your brethen) do not have freedom and opportunity, your freedom is threatened. Such suggestions were what kept these songs from making strong inroads into the mass market.

Finally, we come to the mytheme of the land. Throughout this survey of songs, this has been a variable. Songwriters seem to draw on the mytheme as the times demand. It is very important within the folk-protest movement. The land is, first of all, a necessary adjunct to the mytheme of opportunity. One's potential for opportunity is, in some cases, predicated on one's own ownership of land. (Or it was then.) Land also is a measure of how viable the idea of individualism is in the culture. Do you own your own house? Do you harvest your own food? In other words, do you have freedom and do you enjoy the bounty of the land? In "Sweet Liberty Land" from the 1930s, songwriters Hoffman Hays and John Garden stated that a man is only free "In a land of plenty" where there is "plenty for all." In short, a person's material needs must be met if he/she is to feel truly free; he who has nothing cannot be free in the ideology of the folk-protest movement. As important as this mytheme is to the working community, it is not part of every song dealing with the myth. The songwriters, many of whom were city-born and bred, did not see the sense of extolling the virtues of the earth to their urban audiences. But the land was of utmost importance in the work of one major songwriter from the period: Woody Guthrie.

No single member of the movement—with the possible exception of Pete Seeger later in his career—did more than Guthrie to reestablish the primacy of the landscape in telling the story of America. Having at first hand encountered the Dust Bowl, he understood that the promise and bounty of the land could quickly become the nightmare of the land. In a song like "Dust Bowl Refuge," the vast panorama of the land becomes the backdrop of an Odysseuslike wandering in search of work and home. He describes a family traveling over mountains and across deserts, "From southland to drouthland" and to the sea in search of opportunities for work. We see that those paths carved through the wilderness and Katherine Lee Bates's "thoroughfare for freedom" have now been displaced by images of dislocation. Where once the land signified permanence—as well as the immanence of God—it now signifies alienation and impermanence. Everything is predicated on work: If one cannot find work on the land, one must move and that, in turn, makes the highway one's "home." Tragically, "It's a never ending highway," which says that opportunity and stability are forever slipping from the grasp of the common person.

There is for Guthrie an irony in the idea of the promised land; we have seen evidence of that in his "Do Re Mi" and in "Tom Joad," as he recounts the journey of the Joads from the Midwest to the pastures of plenty in California. But the land is also a source of inspiration and a symbol of the potential for material progress in the United States for Guthrie, as is revealed in his songs dealing with the Columbia River. Written as part of the Columbia River Project after World War II, the songs capture the new sense of optimism that pervaded the folk-music movement following the war. The songs also gave Woody an opportunity to reaffirm the basic tenets of the folk-protest movement's version of the myth by playing to the general public's upbeat feelings about American progress after the war. In "Coulee Dam" he states that King Columbia River is the greatest wonder of the world. He sees in the river and the work to be done on the dam a force to unify the nation: The river and the dam will become something "For the farmers and the factory," for all of us as well. This in turn will make possible the manufacture of a "Flying Fortress," which will "fight for Uncle Sam" as he battles fascism. What is subtly suggested here is that the river is an important component in America's role in the world. Does this mean he is validating the old theocratic ideal? Not really, because at the heart of the experience is the working person making the dam so the Flying Fortress can defend freedom.

Another song, "Roll on Columbia," likewise celebrates the merging of the bounty of the land with the benefits of progress as the Columbia turns "our darkness to dawn." For Woody the Columbia unifies the American experience from "Tom Jefferson's vision" of an empire in the Northwest to the expeditions of Lewis and Clark to the present where "mighty men" labored day and night matching their strength against the river. This might strike us as curious today when we believe that nature should remain pure and inviolate. However Guthrie is largely echoing a view (with many followers even today) that nature and the bounty of the country can be handmaidens to progress. As the Dust Bowl symbolized total devastation, so a rich land symbolized the unlimited bounty and opportunity available to all people. For Guthrie the river comes to symbolize the myth of America: Inspired by the vision of our patriotic forebears and the efforts of the working person, this mighty river, containing all the beauty and bounty of the land, makes it possible for all of us to enjoy freedom and opportunity.

The postwar flush of good feelings that pervaded the folk-protest movement dissipated quickly in the wake of the House Un-American Activities Committee (HUAC) hearings and assaults on communism from other quarters. Although people walked away from the war with a generally positive feeling about the future and America's role in that future, some dark clouds threatened on the horizon. The Holocaust and the bomb made people aware of how fragile life was. These historical events symbolized for many man's infinite capacity for evil and destruction. We had unleashed upon the world, it seemed, forces beyond understanding, beyond all the sophistication of science, psychology, and philosophy. Responses to the twin evils ranged from out-and-out pessimism and a new form of naturalism, to reevaluations of the efficacy of the individual (most apparent in existentialist philosophy and literature), and finally chauvinism: The best way to deal with the issues is to cling doggedly to the country as the last bastion of the four freedoms (freedom from want, freedom from fear, freedom of speech, freedom of religion). Communism, quite naturally, was seen as destructive of these ends.

The 1950s were hard times for the folk-protest movement, as chronicled by Serge Denisoff, Jerome Rodnitzky, and Robbie Lieberman. There was a change in audiences to begin with. Workers were increasingly skeptical of the singers and their philosophy, and the HUAC hearings confirmed their fears. But intellectuals remained and, in time, college students began to take an interest in the music and the ideas that were being sung about. And there was the phenomenon of the hootenanny. Hootenannies became very popular after the war for a variety of reasons. One was that people in attendance drew a strong sense of solidarity from singing along (when and if they knew the words) and just recognizing that they were among similar-minded people. Irwin Silber identified the ingredients that he felt were important to a "hoot"; they included audience participation, topical songs, variety, new performers, and audience composition. Silber states: "The most important quality about hootenannies has been the fact that its audience is composed predominantly of young people—teenagers and college students—who have found that a hootenanny communicates *music, ideas, and a sense of the real America to them*'" (quoted in Denisoff 1971, 114). What was happening then—and this is important for later developments in the 1960s—is that these musicians and this audience found themselves in the enviable/unenviable position of being outsiders, who believed that they were really the insiders, because they felt deeply that they knew the real meaning of America. And the songs reflected this attitude.

The folk-protest movement found that, because of the McCarthy and HUAC hearings, the media were less willing to take a chance on them. The boycotting of Pete Seeger, for instance, is now legendary in pop music annals. The songwriters did have outlets, however, chief of which was the little publication *Sing Out*. Looking back over the issues of *Sing Out*, one finds familiar names—Woody Guthrie, Lee Hays, Earl Robinson, Paul Robeson—and new ones as well such as Peter LaFarge, Malvina Reynolds, and, later, Phil Ochs and Bob Dylan. These were Woody's children in a sense. They carried on his tradition of singing traditional folk tunes wedded to new topical lyrics as well as writing original tunes. The cause was the same: the empowerment of the individual. But to this were added the issues of civil rights and universal peace. Unionism was still occasionally talked about, but, in general, the publication was aimed at mobilizing those with socialist/communist sympathies and those who felt they were numbered among the disenfranchised. As Roslyn Henry's "We've Always Welcomed Strangers" (1951) declares: Columbus was once an alien here himself as were those who landed on Plymouth Rock and Virginia. "And," she adds, there are no foreigners "In a world where ALL belong" (*Sing Out*, August 1951: 4–5).

As with the songs of the thirties and forties, God has litt[le]
do with the new world order. The sense of manifest destiny is communicated through the belief in world peace. But it must be a peace
that is not bought by war. For the folk-protest songwriters of the
1950s, war was not viewed even as parenthetical experience; they
believed that it should not be at all. Jacqueline Steiner's "Peace, It's
Wonderful" (1950), for instance, states that waging war to obtain
peace, as America has traditionally done, is wrong. The ultimate
result of that is all we'll have is a bunch of Washington politicians
working out carving up the map, eating the meat, and leaving the
scrap (*Sing Out* July 1950: 10). One of the dominant characteristics
of the folk-protest movement is their desire to feature the anomalous
aspects of the myth. Thus, we see in this song a highly critical view
of America's role as world leader. The whole issue of its manifest
destiny is debunked in the image of a bunch of greedy politicians
carving up the map as they would a Thanksgiving turkey.

On the other hand, the songwriters of the fifties kept the mytheme
of the patriots pretty much inviolate. Vic Shapiro and Bill Wolff's
"Ballad of You and Me" (1955) uses the mytheme of the patriot-hero
to highlight the importance of the individual. Taking a chronological
approach, the songwriters mention past heroes such as Washington,
Jefferson, Adams, and Paine in reference to the Revolutionary War.
When they cite the patriots of the Civil War, they naturally mention
Lincoln but then include such interesting figures as Harriet Tubman,
Frederick Douglass, and John Brown. There is no mention of Grant
and Lee. These new heroes reflect our growing concern with civil
rights. In the final stanza Washington and Jefferson are mentioned
again and to their names is added that of Franklin D. Roosevelt. The
songwriters say that all these people were important in helping us
maintain our independence, but the real makers of history are those
people standing next to us who want to "build up a peaceful nation"—empowering the individual.

The concern with the role of the individual and with equal rights
led, quite naturally, to a preoccupation with the freedom, opportunity, and equality mytheme. The treatment of the theme, however,
is handled with some cynicism and irony. Some tunes speak of the
hope of having a land where 150 million people are "All free and
equal" ("150 Million" (1951) by Walter Lowenfels and Nathan
Charlieres). But just as quickly songs will introduce lines that point
up the failure of that idealism. In this song, for instance, the song-

The Star Spangled Banner" ("land of the free and
ve") to underscore the tragic dimensions of the death
ee (a black man accused of raping a white woman
in the 1950s) and the whole nation's complicity in
ay, 1951: 3). These lines have been used before, as
nd will be quoted quite often in protest music from
e nineties.

Matthew Hall and Earl Robinson's "If I Am Free" (1952) voices
a similar cynical tone about freedom when their narrator says, "Why
do I laugh when you say I'm free." They take a bit more positive
tack and speak of the freedom road which lies ahead and of a "newly
born star," which will lead them down a new trail to that meeting
place on "Freedom Day." In the case of both of these songs, the
songwriters feel compelled to feature the anomalous aspects of the
country's stand on equal rights and equal opportunity in order to
reaffirm more strongly what they believe is the true mission of the
country. This particular approach to this issue and others will prove
very influential in the folk music revival that takes place in the
late fifties and in the rise of folk-rock in the sixties.

Sing Out and later *Broadside* continued to be important fixtures
in the perpetuation of the ideals of the radical left through the fifties
and sixties. They did not prove immediately successful, partly owing
to the state of the music industry during those years and partly to
the hostile political attitudes felt by many toward the radical left.
The goals of these publications were noble; the editors of *Sing Out*
wrote after their first year of publication: "We have felt that the
true flowering of a people's culture can only come as it reflects and
reinforces the desires and struggles of the people. . . . Many of the
songs we have printed have been used with great success. From Aus-
tralia to New York, across oceans these songs have met the common
needs of people, have joined them in understanding, in common
struggle for a better life. . . . Songs are the deepest feelings of people"
(July 1951: 2).

Sing Out and *Broadside* espoused causes in ways that challenged
the status quo. Many of the songs combine the satiric irreverence
of Tin Pan Alley in the thirties with the earnest desire to change
people's attitudes characteristic of the folk-protest songs of the same
period. Most Americans enjoyed the paradoxical status of being the
world leader but also being isolated from that world—except for our
responsibility for "containing" communism. In following through

on that responsibility, we reaffirmed the underlying assumption of the myth: that we are a good people. Many of the songs of the folk-protest movement did not speak to that sense of national morality. Instead, they highlighted how we had failed in our mission, how we, through our poor treatment of minorities, were perverting the ideals of the "real America."

This was not a message destined to fall on receptive ears, except in small circles, but today these "pioneers" could take satisfaction in the fact that everyone from Janet Jackson to Living Colour to Bruce Springsteen to Sting are echoing the ideas first set down in the *Songs of the Workers*, the *People's Song Book*, Woody's *Dust Bowl Ballads*, and the pages of *Sing Out*.

III

If one were to seek out the ideas that most Americans felt comfortable with in the late forties and fifties, one would probably have to say those of Irving Berlin and Roy Acuff. That may seem at first like a match made in hell—Berlin being the epitome of Tin Pan Alley and the whole musical establishment, and Acuff being dedicated to "hillbilly" music, well outside the musical mainstream. But when it came to America, both men had their hearts in the "right" place for the mass audience. Berlin gave us a tune that provided the right sense of uplift needed to sustain us during the war effort, and Roy Acuff was accorded the honor of being the subject of a Japanese battle cry. During a banzai charge on Okinawa, a Japanese soldier was heard to scream, "To hell with Roosevelt; to hell with Babe Ruth; to hell with Roy Acuff" (Malone 1985, 206).

Country music never dealt much with matters political and only did so when war threatened. Even the output from World War I is quite slim, with Jimmie Rodgers's "The Soldier's Sweetheart" being one of the biggest hits centering around the war—and that was published in 1927. World War II, on the other hand, inspired a body of country songs that fully supported the war effort and, by extension, reaffirmed the myth of America. This should not be too surprising. Country music has a tradition of conservatism. The Civil War songs of the South would, indeed, be quite compatible with the sentiments expressed in the tunes written between 1941 and 1945.

The South was fully behind the war effort and was even more strident at times than the musical establishment in expressing its feelings about the conflict. The emotions expressed, moreover, are dynamic and diverse. Dorothy Horstman writes:

> In the line "God gave me the right to be a free American/And for that precious right, I'd gladly die," composer Bob Miller summed up the patriotic feelings of most Americans during World War II—feelings that overrode the individualism and resistance to regimentation that typifies the southerner. Responding to the high feelings and expert propaganda of the period, southerners perceived it as a truly national effort and gave their all. (1975, 233).

In the above statement, "overriding" the values of individualism and resistance to regimentation seems to me to be going too far. One of the megafunctions of the myth is to reconcile conflicts in the culture. In the case of these war songs, the myth validates the values of individualism and anti-regimentation by appealing to the average citizen's desire for liberty and opportunity. The myth is our ideological defense against threats to those values.

The country music response to the war was similar to that of Tin Pan Alley's but a deeper and more personal feeling courses through the songs. The southerner's awareness of the tragic dimension of life is never very far from the surface in these tunes. There are very few swinging numbers like "Don't Sit Under the Apple Tree." Instead, we find a strong degree of sentimentality in the songs. Consequently, the song "Remember Pearl Harbor" by Frank Luther and sung by Carson Robinson states that we will "kill 100 rats" for every fallen American. This is strong talk, based on the songwriter's feeling that we were stabbed in the back while peace talks were going on. The Southerner accepts the premise that we are good and that goodness has been violated and so we must enter this parenthetical experience, and we must do the job quickly. Bob Miller's "We're Gonna Have to Slap the Dirty Little Jap" (again sung by Carson Robinson) points out that "Uncle Sam is the man who's given a helping hand" to many foreign countries, he is peaceful and believes in the "Golden Rule," but now someone has stomped "on his toes."

One of the most popular war songs and one of the most complete expressions of the myth is Paul Roberts and Shelby Darnell's (Bob Miller) "There's a Star-Spangled Banner Waving Somewhere" (1942). The "somewhere" of the title appears to have a couple of referents: it seems to signify heaven, for, as the lyrics state, only the great heroes of Uncle Sam get to go there. The narrator states he'll see Lincoln, Custer, Washington, Perry, "Nathan Hale and Colin Kelley [a recent air ace] too!" This nicely unites the sense of transcendence with the sacrifice of the patriots. Later we discover that the narrator is "crippled," but he wants to "bring the Axis down a peg" and be a hero. If that happens, he will be assured of a place in "that heaven" where the Star-Spangled Banner is waving. The somewhere could also signify the country itself or any part of the free world. In the second stanza, he talks of the "mad schemes of destruction" unleashed on "sweet liberty" by dictators. He adds that he is willing to die to "be a free American" and wherever that Star-Spangled Banner is waving is where he wants to be living when his time to die is at hand.

We have frequently mentioned the iconic significance of the flag in popular songs. Old Glory functions much the same way in this tune, symbolizing democratic ideals and our patriotic heritage. Similarly, Ed Burt's (Edith Berbert) "Silver Dew on the Blue Grass Tonight" (1943) states, when one fights "for a cause that is right" they keep the flag flying "for those boys who had to die" (Horstman 1975, 244). In another song, "Star and Stripes on Iwo Jima" (Bob Wills–Cliff Johnson), the narrator states that Old Glory is flying over Mount Suribachi and "she always will," which suggests the notion of manifest destiny and America securing the freedoms implicit in the symbol of a flag for people everywhere.

Although "There's A Star-Spangled Banner Waving Somehwere" makes no explicit mention of God's role in the destiny of the nation, it is suggested in the word "somewhere." Similarly, the very popular "Smoke on the Water" (1942) (Zeke Clements–Earl Nunn), made famous by Red Foley and Bob Wills, refers to "heathen gods" who will be overtaken by our army and navy. Other songs, however, were more direct in their evocation of this mytheme. Gene Autry's "God Must Have Loved America" (1941) (Fred Rose–Gene Autry) states that God must have loved America to "make it the land of the free," and that it must have been made from a corner of heaven. This is so remarkably similar to the sentiment of Ernest Ball's "A Little Bit of Heaven" that it is almost disarming. The song also employs the liberty, equality, and opportunity mytheme when the songwriters state that you are welcome here as long as your heart beats true, and that you are as wealthy as a monarch because you live in a land of liberty.

Quite naturally Southerners saw in the mytheme of freedom, equality, and opportunity the principles that allowed them to remain individuals and resist regimentation. This is the spirit that had animated the songwriters of the Civil War, and the songwriters of the World War II carried on that patriotic tradition. Stuart Hamblen, for instance, states in his song "Old Glory" that no foe can prevail over us, because we will defend liberty with our lives. He sees in the colors of Old Glory "all my hope and destiny." One notices here that this is a personal declaration—that is *my* hope and destiny, not the country's. Of course, there is no contradiction here, because if one is fighting for one's own freedom, others will naturally enjoy the same freedoms. Other songwriters paint the fight for freedom in broader strokes. "Smoke on the Water" paints a portrait of an apocalyptic "great destroyer" composed of "fire and flesh and steel" rolling over the "foes" of freedom and turning Japan into a "graveyard." The apocalyptic tone here is in keeping with the vision that Clements had based on a Bible passage about the earth being destroyed by fire (Horstman 1975, 245). Finally, we have "(We'll Write) The Last Page of Mein Kampf" (1944) by Jack Johnston and Will Livernash, which yokes the mythemes of manifest destiny and freedom in the verse where they state that allied nations will free "conquered nations" and restore "each boundry line." The United States then continues to play its role as world leader making sure the "Four Freedoms will forever stand" and that no nation will be subject to slavery.

It should be noted here that country musicians were not a minority in their fervor over the war effort. Woody Guthrie had printed on his guitar, "This Weapon Kills Fascists," and he wrote songs with that instrument that supported the war effort. But it is also true that the expressions of patriotism that came from the country music camp were closer in spirit to Tin Pan Alley than to those of the radical left. This is natural in that the majority of Southerners would have seen the efforts of Guthrie, Seeger, Hays, and the others as a threat to their individualism and not as a liberating spirit. The conflicting perspectives on what America stands for, as embodied in the music of the folk-protest movement and in country music, have remained with us up until the 1990s.

The other voices in America's musical culture would not remain *other* voices for long. The rise of rock 'n' roll music and the emergence of the youth culture of the sixties would work great changes in the popular culture of the late twentieth century. The ideas embodied in the songs we have discussed in this chapter would no longer just bubble below the surface; they would reach a boiling point in the work of a variety of artists. Relatively obscure works such as Woody Guthrie's *Dust Bowl Ballads* would eventually, as Joe Klein notes, become "one of the most influential American recordings of the twentieth century." The records would be played extensively in "left wing schools and summer camps, where the words and simple defiant optimism became part of the curriculum . . . as did the image of a dusty little man wandering around the country with a guitar slung over his shoulder, making up songs that helped people to understand themselves and encouraged them to fight back. It was a powerful, romantic image, especially for kids growing up in the middle of New York City, and it would be central to the mythology of the generation of radicals coming of age" (1980, 169).

Most importantly the blues singers and the folk-protest movement would plant the seeds for a reexamination of the myth of America. In their songs they turned away from the tradition of previous generations, which hearkened to the myth to instill a sense of pride and reinforce or build a sense of community in their audiences. Instead, they looked at the myth more critically. They held it up as an ideal as previous songwriters had done, but they did so to judge it against the reality of their daily lives. In the process, they reified the myth by implying a new vision. The vision spoke to many dusty little men and women who were alienated from the "wealth which you are making" and who were no longer willing to live for "Pie in the Sky." Joe Hill had told them, "That's a dirty lie!" and they were really beginning to believe it.

CHAPTER VIII

"They've All Come to Look for America" The Late 1950s and the 1960s

GEORGE: *You know—This used to be a helluva good country. I can't understand what's gone wrong with it.*
—Easy Rider *(1969)*

The era following World War II, and in particular the Eisenhower years, saw steady growth and, in spite of Cold War fears, a growing sense of sureness about America's place in the world. In fact, it looked more and more like this indeed was the American century. One would still find tunes such as Freddy Grant's "They Call It America (But I Call It Home)" (1952), written during the Korean conflict, which evoked the classic mythemes to reaffirm the myth that had animated our visions for so many years. There were some, however, who, in spite of America's exalted position in the world, questioned what was happening to the country. Some did not see us on the same providentially guided path that Berlin wrote of in 1939; those songwriters, like Phil Ochs, saw America merely as the "cop" of the world, not a beacon of democracy but a purveyor of imperialism.

That Ochs's vision would ultimately prevail is what we wish to explore in this chapter. The early years of rock are largely transitional years in the development of a new myth of America; they are the years when the grandchildren of Woody Guthrie, Leadbelly and Robert Johnson, and Roy Acuff took center stage and made us take a fresh look at the world around us. The birth of the new music gave birth to new ideas, which, like those of the colonial era, were hammered out in the crucible of revolution.

With the arrival of the age of rock, it might be said that the second great "voyage" in search of America began. The music of the first two decades of rock reveal audiences and musicians from all the different fields of popular music grappling with the myth, sometimes recycling it, sometimes attempting to destroy it and redefine it. We will see two versions of the myth of America emerging during the sixties. One version of the myth will highlight anomalies in the existing myth and seek to redefine the role of the individual in the context of a new mythic vision; the other approach will continue to reaffirm the theocratic-enlightenment ideal and in time will begin to sound archly antiquated and even a little jejune.

Let us begin, however, by looking at some of the developments in both rock music and Tin Pan Alley style music of the 1950s.

I

There was every reason for most Americans to expect that Irving Berlin's vision of America as expressed in "God Bless America" would continue to be the "glue" that bound us to our past heritage and pushed us into the future. During the 1950s, in spite of Cold War fears, Americans largely felt in control of their destiny. The ideological foundations of the country seemed sound, and now we had the technological expertise to match it; as Todd Gitlin states, "The idea of America had long been shaped by the promise of opportunity in a land of plenty, but at long last the dream seemed to be coming true. The world seemed newly spacious, full of possibilities" (1987, 13).

As the previous chapter demonstrated, however, these sentiments were hardly universal. The Cold War threat was insidious—all fear and no fight, all tension and no release. It, along with the sense of confidence that permeated the culture, led to a rigidity in the pursuit of maintaining status quo and equilibrium. Morris Dickstein, in reviewing Norman Mailer's writings of the 1950s notes, "Where the fifties theorized about totalitarianism in far-off places, Mailer found a creeping totalitarianism here at home, 'a slow death by conformity,' he said, 'with every creative and rebellious instinct stifled'" (1977, 53). But dissent was there, and getting ready to appear.

We have seen already how many of the sentiments of the Old Left and the folk-protest movement carried over into the 1950s. They were buttressed by voices in the other arts, particularly the poets and novelists of the 1950s. Writers of the Beat Generation found in the myth a suitable subject for their bold verse, and their ideas would influence songwriters of the 1960s. Allan Ginsberg, in one of the clearest statements concerning the myth, declared in his poem "America" (1956), "America I've given you all and now I'm nothing." It is a line that anticipates the vision of Springsteen in his *Born in the U.S.A.* album of 1984. And during this same period, Lawrence Ferlinghetti wrote, "I am waiting for someone/to really discover America/and wail" as part of his waiting for a "renaissance of wonder." In both men's work is the underlying theme that the real America has been plowed under by "fillingstations" and the detritus of industrialism and progress. They began a critical trend, which would continue into the 1960s, of featuring the anomalous aspects of the myth. A number of musicians who would later play important roles in the development of rock music simultaneously began to explore these themes as they came into contact with Beat Generation writers in coffeehouses and on college campuses. In fact, it was in these environments that Robert Zimmerman's political consciousness was forged, first at the University of Minnesota and later in Greenwich Village, where he completed his pilgrimage to see Woody Guthrie and to make a name for himself as Bob Dylan. However, in the 1950s some truly popular songs were being written about America, which serve as a transition to the reevaluation of America in the protest music of the movement.

One of the most interesting songs written about America in the 1950s is "America," from the Leonard Bernstein–Stephen Sondheim musical drama *West Side Story* (1957). The song uses many of the symbols and mythemes of the American dream to poke fun at that same dream. Whatever criticism there might be of the United States is mitigated, however, by the song's humor and the fact that the narrator is basically sold on the country in spite of its faults. The song is revealing, because of the urban perspective it brings to the myth of America and because it also deals with material preferments as being indigenous to the myth.

The song opens with the sentiment that everything is free in America, and then in subsequent verses the narrator deals other aspects of the American experience ranging from automobiles, to the hellos the immigrant receives, to the humorous final verses where they state that the comforts of America will be theirs because they will have "Knobs on the doors" and "Wall-to-wall floors." The fact that there is divisiveness among the Puerto Ricans singing the song further serves to ameliorate the sharp criticism contained in the song. Nonetheless, this continues the tradition of openly criticizing some of the hypocrisies of the system as perceived by newcomers, and it is one of the first to call into question the mythic notion of the melting pot.

The first actual rock 'n' roll song to deal with the myth is Chuck Berry's "Back in the U.S.A." (1959). It, in keeping with rock's rhythm and blues roots and with the values of the youth culture for which it was written, casts the American myth in a more materialistic light. He celebrates the urban experience, stating at the outset that he missed the cities and adding later that he is glad to be back among the highways and the skyscrapers. Like Bernstein and Sondheim's "America," the song also cites the openness, freedom, and opportunity in America by affirming that we have anything a person wants "right here." For Berry, the country means fun, hamburgers, and corner cafés jumping with records playing from the jukebox. Similarly, in his "Promise Land" he mines the mythology of cars and mobility to reaffirm the notions of opportunity in the promised land. His is a youthful vision of the country, and one that completely eschews the heavy overtones of theocratic ideals or the efficacy of the individual. Nevertheless the image is positive and hints at the dichotomy that is to characterize the treatment of the myth of America over the next three decades.

II

We have seen in past chapters that times of crisis seem to call forth songs drawing on the myth of America. Therefore, it should not be surprising that the 1960s not only called forth the myth but forced an entire reexamination of American values. The sixties began with John F. Kennedy's inaugural address, which largely evoked and outfitted American myths for a new generation and ended with Steppenwolf describing the situation in the United States as a "monster" on the loose. The myth of America would undergo a critical examination during the decade, and by the end, the beginnings of a new myth would emerge. Let us look at some of the factors that led to this transformation in our American vision.

First—and, perhaps for the purposes of this study, foremost—there was the change in the American musical diet. By 1960 the musical establishment was completely transformed from what it had been a mere ten years earlier. Rock 'n' roll music was dominant and was moving into an advanced stage, where it would be called plain "rock." What had been thought to be a passing fad joined the ranks of other passing fads—ragtime, jazz, and swing—and brought about an almost complete revolution in popular music. The music was geared to a young audience, now dominated by the burgeoning baby boom sector. Radio, both in the form of portable transistor types and in cars—the site where music and leisure most comfortably met for youth—allowed rock to be an ever-present force in the lives of kids. Paradoxically, however, the emergence of the new myth was most helped by developments in the conservative sector of the rock industry.

By 1960 most of the pioneers of the first generation of rock 'n' roll (Chuck Berry, Jerry Lee Lewis, Little Richard, Elvis Presley) were no longer viable forces in the creation of the music. The airwaves were now controlled by major labels again, who gave us artists and producers, predominantly white, many of whom worked out of Tin Pan Alley's last bastion, the Brill Building in New York. These songwriters penned well-crafted popular songs that owed as much to the style of Tin Pan Alley as to Bourbon Street. They coopted the basic elements of early rock and produced a somewhat homogenous product free of the anarchic elements that had characterized the music and performance styles of the early stars. Although this music found an appreciative audience among white middle-class kids, it also proved less satisfying to those who either liked early rock or who needed more substance in their musical diet. In short, rock no longer necessarily symbolized youthful rebellion.

Simultaneously, into the musical breach stepped the new folk revival. The folk revival was not just a local or purely subcultural event. By 1963 there were TV programs devoted to folk music such as "Hootenanny," and artists like the Kingston Trio, Peter, Paul, and Mary, and Trini Lopez, who had all charted top-forty hits with songs that had generated out of the folk-protest subculture, and live concerts such as the famous Newport Folk Festival were gaining national press and making musical news as well. Then, in 1965 the "phenomenon" of "Eve of Destruction," that seminal statement of social discontent and apocalyptic foreboding, and the popularity of the Byrds' version of Dylan's "Mr. Tambourine Man," helped the folk-rock sound reach a popular apotheosis.

The folk revival was also able to fill what was for some a musical void created by the demise of the first generation of rock heroes and the domination of combined forces of the publishing industry and the record companies. Here was music that was in tune with the growing college-age audience, who found themselves, because of their commitment to the promises in Kennedy's New Frontier rhetoric, taking a more active role in causes like civil rights. Popular artists—Peter, Paul, and Mary, the Kingston Trio, and the New Christy Minstrels—were perhaps not the genuine article, not "true" folk, but their efforts enabled the more "serious" members of the folk-protest movement to become familiar to wider audiences: Bob Dylan, Joan Baez, Phil Ochs, and to a lesser extent legends like Guthrie and Seeger. The work of Dylan and Ochs, up until 1965, was hardly known except to those who happened on their albums by accident or read *Sing Out* and *Broadside*.

Dylan would prove to be the breakthrough artist. His influence was felt, first, as a songwriter in the early sixties, his work being covered by more commercially acceptable acts, and secondly as a performer, when in the midsixties he fused rock with his folk consciousness and gained more fans and more exposure for protest music in general. Wilfrid Mellers has noted of Dylan's musical evolution: "The gradual sophistication of his resources in one sense represents a growth towards conscious awareness; in another sense, however, electrophonic presentation, with Dylan as with other folk artists, implies merging of individual into communal consciousness" (1985, 113).

The community for this music consisted primarily of college students, the fastest growing segment of the population during the sixties. This audience, moreover, was hungry for rebellion, as youth had been in previous generations, and they found in politics and social causes a way to carve out a special place for themselves, as well as a position to take in opposition to their parents' world. Rebellion always centers around dissatisfaction with the world of parents and adults, and in the 1960s this dissatisfaction steadily grew into a full-blown critique of the whole American way. Starting as a move to correct the wrongs done to blacks and other minorities by their parents and grandparents' generations, the rebellion metastasized. Jerome Rodnitzky writes, "Precisely because radicals found it so difficult to confront their adversary in our complex corporate society, the new political battleground became largely cultural and generational rather than social and economic. . . . The idea was to reject and destroy the old culture in order to liberate the individual" (1976,31). Youth—somewhat fancifully—saw a kinship between themselves and the socially oppressed.

In this respect they shared a kinship with the Old Left, which had attempted to establish bonds of solidarity with the common folk and labor—even though many leftists had little actual knowledge of and real experience with the life-styles of these people. Consequently, like the Old Left, the students of the 1960s slowly adopted the stance that had carried over into the fifties and could be seen in the songs of *Sing Out*: It was *Us* versus *Them*. Todd Gitlin notes that the Old Left had also seen the world in terms of We and They. "*We* were different, special. *We*, however isolated in the United States, were part of 'a worldwide community.' . . ." (1987, 73). Youth, similarly, saw themselves as culturally dispossessed as the socially oppressed, saw themselves as victims of the very culture that allowed them the luxury to rebel, saw themselves as alienated from the world their parents had made. Even in matters as "clear cut" as the Good War, the new generation was offered a new perspective. Maybe it wasn't as neat as in *The Sands of Iwo Jima* or *Air Force*; maybe it was more like the world Joseph Heller captured in *Catch-22*: Under that veneer of military and technological efficiency lurked total absurdity. This novel, films such as *The Graduate*, and history itself seemed to confirm Holden Caulfield's notions about the phoniness of the adult world. As a result, youth adopted some of the style of the Old Left, most particularly, as Gitlin notes, a "hostility toward Western imperialism and a sardonic attitude toward America's democratic and pacifistic pretensions" (1987, 74).

The music of the folk revival, especially as it merged with rock music in the midsixties, proved to be the perfect vehicle to express this discontent and this need to carve out a vision for the New World of which Kennedy had said these youths were the stewards. Simon Frith states, "In the 1960s, as young whites, particularly on college campuses, became politically active again, they found in folk music the only expressive form that could be made directly responsive to their political concerns, that could serve the same cultural purpose as black music did for its listeners [an expression of collective experience]; the two concerns and musics came together most obviously in the Civil Rights movement" (1981, 29).

The music attempted to hit at a gut level while at the same time appealing to the audience's need for some intellectual stimulation. Musically, most of the songs follow the typical folk song A/B form consisting of verses and a repeated chorus. Songwriters in classic broadside fashion utilize the form and rhythms of the songs as weapons. In many of the antiwar songs—Phil Ochs's "I Ain't Marching Anymore" being a classic example—there is a reliance upon martial-sounding rhythms and harmonies (Sousa would be proud); moreover, they quote established patriotic tunes (much like George M. Cohan and others had done) but for ironic effect. Accompanying guitar patterns in folk tunes and ensemble work for rock groups will simulate drum rolls—again largely for ironic effect.

Lyrically the songwriters were much more adventuresome. The lyric sensibilities of the folk-protest movement in the 1960s is more informed by literary culture than by oral tradition. Songwriters working within the traditions of the earlier folk-protest movement (i.e., acoustic based instruments, hootenannies, reliance on established melodies) had been generally straightforward in their analysis of America. Dylan and Paul Simon, on the other hand, brought a heightened sense of poetic possibilities to the folk tune, which would influence many later rock artists. This shift in lyric writing style was appropriate considering that songwriters and performers were hoping to reach a largely college-educated audience. Thus one finds flashes of hard-edged wit and irony in many of the songs. For instance, Phil Ochs in his "Vietnam"—amazingly written in 1962—asks why we must die in Vietnam and stating that he doesn't "really care to die for the New Frontier" and adding that we will be making the country safe for "Diemocracy" (*Broadside* No. 14 [October 1962]). The pun on Ngo Dinh Diem's name and implicit critique of the latent imperialism of the New Frontier reveals perfectly the goals and aims of the folk-protest movement in the 1960s.

The key feature of the shift in lyric writing style, however, is that it perfectly complements the shift that will take place in the myth. Fewer and fewer artists assume the mantle of spokespersons; less and less do they paint a vision of America that is the reflection of a community bound to a single cause. More and more they paint portraits of solitary individuals attempting to make sense of their absurdist world. The old folk-style song with its direct message would not be appropriate anymore; what was needed was a medium suited to the individual quest for meaning. The language of poetry replete with allusion, irony, difficult imagery, symbolism, and the entire battery of figurative language was seen to be better suited to the quest of the alienated American and to the needs of the audience.

Ochs's song is illustrative of another aspect of the music of the folk-protest movement and rock music in the 1960s: no solution is offered. In the song he is highly critical of American policy, but he does not offer a corrective or alternate vision. One of the major differences between the songwriters of the 1930s and the 1960s, between Old Left and New Left, is summarized by Serge Denisoff in *Great Day Coming*; the songs of the 1930s "reflected the organizational and collective feelings of 'unity and power' for social change" (1971, 189), with work being a central issue; in the 1960s, however, jobs are obviously not a major issue (or even necessary to the college-student audience), and, instead, "the imperfections of the social order are raised" (190). Similarly, Jerome Rodnitzky notes, "For older singers like Seeger, songs were weapons to be used in a struggle they had already joined. In contrast, younger protest singers tended simply to catalogue social ills without taking part in their cure" (1976, 11–12).

This approach in songwriting perfectly complemented what was going on politically among the New Left. Todd Gitlin writes about Students for a Democratic Society (SDS): "After 1963, in fact, SDS conventions stopped trying to produce sweeping analyses. . . . Successive leadership circles also intuited that if SDS strained too hard to describe the world it wanted, rifts might emerge" (1987, 131).

Lacking an animating *Weltanschauung*, then, what shape would the myth of America take among these new songwriters? In the past, the myth helped audiences reconcile conflicts and contradictions in the culture. But in the songs of the sixties, the old myth can no longer reconcile the contradictions. The struggle for civil rights and the war in Vietnam brought into high relief the contradictions implicit in the myth and showed them to be irreconcilable and the myth to be hypocritical. Earl Robinson, who in the 1940s contributed the lyrics for "The House I Live In," felt compelled to write a parody of his original in 1964. In that parody he again asks what is America, but his response is cynical: It is "Vietnam flim flam," Barry Goldwater, and "A certain word, hypocrisy." Inverting the image of the happy neighborhood from the earlier song, he states that the houses he sees now are on "segregation street," where freedom has been "shackled" for 180 years (that is, from the Revolution to the 1960s). From this we can see that there was a growing feeling among concerned people in the culture that somehow, somewhere, something had gone wrong. The songs written in response to the issues of the day are an attempt to account for the failure of the myth. They raise many questions and give few solutions, but imply a vision. We will attempt to ferret out this vision as we work our way through the different mythemes.

The mytheme of God's role is perhaps the one that is most savagely skewered and finally abandoned in the music of the 1960s. The event that most brought this mytheme into question was, of course, the war in Vietnam. It came to symbolize the hypocrisy of both God's providential role and the concept of manifest destiny. Two folk-protest songs highlight the hypocrisy of the theocratic vision. Shurli Grant's "Are You Bombing with Me Jesus?" (1968) asks if Jesus is with us as we bomb "On the side of Uncle Sam" so we can prevail over the enemy with "mercy." The song also implies that the theocratic vision and manifest destiny are linked in a horrible conspiracy of oppression as she asks Jesus if He will aid us now until we've "crucified" the world. In short, we are not clearing a path to paradise but to martyrdom, and there will no be renewal after the sacrifice. One of the final images in the song reinforces the hypocrisy of the theocratic vision when she notes that the pilot of the *Enola Gay*, who dropped the bomb on Hiroshima, had a rosary in his hand.

In a similar vein, Ian Boyden and Ralph Dale's "Prayer for Peace" (1967) portrays us as the world's most "uptight" Christian land and asks Jesus to bless "each bomb we drop today in Vietnam" and to give us the power to "chasten insubordinate allies" *(Dane & Silber* 1969, 11). Clearly, Jesus is no longer the figure He was for the folk-protest movement of the thirties, forties, and early fifties. He now has come to symbolize the lack of charity and the dangers inherent in believing that God is on our side.

The notion of manifest destiny as an adjunct to the providential role of God was seriously questioned in the work of the folk-protesters such as Phil Ochs early in the decade. His "White Boots

Marching in a Yellow Land" (1965) states that we are fighting in a war that we lost before it began and that where our attempts to free Vietnam may produce the exact opposite: "Centuries of colonies, of slavery and worse/Now lead them to a future of their past all in reverse" (64–65). His "Cops of the World" (1966) scathingly portrays us not liberating others but dominating them; he echoes the national anthem in one line where he notes that we own half the world, "oh say can you see/And the name of our profits is Democracy". He concludes by saying that our message to the world is that you will "have" to be free whether you like it or not (Whitman 1969, 136). Jacqueline Sharpe's "Honor Our Commitment" (1965) makes a similar point when it states that we "truly" promise that if other countries don't obey Uncle Sam, "his troops will visit you" (Broadside No. 64 [November 1965]). Notice that in both songs traditional images/icons have been used to subvert their original meaning: the national anthem and Uncle Sam are no longer symbolic of the "last best hope" of the world for freedom and democracy, but instead symbolize perversion of these ideals. In short, the myth can no longer reconcile the role of God and manifest destiny with the quest for freedom, liberty, and equality.

Of rock songs dealing with these mythemes, Steppenwolf's "Monster" (1969) is one of the most powerful because it interprets the notion of manifest destiny as the United States saying that the "whole world" has to be "just like us" and not as a divine mission wherein we bestow the blessings of democracy on the rest of the world. Similarly, they question the vision of the patriots' efforts and sacrifice by noting that our forebears came here "religious, weary" seeking to build a new vision, but this gave way first to slavery and then to the killing of the redman in our westward expansion. They imply that the country was once animated by the spirit of freedom and justice, but we have to ask, where is America now and "Don't you care about your sons and daughters?" Similarly, "The American Eagle Tragedy" (1969) by Earth Opera implies that our days as a world leader are numbered because the "kingdom is crumbling" as a result of our having killed the "eagle's cry" (i.e., freedom) by extending ourselves "way beyond the shore" (i.e., Vietnam).

In short, the songwriters' message is that just because we are a nation with a vision rooted in Christian thinking, we cannot presume that every war we wage is a moral one. The songwriters of the sixties, unlike their forebears, did not paint the war as a parenthetical experience. The portrait that emerges is that the war is more than parenthetical; it is antithetical to the true aims of democracy and the country. The message of the songs is clear: The traditional myth is really an anomaly, and the audience must now construct a new and more "real" myth of America. It is interesting to note here that songwriters appear to have assumed that there was tacit consensus among the audience about this new vision, for they seldom felt compelled to offer specific parameters for a new myth; instead, its mythemes were implied by highlighting the anomalies of the old myth.

Reflecting back on the songs of the folk-protest movement of the 1950s, one may recall that images of the patriots were an important component in building their vision of the "real America" that Irwin Silber talked about. Such was not to be the fate of the patriots in the sixties. This, of course, only makes sense: If the vision is flawed, so must the visionaries and those who implemented the vision be flawed. Phil Ochs wryly notes in his "Where There's a Will, There's a Way" (1962) that when the original thirteen colonies picked Washington to lead them into battle, he said that if we won, someday we'd have "a World's Fair at Seattle," implying that the logical conclusion to our vision of greatness is sponsorship of a commercial exhibition. He does, however, respectfully evoke the image of John Brown as he tackles the issue of civil rights.

One of the favorite techniques used by the folk-protesters in dealing with the patriots' mytheme is what I call the catalog. In the catalog the songwriter relies upon cumulative effect to debunk and demythologize most traditional beliefs. Tom Paxton in his song, "What Did You Learn in School Today" (1962), has his youthful narrator catalog a series of suspicious truisms that he learned in school such as Washington never lied, soldiers never die, everybody is free, justice never ends, the government is always right, and war is "not so bad." Similarly, Phil Ochs, in his "I Ain't Marchin' Any More" (1964)—a song similar in spirit to Dylan's "With God on Our Side"—catalogs the disastrous effects of wars throughout American history, showing in the process that all that heroism, all that we've "won with sabre and gun," was hardly worth it. And finally, in a rather oblique reference to our patriotic past, John Prine declared in the early seventies that "Your Flag Decal Won't Get You into Heaven Anymore." Once again, as with the notion of manifest destiny, the songwriter chooses to highlight the anomalous aspect of the mytheme, chooses to show that it is not grounded in reality and that to believe the myth is to believe in a falsehood. Nothing is holy now, including George Washington.

If there is one mytheme that largely remains inviolate, even into the 1990s, it is the one dealing with the ideas of freedom, liberty, and equality. There is consensus among the songwriters that reification of the American Dream and the renewal of the American spirit must be predicated on this mytheme. We have seen in the past that these ideas have been interpreted in differing manners, but everyone is in agreement that they are the heart's blood of the myth of America. Therefore, it is the evocation of these mythemes over the next three decades that seems to enrage songwriters most, for they agree that the course America is on is destructive of these basic principles. Early songs, such as Malvina Reynolds' "Are You Walking There for Me?" (1964), affirm the quest for equality by stressing themes of brotherhood and by stating that even though people may be separated by long distances they are bound by "the selfsame flag," which flies over us all; therefore when someone puts a gun in your face or beats you "they beat me." The Christlike imagery here is very reminiscent of the folk-protest songs of the previous two decades, especially in the yoking of patriotic imagery with New Testament philosophy. She also ends the song by asking where she'll find the courage to "make Freedom's dream come true?" and suggests that it is possible because there are heroes out there today as great as any in history "walking for you and for me" (*Broadside* No. 48 [July 1964]: 3). The song owes a lot to the music of the previous generations in its uncynical affirmation of the mytheme and in its evocation of the image of Jesus as symbol of martyr for the common person.

Previously we have seen songwriters turn a cynical eye on American attempts to bring freedom to foreign climes while it goes a-wanting stateside. The indictments were forceful, but they also held a conciliatory note. Not so in the sixties. The war in Vietnam highlighted this perceived hypocrisy of our claims to be a free nation who safeguarded the notion of freedom and equality for all. The sentiments ran from the simple: "I ain't going to Viet Nam/That Free World Jazz is all a sham" (1967) (*Dane & Silber*, 1969, 61), to the more comprehensive, such as Jim Bowder's "Who's in Charge of Killing in Vietnam" (1968) which mockingly tells the audience that they can join the "holy war" and save Vietnam, but he adds that he will not kill for freedom when "It's dying where I am" (113).

The message is the same as the one we heard after World War II and into the 1950s. The songs almost universally point out that we are forcing freedom down people's throats, that they have lost their ability to determine for themselves what they want, and we are less free for doing this to others and that it will be a bitter harvest we reap at home. As Judith Wieder wonders in her "So What's the Big Blonde Boy of Freedom Doing Now" (1967)—the title of which suggests strongly a Hitleresque and Aryan dimension to our role in Southeast Asia—how can everything possibly turn out well when we're done "scarin' the hell outa anyone not willin' to submit to freedom" (*Dane & Silber*, 1969, 86–87).

Finally, the mytheme of the land plays an important role in the reevaluation of the myth of America in the 1960s. Some songwriters extol the beauty of the landscape and see in it the promise of the patriot's vision of freedom and our goodness. These songwriters are largely following in Woody Guthrie's footsteps in affirming the land's central role in determining the efficacy of the individual. One of the finest songs to deal with this mytheme is Eric Andersen's "My Land Is a Good Land" (1964). It is part celebration and part cautionary tale. Andersen says, "This is a song I wrote to Woody Guthrie, who knew the land could bleed too" (*Broadside* No. 41, [March 10, 1964]). In a reversal of trend, Andersen unabashedly states in the opening stanza that the land's fields and rivers were "blessed by God." He uses the land as a metaphor for the ideas of bounty and abundance, adding that it contains "good people." He also sees the land as a unifying force that binds man and animals in a shared inheritance (it's a song made up of "many men's hands and the throat of a hummingbird"). Finally, he reiterates the concept that the land is symbolic of freedom because, like freedom, it can't be bought with money. Thus, for Andersen the land largely reaffirms the basic myth: The country is blessed by God and binds us together in a quest for freedom. One senses that he lives with the Romantic dream that the landscape will have the palliative effect it did for Katherine Lee Bates and that by recognizing its inherent goodness we will recognize the good in each and everyone of us.

The other perspective on this mytheme, however, is bleaker. Dylan and Paul Simon do not see the vastness and boundlessness of the land as signifying bounty and regeneration. What they do in their songs is force one to confront the "dubious" aspects of the landscape (to borrow a term from Leo Marx). Another perspective which we will see hinted at, especially in the seventies, highlights the devastation of the land as a metaphor for what is happening to the character of the people.

If then, the old mythemes are failing or are found wanting, what is the solution? Some songwriters, carrying over sentiments from the fifties, saw America affirming its commitment to freedom by working for equal distribution of the bounty and working for world peace. Others, like Phil Ochs in his "Power and the Glory," sent out mixed messages. In the song he uses an apparently ironic Yankee-Doodleish accompaniment of fife and drum to survey the states and land and ask, "Who could ask for more?" He then reminds us that our power rests on freedom and our glory rests "on us all." He affirms the egalitarian mytheme when he states that we are only as rich as the poorest person, and he evokes the symbol of the land to emphasize the bounty we have. His version of the myth largely reaffirms those earlier visions that America is a community bound by principles that reaffirm the goodness of humanity. Others, like Laura Nyro in her "Save the Country" (1968), saw love as the solution to building "the dream," saving the people, the children, and the country. Jody Miller, in her "Home of the Brave" (1965) by Barry Mann and Cynthia Weil, saw the answer embodied in the national anthem with a distinctly sixties spin. "Home of the Brave, Land of the Free," she asks, why won't we let him be "what he wants to be." This sentiment slightly predates the great "do your own thing" explosion of the late sixties. Oddly enough, however, it is Miller's somewhat glib answer to the nation's dilemma that is explored in the work of Dylan and Paul Simon, who see the solution as residing in the individual, but the individual plays a different role in their music than he/she did in the music of the folk-protest movement of the previous three decades.

In the past, the individual achieved a sense of purpose and a oneness with the American community through solidarity with other individuals. This solidarity could be achieved either through simply believing that one shared in the manifest destiny of the nation or through affiliation with the "one big union." In some cases, the sense of solidarity could be achieved by seeing oneself as part of a community sharing a need for meaningful work, or by standing with others in the pursuit of civil rights or world peace. In the 1960s the individual's quest is a solitary one, ironically, achieved by sharing a bond of alienation with others who are similarly alienated. The message is that we are all outsiders in America. The myth has failed as a communal enterprise, and only by standing outside the main-stream—outside the myth if you will—can one really encounter the true meaning of America.

Dylan and Simon built their consensus by creating narrators or personae to whom they felt their audiences could relate—individuals who wandered on the borders of an absurdist technocracy, which threatened them with a loss of freedom, equality, opportunity, and individuality. This image of the outsider, a romantic one in Ameri-can culture, proved to be the locus of the reexamination of the myth of America and the key concept in the continuing attempt to create a new myth through the next two decades.

The major force in this paradigmatic shift is Bob Dylan. His voyage toward becoming the troubadour of youth's protest and political awareness began in his home state of Minnesota. After pursuing a rock 'n' roll career, he latched on to the music of Woody Guthrie. His pursuit of that mythic figure drew him, first, to the University of Minnesota where he soaked up "folk" music and radical Midwest-ern politics, and then to New York, where he hoped to meet Woody. In New York he quickly gained an enthusiastic and avid following among musicians, such as Dave Van Ronk and Joan Baez, and people from the media, most notably Robert Shelton of the *New York Times*, who wrote a glowing account of Dylan and his music. It was only a matter of time before that most perceptive of all record-industry men, John Hammond, signed Dylan to a recording contract with Columbia. Hammond wisely persuaded Columbia to allow Dylan to "do his thing" (i.e., record him with only guitar and harmonica accompaniment), and the rest is history.

In his individual songs Dylan does not deal with the entire myth as many of the other major songwriters surveyed here do, but, in-stead, he selects a different mytheme or two in each song to use as a point of departure for his assessment of the American experi-ence. Moreover, Dylan is guarded in his statements. Both Dylan and Simon would have been the first to state that they didn't speak for any one. What they did was *create the illusion*, through the charac-ters of their narrators, that they did indeed speak for their audience. For instance, in his "A Hard Rain's a Gonna Fall" (1963), even though he proclaimed that he would be spokesman for the causes and injustices he saw impending, he actually just asks rhetorical questions. "Blowin' in the Wind" is a perfect case of this rhetorical strategy, where almost every stanza begins with the phrase, "How many?" The burden of supplying the ideology falls to the listener. The listener becomes the mythmaker by participating in the song, either through identification with a narrator or as part of the "dialogue."

The listener finds in the process that he/she encounters a dissonance. The ideology is not pat; it may be rooted in the myths of the past, but that does not ensure its validity or efficacy. Dylan, taking his lead from the other songwriters in the folk-protest movement, approaches the myth through anomaly-featuring by highlighting a characteristic or characteristics that seem to contradict the established ideology. Previously anomaly-featuring was largely confined to a subculture; in the sixties, largely through Dylan's efforts, it is the anomaly that becomes reified as the new myth or ideology.

One of the dominant examples of anomaly-featuring in Dylan's music is the role of God in the country's destiny. The notion that there is a collective theocratic ideal and a providential figure guiding the country gives way to a bleaker examination of the lonely individual, bereft of God and collective identity, wandering a country that seems to have lost its ability to regenerate the individual. God is portrayed either as a paradoxical figure in the country's history or not mentioned at all. This opens up a corollary problem in regard to the megafunction of transcendence. How does one achieve a sense of transcendence if God either does not exist or is no longer on our side? Where do we seek a higher meaning? The answer has already been partially answered in Woody Guthrie's "This Land is Your Land": One achieves a higher meaning of what it is to be an American by realizing what the free individual can do for himself and others and by understanding the symbolism of the land itself. One of the more intriguing aspects of the songs of the 1960s and 1970s is that the mytheme of transcendence becomes a quixotic or at best mercurial subject in the songs.

A perfect example of Dylan's anomaly featuring is his "With God on Our Side" (1963), wherein he takes the mytheme of manifest destiny and the role of Providence in shaping our country and turns it on its head. As narrator, Dylan plays the role of the American innocent asking questions and questing after truth. He states that his name is nothing and his age means less; he then informs the listener that he comes from the Midwest. He is most definitely the inheritor of Woody Guthrie's modified populist vision here, identifying the locus of his consciousness as the heartland. In the heartland, he tells us, he was brought up to "abide" the laws and to believe that his country "Has God on its side." In short, he is saying that we were brought up, educated, and conditioned to believe the Irving Berlin version of America.

He then undertakes a Whitmanesque catalog of wars and injustices in which someone probably felt that God was on his/her side. He rewrites the myth of the west and the frontier as he sings of how the cavalry charged and the Indians died, but the reason was that "the country was young" and had the confidence of having God on its side. The understatement in the lyrics is crushing, and the irony is almost brutal, considering the past images of God presented in popular song. He implies that the excuse for the slaughter of the Indian was our innocence—an innocence protected by Providence—but then, in the context of the entire song, we discover that that is no excuse at all: Judas Iscariot probably had God on his side.

Dylan, in these lyrics, attempts to show that, contrary to the myth, the power of God in shaping the country's destiny was perhaps not a regenerative force nor the antecedent for establishing the "throne of freedom." It was, quite to the contrary, but a cloak for just another form of oppression and tyranny. What then does a person do if the hand of God is removed from our destiny? For Dylan, as for Guthrie, the answer lies in the individual. His last stanza returns to the narrator stating he's leavin' (destination and reason not clear) because he is "weary as Hell" and feeling confused. In this stanza he perpetuates Woody Guthrie's theme of the wanderer, but for Dylan that wanderer is not the happy-go-lucky populist radical. The narrator's "leavin'" signals the beginnings of the alienated-individual mytheme that will dominate the myth of America in popular song over the next two decades. Finally, he ends the song on a bitterly ironic note as he states that, if God is indeed on our side, he will stop another war. This, of course, rings hollow in light of the catalog of abuses he has just chronicled.

The alienated individual had been a phenomenon for well over four decades in literature, American and Continental, but his appearance in popular music was more gradual. Dylan was the dominant force in defining the nature of the individual in America for future songwriters. For instance, in "Bob Dylan's Dream" (1963) the train ride west, instead of being a symbol for the potential of the country, is the beginning of a journey toward alienation and dislocation (we will see a similar trip in Paul Simon's "America" [1968]). He writes of people with "haunted hearts" who think they will never get old and who will "sit forever in fun." But this is not to be, for over the years, he notes, many gambles are "lost and won" with these friends taking different roads, "And each one I've never seen again." That feeling we observed in previous songs about the American experience—that the myth is a shared ideal—is inverted in Dylan's vision of the country.

In another song, "Bob Dylan's 115th Dream" (1965), the vision becomes surrealistic as he states he sees Captain Arab going to sea, obviously Melville's Captain Ahab. The song seems to suggest a preface to a journey: Is it the journey of the Pilgrims, the journey west, the journey of Woody Guthrie's outsider-wanderer on his quest to discover "his" land? All these are suggested but in a very surrealistic fashion and in a manner that features the anomalies. For instance, he begins by talking about how he barters with the Indians but ends up throwing them in jail for carrying harpoons. Later on he brings into question the ideal of communal purpose and unity, and features an anomaly in the mytheme of the open land of opportunity when he writes of going up to a house "With the U.S. flag upon display" and asks if they could help him out; instead, the man tells him to get out, or he'll tear him "limb from limb." In the final stanza as the narrator prepares to leave the bay he sees three ships, and when he asks the captain why he isn't driving a truck, he finds out that the captain is Christopher Columbus.

Dylan is clearly trying to show, much as the Beat poets did, that time is out of joint; our journey is not one of progress, and we are not individuals on a quest for new opportunity under the guiding hand of God. For Dylan, when we make that return to the past— and the original sense of discovery that gave birth to the United States, we find instead the death of community and only the perseverance of the individual. The individual, however, is not a rugged self-reliant type; he is, rather, a wanderer, no longer the symbol of great beginnings, but instead symbolic of someone cut off from the collective destiny willed by God. His individuality is riddled with a sense of irony and loss. We are no longer in the presence of the American Adam, but we see, instead, that this figure wandering the "ribbon of highway," like Ahab, has the mark of Cain; he is the alienated man seeking a place east of Eden.

What is poignant in these songs (in retrospect) is that all this was being sung during a period of growing political collectivism. The sentiments seem at times to belong more in the "me decade" of the seventies than in the sixties—and, in fact, they will reappear in the seventies, sung by others. What Dylan gives us, however, is a new look at the role of the individual and a new notion of transcendence within his mythic vision. For all of his anomaly-featuring in discussing the myth in his music, there is a sense of transcendence: The lonely, isolated individual finds a higher meaning by being cut off from the collective identity and Providential vision. For by being cut off from that vision one will avoid the hypocrisies of the vision and in turn can forge a clearer, more honest, truthful, and real vision of what America is. For Dylan and, in the final analysis, for his audience of rebellious teens and young adults, the heart of the country lies outside the traditional myth.

As the 1960s progressed, youth would, indeed, live out the vision of America that Dylan had painted earlier in the decade. The many gaps—generation, communication, and the like—that split the country were clearly anticipated in Dylan's music. Like radicals from prior ages, 1960s youth saw in the image of the outsider a romantic articulation of the natural feelings of alienation that are part of being a teenager and young adult. Dylan gave their disenchantment and sense of disenfranchisement a heroic dimension. Dylan's Captain Arab speaks as eloquently about the youth culture's quarrel with authority and "the establishment" as Herman Melville's Captain Ahab speaks of the nineteenth-century man's angry quarrel with God. Todd Gitlin, in a discussion of Dylan's "Mr. Tambourine Man," makes a statement that can easily be applied to Dylan's "America" songs:

> Thus did Dylan lilt of absolute liberty in an infinite present time severed from the past: this was the transcendentalist fantasy of the wholly, abstractly free individual, finally released from the pains and distortions of society's traps, liberated to the embrace of nature and the wonder of essential things, in an America capable of starting the world again. (1987, 200–201).

Note that Gitlin hearkens to one of the venerable mythemes, regeneration. If youth did indeed see in Dylan's vision, and in his outsider-wanderer hero, the renaissance of a new American Adam, their perceptions would be altered by the late 1960s. The political realities and deeply ingrained myths held by the mainstream culture grew increasingly hostile to this new counterculture. The aftershocks from 1968 alone were enough to stagger the most idealistic. Not surprisingly, by the late 1960s and early 1970s, the heroic dimension of Dylan's vision had given way to the bleaker side, the anomalous side, of the myth.

By then the most eloquent spokesman for the myth of America had come to be Paul Simon. Two of his songs, "America" (1968) and "American Tune" (1973), draw heavily on the traditions of Dylan and Guthrie. With great effectiveness Simon utilizes the first person narrator to establish the role of the individual in the quest for America. His songs, like Dylan's, speak of loss and a corresponding wandering search for the country. Early in "America" a young couple board a Greyhound in Michigan bound for Pittsburgh; the young "lovers" are planning, in a quaint evocation of nineteenth-century sentiment, to marry their "fortunes together." We find the boy's fortune is "real estate," which he has in a bag; again we see here a good example of anomaly featuring as he inverts the traditional images associated with the myth. One's real estate is no longer one's private property; the individuals in this song, in fact, have no home. Like Dylan's characters, they are cut off from the archetypal images of the land and the "home sweet home" of Irving Berlin's generation.

Eventually the couple sink into separate activities; she reads a magazine, and he sinks into a lonely reverie and looks at the scenery as the moon rises "over an open field." The image of the land here is not one of regeneration or even the bountiful symbol of individual freedom as suggested by Guthrie. Instead, it is a symbol of loneliness and alienation, of an expanse that exists between individuals. This point is made very clear when, after looking at the scenery, he says to the sleeping girl beside him that he is "lost" and "empty and aching," but he doesn't know why. Simon's favorite theme is the breakdown in communications; here, taken in tandem with the image of the lonely landscape, it further suggests the loss of community and the alienation of the individual. In the final stanza, the image of the landscape is juxtaposed with an urban image as his narrator counts cars on the New Jersey Turnpike,* and stating that

*If you're wondering why this pair is taking such a roundabout route to Pittsburgh, you'll have to ask Paul Simon.

"They've all come/To look for America." Simon here depicts the solitariness of the quest by using the symbol of the automobile and commuters on their way to work. One may be reminded here of Ferlinghetti's and Ginsburg's devastating images of the highway in contemporary America and our headlong rush down those thorough-fares toward materialism and nothingness. Guthrie's "ribbon of high-way" is transformed from a path of freedom and opportunity for the individual to a symbol of the mass of men leading desperate lives. The quest has become the grind; we are well past that moment when we cleared a path through the "desart" to paradise. Work, furthermore, has lost its efficacy as part of the myth. Henry Steele Commager has written:

> With the passing of the necessity for hard work, the old Puritan idea that work was a virtue and idleness a vice went glimmering, while prosperity, the easy speculative profits of the twenties and the forties, government responsibility for security, high income and inheritance taxes, the vicissitudes of economy and fluctuations in the value of money, all combined to make other Puritan virtues like frugality and thrift seem outmoded. (1950, 433)

What Commager chronicles above in 1950 did not fully enter the popular consciousness until the 1960s, when parental values (hard work being one of them) were seriously questioned and threatened. Simon just happened to be the songwriter who captured the feeling and articulated it for youth in the late 1960s.

In this song the narrator, from his observation point on the bus, has come to the realization that he is alienated from the symbols traditionally associated with the myth (i.e., the land, real estate), and he is alienated from the contemporary average American's notion of the myth (i.e., success in the form of a job). By the late sixties work no longer suggests opportunity and regeneration but merely survival and perhaps even loss.

Work also plays an important role in Simon's "American Tune" (1973). Where Guthrie's wanderer ambled happily outside the traditional myth and often contemplated the necessity of work as part of the myth, Simon also has made it an important variation on the mytheme of opportunity and freedom. In "American Tune," more-over, the despondency hinted at in the closing lines of "America" is fully realized.

The song uses for its primary melodic idea, interestingly enough, a Bach chorale (sometimes sung as "O Sacred Head Surrounded"), which evokes the hymnlike melodies of the founding fathers and early songs about America. And he makes an immediate association with the Pilgrims in the line about it being hard to be happy "so far away from home." This perspective is then yoked with a contemporary sentiment in the lines where he states that he doesn't know a person "who's not been battered" or "feels at ease" and adds, "I don't know a dream that's not been shattered/Or driven to its knees." This is followed up by an understated line, "But it's all right." These words struck a poignant chord in listeners reeling from the shocks of Kent State, Altamont, Vietnam, and the Nixon landslide in the 1972 election. Furthermore, in the above lyrics, one hears echoes of Dylan's songs in the lines about friendship. The shattered dream idea and the line "I wonder what's gone wrong" clearly invert and enunciate the anomalous aspects of the Paradise and Edenic my-theme of the earlier songs. The allusions to the failed dream song also seem to evoke E. Y. Harburg's "Brother Can You Spare a Dime" (1932) and foreshadow Springsteen's songs of the late seventies and early eighties.

As in "America" a journey is the central action and symbol. In the bridge of the song, he has a dream sequence in which he states he dreamed he was dying; his soul rises to look back on him. He then says he sees the Statue of Liberty sailing away to sea. The image suggests that the dream has been cut adrift and wanders, no longer connected to the land, much as the narrator is no longer connected to the dream. In the last stanza the Pilgrims again figure as the narrator sings of those who came on the *Mayflower* and those who sail the moon (i.e., another "new frontier" and the extension of our belief in manifest destiny); he closes with a reference to those who come "in the age's most uncertain hours" singing an "American Tune." He is seemingly trying to make a universal assumption about Americans and how this song of our American spirit seems to come forth during times of trial, but Simon does not see regeneration after the trial as the Pilgrims did.

He ends the song by stating that we can't be forever blessed, and adds that tomorrow is a working day and he's "just trying to get some rest." Simon again ends a song by looking to work as the most immediate realization of what it is to be an American. The song suggests that the narrator is reconciled to his condition, but work for him is no longer an edifying or transformational force (as it would have been for the radicals of the thirties); it is merely necessary for survival. Work, for Paul Simon, has become symbolic of a dull, blind, persistent quest for the myth. The journey does not clear a path through the "desart" to Paradise, but merely takes us back to the daily grind.

III

By the decade's end an interesting paradox haunted popular music and the culture in general. As youth moved toward achieving a dream of participatory democracy and mobilized themselves in a number of collective concerns (from peace to communes), the value of the individual became paramount. The America of Paul Simon and Bob Dylan was one where only individuals could survive outside the system. In this way they carried on a kinship with the Old Left, which also achieved a sense of solidarity through their "otherness." The America that youth now envisioned was one which stood in opposition to the forces that would undermine the common bond of humanity: the "war machine." They sought to find a new sense of moral progress to counteract the material-technological progress. This moral vision, however, did not include God; they wanted no new theocracy. Reason and reality, in terms of exploding the myths of the past, were the rules, reaffirming humanistic values.

There were still those who believed in the old myth, and by an even greater irony, these people also appeared to be the outsiders: the country and western musicians. As with the Civil War, each side believed that it spoke for the "real" America. Rock musicians, speaking to students and radicals, were united in their doubt, uncertainty and alienation. The country musicians speaking for a working-class and rural audience, were united in their affirmation of the theocratic ideals of the original myth and in their distrust of college-student protesters, whom they perceived as nothing more than a bunch of overprivileged whiners. Their songs echoed Stephen Decatur's famous toast: "My country, in her intercourse with foreign nations, may she always be right. But right or wrong, my country."

There was not a lot of activity out of Nashville during the fifties and sixties regarding the myth. There was no real need for it. Johnny Horton's "Johnny Freedom" from the early sixties and written for the Freedomland, U.S.A. Exposition by George Weiss and Jule Styne (yes, he of *Gypsy* fame), takes the classic country music worm's-eye view of the common person as the fighter in every war and the pioneer on every frontier. He is the "spirit of America," a Yankee Doodle Dandy, and the Lincoln "of the day." It is a little bit of Woody Guthrie, Roy Acuff, and Irving Berlin.

The event that brought the country music perspective on the myth to the fore was Vietnam. As Bill Malone notes, around 1965 and 1966, as student demonstrations began in earnest, more country musicians threw their songwriting efforts behind the war effort (1985, 318). Like their Civil War and World War II forebears, they largely affirmed the basic principles of the myth. Warner Mack, for instance, states, in his "Pray for Your Country" by Warren McPherson, that because this land was "made for liberty" and allows each of us to make our smallest dream a reality, we must answer "freedom's call." He employs the mytheme of the patriot's sacrifice as he reminds the listener that those who have "yellow" in their veins should recall those whose red blood was shed "in freedom's name." Reminiscent of the songs of the Revolutionary War and Civil War, he resurrects the theme of the outside threat; in this case, to avoid this conflict is to cave in to those who wish "to see us fall." Therefore, in an evocation of manifest destiny and God's providential role, he concludes that we should pray for our country, "And let God's will be done."

Not all the songs are as comprehensive and sweeping in their use of the myth. Most songwriters/performers draw on two or three of the mythemes to make their points. In keeping with the fundamentalist values that pervade Southern culture, the name of God appears often. Bobby Bare's "God Bless America Again" (1970) recalls Irving Berlin in the title and is a good measure of where the country performer thought America had come to: We need to get back Berlin's original sentiment. The song does not do much with the myth other than to remind the listener that God blessed America way back in the beginning and to imply that we should not abandon that heritage. Even the "Battle Hymn of Lt. Calley" (1971), which basically describes My Lai as a rather routine fire fight, notes that the soldier who was part of the massacre will appear in front of his Maker and will be able to say that he "never left his gun." The song ends with an echo of "The Battle Hymn of the Republic," leaving the listener to ask, "Who's truth is marching on?" Calley's or God's? Of course it is a rhetorical question because Calley's truth *is* God's.

Manifest destiny also figures prominently in the songs of country musicians. Tom T. Hall's "Hello Vietnam" (1966) echoes a couple of sentiments we have encountered in previous war songs: First, there is the call for total war. Hall says freedom must be saved at "any cost" and that the "world will learn" that fires we don't put out will burn bigger. Second, and more important, is the role we have to play in maintaining freedom: If we don't stop Communism in that land, "freedom will start slipping through our hands." The suggestion here is that we are the embodiment and primary—if not sole—dispensers of freedom in the world, and the entire responsibility for maintaining it is ours. Another less direct suggestion of the mytheme is in Kris Kristofferson's "Vietnam Blues" (1966), in which the narrator states that he doesn't want to die, but he is not going "to crawl." The audience might see here an implicit declaration of superiority or of dominance that we must not relinquish.

The country artist also drew heavily on the mytheme of the patriot's sacrifice in countering antiwar feelings. Dell Reeves' "The Private" by C. Putnam and J. Barlow mixes a bit of Johnny Freedom in with the sacrifice of the patriots by using the "lowly" private as a symbol of patriots throughout our history. Reeves tells us that the private is always there to point the gun at the heart of "the things that free men hate"; he reminds us that he was there at Valley Forge, in the Great War, and now in Vietnam. The effective part of this is that by investing the private—that is, the common fighting person—with heroic status, he allows all listeners to feel a sense of ownership in heroism. Similarly, Stonewall Jackson's recording, "The Minutemen Are Turning over in Their Graves" (1966) by H. Howard, which almost says it all in the title, also tries to bring the patriot's sacrifice into the realm of the personal for the listener. In the song he says he is grateful that the people protesting the war weren't around at Valley Forge and that Washington and Jefferson must be "crying tears of shame." He ends the song by first offering up a prayer that "pacifists" not serve in Washington and then with a final bewildered comment that he can't understand why someone won't defend his home. Again, the symbol of the home gives the war a more personal dimension.

Another song that effectively utilizes the patriot's mytheme is Bill Anderson's "Where Have All Our Heroes Gone" (1970). Similarly, Paul Simon had asked in "his Mrs. Robinson" (1968) where heroes like Joe DiMaggio had gone and added that the nation was turning "its lonely eyes" to him. But there the wit mitigated some of the serious intent. Not so with Bill Anderson. He announces that America is "still my Home Sweet Home," which is a direct borrowing from Berlin and then largely catalogs our past heroes such as MacArthur, Roy Rogers, Gene Autry, Charles Lindbergh, John Wayne, Gary Cooper, and Ike to illustrate how far we have fallen from our transcendental aspirations. He adds toward the end that when Churchill held up two fingers it meant peace (actually it meant "V for Victory") and "not let your enemy have it all." One detects in these songs the sense of outrage that protesters were betraying the country, betraying the original vision that had made us great, and jeopardizing freedom here and abroad. (The protesters, on the other hand, felt that the original promise had been betrayed long ago.) Many such lyrics were oversimplification, but they were aimed at an unsophisticated audience, which thought in general symbols.

Finally, there are the songs of Merle Haggard, which almost stand in a category by themselves. The tunes, most especially "Okie from Muskogee" (1969), have come to be emblematic of prowar forces in the late sixties and early seventies. Oliver Stone in his 1986 movie *Platoon* has Bunny and others in Sergeant Barnes's "camp" listening to Haggard's song, and Phil Ochs tried during the seventies to turn the song's sentiments on their head when he sang it in concert. For all its numinous presence in the musical culture of America for the last twenty years, it actually says little about the myth of America. There is one reference to Old Glory waving over the courthouse, an image which, I would assume, suggests that the country still believes in law and order (a sentiment which was very real at this time as it formed a major plank in Nixon's presidential campaign). Oddly enough, he follows up this image with a verse about white lightning being the biggest thrill of all, but I am sure he would not look as kindly on the "innocent" pleasures of other popular illegal substances of the day. And in the only real evocation of the myth, he states that we don't burn our draft cards, "'Cause we want to stay free."

His other major song, "The Fightin' Side of Me" (1970), is more directly concerned with the central themes of the myth. For instance, he states that people (i.e., protesters) will end up on his fighting side when they run down a "way of life" that our fighting men have died for. His solution to this dilemma is similar to the one

Paul Dresser offered some seventy odd years earlier: "If you don't love it, leave it!" Furthermore, he sings, if these "squirrely" guys don't believe in fighting, how long can we "count on being free?" Finally, he employs the Christian imagery of the land of milk and honey as he notes that these people who run down the country are really hypocrites: They love our "milk and honey," but they "preach" about "some other way of livin'." Perhaps more than the sentiments in these songs, it is the voice that Haggard projects that gives these songs their power. John D. McCarthy, Richard Peterson, and William Yancey note in their essay, "Singing Along with the Silent Majority," that these songs "are symptomatic of the emergence of an explanation of troubles for those who have been apparently left behind by the systemic changes which taken place over the last decade [1960s]. Yet in this case, the blame for failure is not placed upon the system— this would not fit in with the strong belief in the American dream—but rather on the agents of social change [i.e., welfare, education, protesters, hippies, weak leaders]" (1972, 62). Most country musicians exited the turbulent sixties convinced that they had literally and figuratively kept the faith.

Finally, there is the occasional country song that seems to make concessions to the "new consciousness" rising among the young. A case in point might be Tom T. Hall's "America the Ugly" (1968). In what seems like a radical reversal of his earlier thoughts about America in "Hello Vietnam," the title suggests that Hall will undertake a withering reevaluation of the meaning of America as it has been perpetuated through tunes like "America the Beautiful." And, to a certain extent, he does. He tells the story of a foreign photographer who comes here to photograph Uncle Sam's "progress." The photographer gets off the boat and immediately heads for the Bowery, where he observes the "hopeless, hungry living dead" and those who would sell their souls for cheap wine. Next, he goes to Appalachia, and there sees hungry and ragged children, pregnant women, and "good men" with nothing to do; he adds that we'll probably try to tell the photographer that "it ain't so." Finally, he goes to a Medicare center where he sees the younger generation dumping the older citizens because they didn't want them "in their hair." He concludes by singing about the poor man who is daily working it out while mighty rich men live "high"; this, he warns us, will be bring a "gleam to the enemy's eye," remonstrating with the listener that when the heart gets hard the country will fall. On the surface he is, like the protest singer, asking for a more humanistic America, but this masks the underlying desire that we remain strong so foreigners and outside threats do not think we are an easy mark. There is a slightly schizoid quality to the message, but this quality seems perfectly logical and natural in a decade of flux, change, and uncertainty. This song is nonetheless an attempt to reconcile the troubling currents of the times; it fails as a strong mythological statement because it offers no sense of transcendence. It merely forces listeners into a defensive posture, where they are forced to state, "Let's make things better so we don't get pushed around." In the final analysis, chauvinism overrides humanism.

It might be said of the 1960s that the decade offered no solutions for today and little hope for the future. The dichotomous vision of the myth that was present at the beginning of the decade was still present by the decade's end. What was different in 1970 was that Irving Berlin's version of the myth had been replaced by Woody Guthrie's by way of Bob Dylan. Woody's grandchildren had clearly taken center stage (in the case of Arlo, his children), but there was a difference in the element of hope and transcendence. Woody saw something greater in the land than the mere pursuit of individual desires. Dylan lacked that faith in the solidarity of individuals.

What hope there was seemed to lie within the province of the individual who had adopted an existentialist philosophy. This individual, unlike the individual depicted in earlier protest music, could not expect to be regenerated. There was nothing greater than the self, and the only way to preserve the self was to remain outside the mainstream, to repudiate the myth. And unlike the individual of the folk-protest movement, who undertook wandering to secure opportunity, the individual of the 1960s songs undertakes his/her wandering to find (perhaps rediscover) the country and some sense of community. The wandering, however, proves to be a dead end and brings us back to highways, routinized work, and a meaningless grind.

The other search took us overseas in pursuit of our manifest destiny. When Americans went looking for America, they were left with a question for an answer, a question which Norman Mailer used for the title of a novel: *Why Are We in Vietnam?* Country musicians, relying upon the established myth, were able with some certainty to answer that question; the young intelligentsia, relying upon the version of the myth that had been spawned in the thirties and kept alive in the underground in the fifties and early sixties, also had an answer: We were there because of some larger flaw in the national character; the war was a metaphor for the failure of the myth. God and our own misguided belief in our manifest destiny had led us to a small, steamy country, where we were fighting a war that was —according to the songs—oppressing and destroying a people and their country (we similarly saw our own land plundered for the war effort) to make them free (and therefore robbing them of the very thing we believed we traditionally fought for: self-determination). Thus, the war came to symbolize the oppression of African-Americans and other minorities that was taking place on the homefront. The war was also robbing young Americans of their freedom and chance for opportunity. It was the triumph of technology over humanity, and this was wrong. The central tenet of the folk-protest movement, ever since the 1930s, was to move human beings to the center of the American experience, to reaffirm the sanctity of the individual. That sacred hope was now being violated.

We, of course, can see this all in retrospect; we can piece it together from the musical tapestry. At the time, however, it was pretty much confusion and inchoate feelings that were mined in songs, to quote Jerome Rodnitzky, that "called not for solidarity but for diversity; they did not point out specific social ills, they depicted general absurdity.... Popular music with vague protest themes made some converts subtly. Youths, first attracted by the music, often later imbibed the style and finally perhaps read something of personal significance into the lyrics" (1976, 33). This may indeed be true, but the songs also spoke to the need for youth to rebel and to have some foci for their anger and for their need to make the world anew; that the rebellion took place in the arena of politics and protest made the rebellion seem all the more important.

Perhaps it was the rebellion itself, the engagement with large issues, that provided the sense of transcendence. Perhaps the mere questioning of the monolithic forces of the military-industrial complex bound these disparate individuals to something greater than themselves. They believed in utopia; they just expressed it in dystopian fashion. Hence the songs have an urgency and communicate a desire to change, to destroy if necessary, to turn away from the cant and the seeming hypocrisy, and to join Dylan in finding a place to wait out or halt that hard rain that was gonna fall. In their quest to find a new America, the songwriters of the sixties may have failed, they may have raised more questions than they could answer, but then, they needed to remind themselves that the storm-tossed journey to Plymouth was but the first leg of the journey for those first revolutionaries and rebels.

CHAPTER IX "**You Can't Be**
Forever Blessed"
The 1970s

Maybe the American
Dream is in the past,
understanding who you
are instead of looking to
the future: What are you
going to be? 'Cause
we've kind of reached
the future. I'm not just
talking about nostalgia.
I'm talking about finding
familiar guideposts.
Maybe this is a period
of reflection.
—*Vine Deloria, quoted in*
Studs Terkel's American
Dreams: Lost and Found
(1980)

Toward the end of Dennis Hopper's *Easy Rider* Wyatt (Captain America) and Billy are preparing to make the final leg of their journey to "retirement" in Florida. As they talk Wyatt remarks, "We blew it." Billy is, of course, incredulous; he tries to remind Wyatt of what they were trying to achieve: "That's what it's all about, man. . . . I mean, you go for the big money, man—and then you're free. You dig?" Wyatt's only response is, "We blew it." Both men go to sleep oblivious to the holocaust that tomorrow will bring.

Is it a metaphor for the sixties? Did we blow it? Americans standing on the brink of the new decade of the seventies may have, like Wyatt, sensed that they blew it, that the dream lies in the past and was now slipping out of their grasp like the Statue of Liberty slipping out to sea in Paul Simon's "American Tune." And they could only wonder about the future and hope that it wouldn't result, as it had for Wyatt and Billy, in a holocaust annihilating the dream completely.

Thus, in the 1970s Americans, including songwriters and performers, would be taking a new look at America and asking some hard questions about it. Was it, as Artie Kaplan suggested in his 1972 song, "The American Dream" (Norman Simon–Artie Kaplan), a place for him to be what he wanted to be or just "a fantasy?" The songs of the seventies show a culture struggling to build off what happened in the 1960s. On the one hand, there is a perpetuation of the tradition of protest where songwriters continue to chronicle the failure of the American system, and on the other hand, there are those songs that attempt to offer a solution and a new vision.

A number of events shaped the different approaches to the myth of America in the songs of the seventies. The decade opened with the killing of four students at Kent State University in Ohio. Next, the country watched as a "third rate burglary" resulted in the resignation of a President for the first time in our history. Shortly after, we witnessed our rather indecorous withdrawal from Vietnam—a far cry from those old newsreels of ticker tape parades.

Almost simultaneously, we faced the specter of diminishing natural resources in the oil shortages and embargoes, which proved two things: We exercised even less control over world affairs than we thought, and we were not as mobile (long gas lines) as Americans like to be. Finally, we were given an ignominious decade-ending shock with the storming of the American embassy in Teheran and the seizure of American personnel.

We found that the solution for it eluded us; all our past historical referents and responses failed us. Jimmy Carter perhaps sounded the note for the decade when he told us that we were suffering from a malaise. Accurate as that may have been, it was not what Americans wanted to hear. Dreams of greatness are not animated by specters of feeling faint.

As a result of events in the 1960s and the above-mentioned events three dominant themes emerged in the culture of the 1970s, influencing how songwriters approached the idea of America. They are, first, the feeling that we were living in an "age of diminishing expectations" (articulated most fully by Christopher Lasch), second, our growing inability to wield power or even will to power, finally, the new individualism, addressed first by Tom Wolfe in his essay on the "me decade."

Events of the seventies pointed clearly to an age where things were not going to be as lush, plush, and rich as they once had been. Diminishing expectations were evident in higher interest rates, our inability to "win" a war, and that certain resources were just not as readily available (hence, at our command) as they used to be. Christopher Lasch noted that, "Today Americans are overcome not by the sense of endless possibility but by the banality of the social order they have erected against it" (1978, 11). In short, people had begun to question those progressive ideals (universal education, welfare capitalism, scientific management of both industry and government) that had fueled our social and economic machinery for the previous forty years. There was a feeling that we had to turn our backs on those myths that had promised abundance and fullness of life. The seventies then established a climate where Americans, even more so than in the sixties, had to wonder if the best were in our past.

Because our past had been dotted so regularly with displays of our power to effect good in the world, the contractions of the seventies proved particularly painful. America's position as a world leader continued, but we seemed less the power than we had been. Vietnam had forced a real examination of the whole notion of manifest destiny. It seemed that not all countries wanted or were ready for the blessings of democracy—at least not as we defined it. In fact, not only did they not want it, but in certain quarters we were attacked as the "Great Satan" of mankind. This was especially distressing for generations of Americans who had believed the myth of America, which upheld the notion that we were the last best hope of civilization. Now we seemed like a conflation of absurdist dramas.

Finally, there was the state of the individual. The songs of the sixties as we have seen, put an entirely new spin on the old theme of the disaffected individual. The seventies continued to refine and define the role of the individual in an age when individual opportunity seemed to be diminishing. The participatory democracy of the sixties had yielded solid results in that the draft was ended. Consequently, student protest quickly faded (although the war went on), and campus life returned more or less to normal.

Underlying the songs of protest in the 1960s was the tacit assumption that the audience shared a common vision of the "real America." The individual achieved a sense of empowerment and shared purpose through joining similarly alienated individuals who stood outside the system—that is, the community formed itself around opposition to the myth.

In the seventies, however, there wasn't the assurance that one would achieve a sense of solidarity by banding with other alienated individuals. Jim Curtis states: "But a major lesson which we learned in the sixties is that we could not have involvement in depth [this is a phrase from Marshall McLuhan] with America as a whole. Our country is too big, too diverse, and too complicated for that. So we decentralized our experience of America in multiple smaller groupings of like-minded people" (1987, 241). People talked about working for change "through the system." A minor measure of the insecurity we were feeling is the spate of religious or pseudoreligious songs that enjoyed popularity in the first couple of years of the decade: "Amazing Grace," "Put Your Hand in the Hand," "Jesus Is Just Alright," "The Lord's Prayer," "Bridge Over Troubled Water," and—perhaps most dubious of all—"Let It Be." There was a rekindling of evangelical fervor wherein one—in keeping with the general tenor of the "me decade"—could establish a personal relationship with the Savior. If one was uncomfortable with this route, there was the exploding human potential movement, which offered a personal growth program for almost anyone. Jerry Rubin gave up revolutionary consciousness for money consciousness, and the "me decade" was in full swing.

The "me decade," however, did not really produce a renewed consciousness about the role of the individual in society; one finds no sense of individual empowerment in the popular arts, but, instead, either a hardened cynicism or—a survivalist mentality. Songwriters either slipped into a world-weary cynicism, or they extolled the merits of survival. In the other popular arts, ranging from historical romances to TV series, to have survived hard times is a major achievement. "The Waltons," for instance, transformed the Great Depression into something of an allegory for our own "hard times"—if that family could do it, so can we.

Consequently, we shall see in the music a pull of opposites—between a need for an integrative vision of America that offers individuals hope for a future (and a return to the "glories" of the past), and a genuine skepticism bordering on contempt for America and what it has become. This division continues the pull between what Ferlinghetti saw as a need for a renaissance of wonder and Ginsburg's more nihilistic vision, where the individuals had given their all to the country but now it had forgotten them. The division seemed even wider in the seventies than it had in the sixties, and for a songwriter to reconcile these polarities would be difficult. Paul Johnson titled his chapter on the sixties "America's Suicide Attempt," and it seems that some of those suicidal tendencies extended over into the seventies.

Events in the music industry in the 1970s paralleled the culture at large. The decade began with the breakup of the major groups—in a sense, a symbol for the breakup of participatory democracy. Simon Frith notes:

> Young people in the 1960s had experiences (experiences of war and politics) that intensified the conflict between public and private obligations, between freedom and responsibility, and it was these problems that rock, more than any other form of expression, addressed and made plain. . . . The 1970s meant a moralization of youth and rock too, as college students expressed, once more, a sober concern for grades and careers, as teenage culture was reestablished around new conventions of drug use and sexuality, as youth leisure, on campus and off, became again simply a matter of partying. (1981, 195)

The retreat into the "Me decade" was complemented by the emergence of the singer-songwriter. Groups gave way to solo acts, and rock gave way to a series of trends.

As the youth culture seemed to break apart on the Scylla and Charybdis of Woodstock and Altamont, the music also seemed to be fragmenting. The seventies was the decade of the trend or movement. Refinements in styles were hinted at in the last two years of the sixties, such as art-rock, country-rock, heavy metal, funk, jazz-rock, glitter-rock, and so forth. But no one style held the stage; no one person or group seemed to be able to focus the creative energies of the music and lead as the Beatles and, to a lesser extent, the Rolling Stones had.

In spite of the changes that were taking place—and the sense that protest would lead one, at its worst, to death or, at its least, into nothing more than a hollow exercise in street theater—the protest tradition carried on in subtle ways. Jerome Rodnitsky feels that the protest songs written around and after 1966 were largely 'do-it-yourself' protest songs which, in their attempt to be all things to all people, had less power but may have been more influential "because of the simple weight of numbers and their matter-of-fact presentation" (1976, 16). As we shall see, the flame of protest flickered with some regularity throughout the first half of the seventies, but gave solid evidence of its staying power in popular music with the emergence of punk in the late seventies. Just when one thought it was safe to don a white polyester suit and boogie on the dance floor, there arose in England and America a new generation of musicians who, like Stephen Dedalus, saw history as a nightmare from which they were trying to awake. They sent out a message of new beginnings. There were suicidal overtones to the message, a nihilism that was discomfiting to some, but the music served as a reminder of the essentially revolutionary character of rock and of its ability to animate and agitate for change. For many who viewed the disco craze as the virtual end of history, punk offered the hope that in the midst of death there is life.

I

We will begin our survey of popular song of the seventies by concentrating on the music of African-Americans. Of course, the sixties was the decade in which black music broke through into the mass market with a vengeance. The emergence of "soul" coincided with a growing awareness on the apart of the burgeoning youth culture about civil rights and the role that members of their generation were playing in that struggle. The rhetoric of the civil rights struggle struck a responsive chord in many Americans (white and other races) and the music pulsed with an energy and authenticity that was missing from much of the offerings of the major labels. Consequently, soul music, generating largely out of Motown and Atlantic records, found an appreciative audience among a community who saw all forms of rock music as essential to their identity as a community. Soul music was perceived by many young people as a bridge to understanding black culture. It was their way to share in their "brother's" struggle for full and equal rights.

Up until the age of rock, African-American musicians and songwriters seldom engaged in direct protest. Much of their music, be it the blues or spirituals, contains an element of protest, but direct attacks on institutions or agitation for revolution was isolated and rare. This changed in the midsixties, when protest in general was becoming an important part of youthful rebellion. Still, it took galvanic public figures such as Martin Luther King, Jr., to allow the music to make it into the mass market. The issues the songwriters deal with are much the same as those that were dealt with by Delta bluesmen in the previous three decades, but they were expressed in bolder terms and included broader concerns—concerns such as, what is America's responsibility to its black citizens?

One searches in vain through African-American music for songs that attempt a comprehensive critique of the American experience. For the African-American, the idea of America is largely embodied in two major themes: opportunity and equality. Seldom does the African-American songwriter deal with the themes of God's providential role or that of manifest destiny. Some of this may have its origin in the black religious experience, where ideas of destiny, God's plan, and the whole notion of the promised land (or the land of milk and honey) are conditioned by religion. Thus when the African-American talks of the promised land, it is not the *new* Canaan, but the real Canaan of the bible.

Nor does one find many allusions to the land as the source of bounty and goodness and the seedbed for the ideas of freedom, equality, and opportunity. First, the African-American's bond to the land is a tenuous one at best. As slaves, they worked it, but could never own it. The legacy after the Civil War was one largely of sharecropping, where once again they would not necessarily see a strong sense of opportunity or renewal. The traditions of black music, moreover, especially in the blues, portray African-Americans as uprooted and constantly moving; that "hellhound" that prompted Robert Johnson's wail, "Got to keep moving" could be discrimination as well as a woman. Thus, the land holds no special symbolic import for the African-American. But the city does. The city becomes the site where the struggle for freedom, equality, and opportunity is played out; it provides African-Americans not only with a sense of place but also with a symbol or benchmark whereby they could measure the degree to which they had achieved their dream and been integrated into American society.

Thus the myth of America, as it emerges in African-American music, is for all intents and purposes the American Dream or the Myth of Success. The ownership of certain items is symbolic of attainment of opportunity and equality. Good neighborhoods/homes and good jobs mean that they have achieved what others Americans have. The music of the sixties and early seventies shows the African-American placing some faith in the basic values of the dominant culture. The songs reveal an attitude that what the white ruling class has (both in actuality and potentiality) is desirable; there is no need to set oneself apart from that dream.

The roots of their culture had to be preserved, however, and this was achieved through a reaffirmation of the gospel and blues roots in the development of soul music. These two musical roots were perfectly adapted to the African-American's treatment of the myth. In the blues songs, a tradition of protest embodies the spirit of resistance and a complementary assertion of one's identity and strengths. In the gospel song is the spirit of affirmation and hope for the better world. Curtis Mayfield, who wrote some of the best protest songs of the late sixties, said that he saw songs such as "This Is My Country" and "Choice of Colors" as, "'songs of inspiration, songs of faith'" (Alexander 1972, 194). Similarly, Ian Hoare notes of the changes in socially oriented black songs in the sixties:

> These changes were directly related to the ways in which soul lyrics about love differed from blues lyrics about love: the earlier emphasis on desperation and loneliness was replaced by a move towards inspiration through solidarity—an optimistic group-consciousness that bore many faces of Christian faith but was very much about *this* world. (1975, 206–207).

The music, then, allowed African-Americans to stake their claim to a portion of the dream while preserving a sense of their own special cultural identity.

The protest music that emerges during the sixties and seventies questions some of the fundamental mythemes, but, unlike the music of the folk-protest movement, it also offers some hope. One of the themes is the hope that America will someday soon be "color blind." William Oliver and Gladys Foreman's "Hymn to the Freedom Riders," "How Long? How Long?" (1962), for instance, asks a series of rhetorical questions of God about when the world will be color blind. Hope is also held out in the form of love. The word "love" is one that had much currency in the late sixties; it was the central principle of hippie ideology, and it insinuated itself into most songs dealing with hopes for the future (i.e., "All You Need is Love" by the Beatles, "Get Together" by the Youngbloods, etc.). One of the most affecting moments in the film *Monterey Pop* (1967) is when Otis Redding asks of the crowd, "We all love one another, don't we?" This, of course, was during that period when Sly Stone was also able to say to his audience, "Thank You for Lettin' Me Be My Self Again." Finally, there is a theme in African-American music of achieving a sense of equality and opportunity (or at least less divisiveness) through the powers of music. George Clinton called for one nation under a groove, and Stevie Wonder's "Sir Duke" almost paints a portrait of a utopia united by people feeling the music "all over"—in short, music is the one constant in an otherwise chaotic world.

Protest, however, also followed the lead of the folk-protest tradition, and it is this tradition that seems to have survived and retained most of its vitality into the eighties. In their call for a share of the American Dream, the African-American songwriters use some of the mythemes of the myth of America as reference points. For instance, Curtis Mayfield's "This Is My Country" (1968) questions the attitude that African-Americans don't have "a right" to say it's their country. He alludes to a different group of patriots, a group who will speak to the souls of African-Americans, when he notes that they have endured slavery for 300 years. He adds that too many have died protecting his pride for him to go "second class." Slavery, of course, suggests not only the sacrifice of his forebears but implies the struggle for liberty and freedom; while the image of second class implies not only equality but opportunity as one struggles to have the best. He then appeals to the better nature of his audience by assuming that they will give him "consideration" but is quick to follow this up with a cautionary note, reminding listeners that there are really only two paths we can take: to allow African-Americans to "perish unjust" or to live equal as a nation.

I noted earlier that in black music the mytheme of the land is replaced by that of the city. Beginning in the late sixties, as actual American cities were going up in flames as the result of racial discontent, the city figures more and more prominently in soul music. This is not the city of "Up on the Roof" or even "Summer in the City" fame. This landscape inverts the mytheme of the land to expose the American nightmare. There are no images of abundance and plenty, only blight and despair. Where the land offers images of expansiveness and hope of renewal, the city forces individuals to look at their immediate condition and then summon what resources they have to transcend the blight. The answers are usually not encouraging.

The Temptations' "Cloud Nine" (1969, Norman Whitfield–Barrett Strong), for instance, describes a person born and raised in a one-

room slum apartment where there is no food and only "hard times."
The father doesn't know the "meaning of work" and does not respect
the mother. The narrator cannot find a job (failure of the myth of
opportunity), and so he takes to Cloud Nine, an obvious reference
to drugs. Sadly and ironically, it is only on Cloud Nine where the
narrator can achieve the dream, for there he can be who he wants
to be. On Cloud Nine every man is free, but this, of course, is
achieved by being a "million miles from reality." The final stanzas
of the song suggest that there is a subtle shift in thinking about
the hopes for the future as the songwriters note that on Cloud Nine
one is free as a bird and there is no difference between night and
day (color blindness), and the world of Cloud Nine is one of "love
and harmony." In the context of the song, the ideas of love and harmony, which had animated so many hopes previously, strike a dis-
cordant note and ring with a harsh falsity. Furthermore, there is a
more tragic irony implied here: In order to achieve the dream, one
must follow a path that leads to self-destruction. There is definitely
a change stirring in the African-American's relationship to the myth.

This change is further fueled by two other songs, the Temptations'
"Ball of Confusion (That's What the World Is Today)" (1970, Norman
Whitfield–Barrett Strong) and War's "The World Is a Ghetto" (1972).
Both songs offer no hope. They are clearly in the tradition of the
folk-protest movement of the late sixties and early seventies, which
continued the attack on American traditions and values. The point
of both songs is clear: The world is a mess. Politicians "rap on"
with the old lies about setting people free, but in actuality, nobody
really knows where we are headed (the notion of manifest destiny
has absolutely no credence here). The Temptations' song features
powerful "rap" sections, where they catalog the contradictions that
seem to be pulling apart the very fabric of existence: "Segregation,
determination, demonstration, integration, aggravation, humilia-
tion, obligation to our nation." The point here is that there is no
one principle that carries the day, only the contradictions, the result
of which is, as a final stanza suggests, the cities "aflame in the
summer."

War's song similarly points out that there is no abundance or
plenty in the city (or world for that matter); it is, instead, a blighted
landscape, which offers no hope for those searching for something.
It is interesting that the sentiments expressed are much akin to those
of Paul Simon in "America" and "American Tune," but they have

moved the stage to the inner city instead of the "open field." The city becomes a metaphor for the self: The narrator, employing symbols that previous songwriters have used to reaffirm the efficacy of the myth, wonders when he'll find "paradise," a home and happiness; his conclusion is that, if you do find it, you'll just have to "give it up." In short, the quest for those things that make one an American will more than likely end up a hollow journey through a blighted urban landscape searching "for a place," weary-eyed."

In the seventies the pull between an anger born of despair and an attempt to reaffirm the African-American's quest for a share of America characterizes the songs. Marvin Gaye's seminal album *What's Going On* (1971) catalogs a series of social ills, but offers the corrective in a reaffirmation of love and reliance upon God. This is not exactly the Old Testament God of past songs dealing with myth; this is the God of mercy who knows where we're headed and whom we must have faith in if things are to be all right. In short, the reliance on God here owes more to the tradition of gospel music than to Irving Berlin.

On the other hand, the Chi-Lites believe that the solution is in empowering the people. Their "Give More Power to the People" (1971) mildly echoes socialist sentiments as they decry the concentration of power among a wealthy elite, who lie about the "people's money" and then throw it away. They focus on the ills of hunger and killing, and note that the response of those in power to these problems is to make a promise and then throw the money away. Finally, they repudiate the mytheme of opportunity by showing the *Catch-22* nature of economic opportunity: Just when you think you are little ahead, you find the price of living has gone up—so you are, in essence, right back where you started. In the final analysis, the Chi-Lites reaffirm the late sixties position that opportunity is becoming more elusive, and only when people are empowered, may we see a return to the principles of freedom, equality, and opportunity.

Similarly, Stevie Wonder's album *Innervisions* (1973) sets out the problems affecting African-Americans in the early seventies, but he always holds out some promise. In his "Living for the City," for instance, he employs the image of the city to illustrate the desperate need for change. He paints a portrait of Dad and Mom working long hours and at menial jobs just to get "enough for the city." He adds in a later stanza that there are no jobs for African-Americans and that voting seems to offer no solutions. He introduces a little playlet where a country boy gets duped into running some drugs and gets busted for ten years. The conclusion to the whole song is that we have to "make a better tomorrow."

This idea of a better world is expanded on in his "Visions," where he sees a people walking "hand in hand" and wonders if he is seeing the "milk and honey land," where people truly feel like they're free. But he also asks if this is just a vision and if we can only reach this utopia by finding wings and flying away to this vision in our minds. It is roughly the same message as contained in "Cloud Nine," but it is marginally more hopeful because the attainment of the vision is not linked to something that is going to destroy the individual. He does, however, offer a positive antidote to this situation in his "Higher Ground" where, like Marvin Gaye, he encourages the listener to turn to God—specifically Jesus. The song's opening apocalyptic imagery serves to underscore the need for Jesus's friendship. The one assurance we have, according to Wonder, is that Jesus loves America and that we are all the "Jesus Children of America." Thus Wonder establishes the common ground for our brotherhood and our only hope to really see that milk and honey land he spoke of in "Visions."

Other songwriters echo Wonder's hopes for brotherhood in the seventies. Solomon Burke's "I Have A Dream" (1974) returns us to the early sixties and King's great "I Have A Dream" speech. His message is that equality (walking "hand in hand") is our destiny and that liberty and freedom can only be achieved if we "get it together." The forces behind getting it together are love and peace. The decidedly sixties mentality that pervades the song makes it seem slightly anachronistic, but it shows the power of the African-American patriot (i.e., King) to continue to animate the African-American vision of America. Another song that makes love the answer is Harold Melvin and the Blue Notes's "Where's the Concern for the People?" (1977), which largely catalogs the usual social ills (hungry children, "brothers" fighting among themselves, pain, misery) and asks where our concern and love for humanity is. It remains as a question and, couched as the sentiments are within a disco format, the ideas seem almost secondary to getting people into a dance groove.

We see then that throughout the seventies a large number of popular and influential African-American songwriters struggled to find a message of hope in a world that militates against that. Songwriters attempt in their reworking of the myth to reconcile the need to preserve a separate cultural (subcultural) identity with a need to be assimilated into the mainstream of American Life. The African-American depicts America as a place where freedom and opportunity should be available to all, and a place where they are entitled to share in that experience on the basis of their history and contribution to our culture and through the efforts of their own "patriots" such as Frederick Douglass (who was cited more often in the protest songs of the early sixties), Martin Luther King, and, as is the case in one song, Malcolm X.

The more troubling undercurrent that exists here, however, is that maybe this place does not exist. If it does, it may only be in your mind or in a drugged state or, as Curtis Mayfield suggests, "Underground." In that song he suggests that because the surface has "truly become a vast wasteland" brought on by our own urge to self-destruction, we may have to go underground, where there is no sight (i.e., a version of the color-blind notion) and where we can only judge one another by "what is right." This is never spelled out other than to note that underground everyone is black. So, on the one hand the song reaffirms that equality is the answer, but it argues as strongly that perhaps the answer lies outside the system as we have it. The rappers of the 1980s would pick this idea up and carry it to the next phase.

II

Turning to other music of the seventies, we find a similar situation to that in African-American culture. The cynicism carries over, but there are also occasional attempts to reforge a new vision of America that reconciles some of the classic symbols of the past with the new consciousness spurred by the radicalism of the sixties.

In general, however, the tone throughout the decade is largely cynical. Steve Miller's Chuck Berryesque "Living in the U.S.A." reminds us that we are living in a "plastic land" where we do our best to keep free, but where the greatest wish seems to be that somebody just get "me a cheeseburger." Similarly, Don Harrison's "American Dream" (1977) denounces the materialistic drift when he states that as a young man he had a dream that included God, rainbow skies, and diamond seas." But now he is replaced by a machine, leaving him with the feeling that all they did was use his life and take his money.

The dominant theme of most of the songs of the early seventies is that the ideology of the past (our former myth) is bankrupt. A number of songwriters evoke the classic symbols of the myth to illustrate the disparity between the dream and the reality. Richard Farina's "House Un-American Blues Activity Dream" (1971)—which seems more a part of the sixties"—alludes to Berlin when he says that "God Bless America without any doubt," but all that means for him is that it is time to get out. He alludes to the "Red, White and Blue" making war on poor people (which could refer both to minorities in the United States and to the Vietnamese) while justice is sitting on a heap of "manure." The final measures imply that by falling back on the ideology of the past (saying our prayers and pledging allegiance to the flag), we delude ourselves into "feeling" all right about things.

John Prine's "The Great Compromise" (1972) takes a similar view of the state of affairs as he describes America as a honky-tonk waitress, a girl who was "almost a lady." The word "lady" recalls the lady in the harbor, the Statue of Liberty. The lady, as Prine describes her, blossoms in beauty but spends every penny she owns to see the "old man in the moon." He goes on to state that she betrays him at a drive-in (a metaphor for Vietnam), and as the last verse states, now she is just a "sick woman," who writes all the boys love letters. Nonetheless, he still wishes she was his girl. The chorus of the song ties together the verses as he describes himself falling asleep under Old Glory and awakening at the "dawn's early light"; but when he wakes, he realizes that he was just a "victim of the great compromise." Obviously, compromise is no value here; it is, instead, perceived as the betrayal of promises and trust. The message that emerges—and one that anticipates the songs of the eighties —is that one's faith in the institutions and beliefs of the country will lead to disappointment. The other nagging notion here is that the best of what we were is now behind us, brokered away in blind pursuit of our manifest destiny, symbolized by our ventures into space and into Vietnam. Prine and Farina, continue the tradition begun in the sixties of suggesting that these original ideals do not define the "true" America but are actually anomalies and in fact have led us to destroy the same ideals we originally purported to believe in and offer to the rest of the world.

The greatest song to capture the anomalous aspects of the old myth is Randy Newman's "Sail Away" (1972). Newman's vision, like Paul Simon's, is redolent with irony. The song has an easy gospel hymn feel to it, which belies the "sneaky" sentiment in the lyric. That gentle gospel feeling is suggestive, as it is in African-American soul music, of hope. The song presents that spirit of hope by showing how the promise of the new land is embodied in the wonderful food to be had and how they won't have to run through the jungle and scuff up their feet. The jungle image immediately alerts one to the implications of the promise; in previous songs we have had the wilderness, the desert, the thoroughfare of freedom, but this is the first time we have encountered the jungle. What is Newman doing here; where is this journey taking us? Are we traveling, like Conrad's Marlowe, into "the heart of darkness"? We soon find out, as in the chorus, when the narrator talks about coming into Charleston Bay, we realize that the voice is that of the slave trader. Greil Marcus has written: "Newman has presented an American temptation— tempting not only the Africans, who became Negroes, and went on to create the music that finally tossed up Elvis Presley, rock 'n' roll, Newman, and his audience, but tempting America to believe that this image of itself just might be true" (1982, 127).

Newman draws on a number of symbols indigenous to the myth to illustrate the promise. He notes in the first stanza that they will sing about Jesus and drink wine all day, implying the ideas of religious freedom and the leisure that are attendant upon that seminal freedom. He notes as well that there are no lions and mamba snakes, the last being a fine Edenic image. And finally, he uses images of food (watermelon and buckwheat cakes) to suggest the bounty of the land and, consequently, the plenty of the land. In the second stanza, he again enunciates that every man is free "to take care of his home and family," an image suggested in earlier songs dealing with the myth. As in prior songs, the images suggest a bountiful existence, but, unlike other songs, where the images suggest a positive transformation of the individual's life and movement toward the realization of the individual's potential, the images here become the rationale for the dehumanizing institution of slavery. The symbols are powerful, and may explain a number of ills and contradictions in society. Greil Marcus states:

> The song transcends its irony. It is, in the end, what America would like to believe about itself, and what ten years of war across the ocean

[Vietnam] and ten years of bitter black faces will never let it believe, even in secret: that everything America did was for the good. Better than good: that God's work really was our own and meant to be. That we brought something new and precious into the world, a land even the most miserable slaves would recognize as Eden. (1982, 128.)

By featuring the anomalies of the old myth, the new myth, and most especially the mytheme of the Edenic new world, has come to represent the disenfranchisement of the individual and not his efficacy. In Newman's song it is difficult, if not impossible, to gather a sense of transcendence. Individuals are not exalted and made heroic by their alienated state. This vision is almost totally ironic, and there is, in fact, a paradoxical dilemma here: As Newman's song speaks of transcendence, it actually negates the notion. The message is that perhaps we should not look too hard for Eden, and that the promise of transcendence is perhaps itself a trap.

Two songs that highlight anomalous aspects of the myth, but also suggest that there is an affirmative message in our past and in the original myth are Don McLean's "The Statue" (1977) and Neil Sedaka's "The Immigrant" (1973). Both evoke either implicitly or explicitly the symbol of the Statue of Liberty as a controlling image to suggest the mythemes of liberty, equality, and opportunity. These songs, however, imply that we have somehow lost our way. McLean suggests that there once was a time—but provides no specific time frame—when we welcomed strangers and were kind to those who came here for their "moment to be free," and we were "faithful" to the words on the base of the statue. The narrator goes on to say that now, because her eyes are "carved in steel," she cannot see and is not warm toward those who come here or even toward himself (i.e., those who already live here). The narrator concludes by saying that the dream is gone, and the torch hasn't been passed. Nonetheless we "still wait," and, he adds, if he could give her life as God gave it to him, she would be able to see what "they" have done, referring to the "gentle" dead who loved her and died for her. McLean's song, then, basically affirms the basic tenets of the myth but masks them by highlighting the failure of the promise.

Neil Sedaka similarly focuses on the immigrant's experience as being emblematic of the myth. He notes that people in the past came here to live in the "light of liberty"—an image reminiscent of the songs of the Revolutionary War—and because there was room for everyone. But now it seems that we don't want strangers here anymore because one can no longer "marry fortune to promises." In the final stanza Sedaka poignantly depicts the immigrant turning away, but remembering that once he heard a "legend," which talked about a "mystical magical land called America." Again, the greatness of the country lies in the past. Sedaka also reaffirms the traditional myth in a way by emphasizing that it was once true—as opposed to Farina and Prine, who hope to show that the whole mythology is basically fraudulent—a point which is given strength by his allusion to the country's numinous reputation as being magical and mystical.

There are others as well who tried to look through the seeming failure of the system and the myth to salvage some principle or belief. Johnny Rivers' "Come Home America" (1972) calls for us to pick up the "dream" we left behind. He reaffirms the egalitarian ideals by noting that rich and poor, black and white can come home to America. His final message is that the people should be given their voice and that we need to answer our "brother's need." It seems a recycling of the old myth.

Arlo Guthrie's "Patriot's Dream" (1976) written in our Bicentennial year, basically says we need to "rekindle" the dream of the patriots. His depiction of our current situation is that tyrants are breeding, and the just are being imprisoned. The suggestion here, as in McLean's song, is that the fire has gone out, and we need to recall the principles that inspired the patriotic forebears. These are not spelled out, but we are cautioned that time is running out, and we need "sweet destiny" to arise.

Harry Chapin to his credit does not blindly recycle old nostrums or completely trash the past. He is one of the few to offer a new slant on the myth. His "What Made America Famous" (1974), in typical Chapin fashion, spins a fine tale about two segments of a community—hippies on one side and patriotic firefighters on the other—who are brought together through tragedy. Chapin paints a portrait of a town that looks like a page ripped out of Earl Robinson's "The House That I Live In" except that things are only fine on the surface. The house that the lazy, long-haired dropouts live in is a slum containing blacks, welfare cases, and "love children," in short, society's outsiders. On the other hand, we have the volunteer firefighters, who see themselves as the types who made America famous, but who also spend their free hours at the station watching dirty movies. Meanwhile, the outsiders go out of their way to draw a swastika on the firehouse door, an act that leads the narrator to allude to "America the Beautiful." It is, however, delivered with an anger meant to suggest how much we have bastardized the ideals iterated in that hymn. The act is clearly not one to make us proud.

Throughout Chapin employs a chorus, which repeats the line, "Something's burning somewhere." This finally makes sense in the climax of the song in which a fire ravages the outsiders' slum apartment. Some of the firefighters just want it to burn, using the cynical excuse that they just cleaned the chrome on the engine, but one of the men, an overweight plumber, takes the initiative and helps rescue the narrator. The narrator's statement that he never thought he'd be happy to see that fat man's face is a preface to an epiphanic moment when he realizes that it is not his particular view or the fireman's view that made America famous, but the mutual toleration of each other's ideas. His warning about something burning may recall James Baldwin's *The Fire Next Time.* To Chapin's credit, his belief that toleration—as a preface to a renewed sense of brotherhood and cooperation—may be the destiny of the country does offer a new vision and one that is not only consistent with the ideals of the past but also looks to new horizons.

Finally, a few songs focused attention on the mytheme of the land. One might have assumed, with the interest in ecology that blossomed during the seventies, that this mytheme would have played a more important role in the songs dealing with America. Instead, the songs of the seventies, tended to focus on the ideological components of the myth, and those elements of the old myth that spoke to the need for regeneration of our collective soul (i.e., through belief in God's role, joining the succession of patriots, and the land) received little attention. There was also a feeling in the culture that the land had limits and perhaps should not be viewed as unlimited bounty—in fact, that view had proved to be its destruction. Americans were once again caught in the "Ball of Confusion" created by the paradox of the myth. By exploiting the land to achieve the goals of freedom and opportunity, we ended up destroying the very wellspring of those ideals. The age of diminishing expectations gave the lie to the tradition of plenty and abundance.

Perhaps the most eloquent spokesperson for the role of the land in the myth was Buffy Sainte-Marie. Coming out of the folk-protest tradition, she crafted songs that drew on her Indian heritage to speak to the needs of the new generation. The popularity of such books as *Bury My Heart at Wounded Knee, Black Elk Speaks,* and, to a lesser extent, Carlos Castenada's "Don Juan" series showed that Americans were looking to another part of our "heroic" past to reclaim values. The Indian offered youth another instance of outsiders (Indians driven from ancestral lands and homes) who were actually the insiders those who were closest to what really defines an American. Buffy Sainte-Marie's first "American" song, "My Country 'Tis of Thy People You're Dying" (1970), in fact, follows in the tradition of Dylan and Phil Ochs by questioning the history of the country, stating that maybe it didn't begin with Columbus and that those heroes whose exploits we extol maybe are not so heroic. In fact, she adds in a later verse, that the biggest, boldest, and best are little more than "leeches," who have perpetuated the program of genocide that she believes is part of the "country's birth."

Like other artists of this time period, she calls into question the whole myth of national destiny by making the original mytheme of the patriot's sacrifice appear to be the anomaly. Instead, this allows her to identify where the real sacrifice lies: In the "bargain" for the West, the white nation got fat while the ground from the Grand Canyon to the "craven sad hills" spills forth with losers. We see here how the land is not necessarily the landscape of alienation but a metaphor for the sacrifice of the native American; the land, then, is symbolic of the destruction of the people, hence the title of the song, "My Country 'Tis of Thy People You're Dying." Her message is that the promises of the nation—those contained in the Bill of Rights, in the blessings of civilization, in the wars we have waged (the eagles of war were nothing but "carrion crows")—have resulted in little but the genocidal elimination of those who were most intimately bound up with the promise the land had to offer. As a result, we now have a country where the past crumbles before our eyes, while the future holds nothing but threats. Again, as with other songs from the period, there seems to be no way out, no possible redemption except to restore the land to the people.

In later songs, Sainte-Marie's tone is modulated slightly, and she seems to be seeking some sort of resolution to the conflicts broached in her earlier songs. "Sweet America" (1976) leaves behind the anger for a more elegiac tone, while in "America My Home" (1976) she seems to return to the land to seek some healing. Published during the Bicentennial year, the song reaffirms that there is a goodness residing in the land, but it also reminds us that our two hundred years have jeopardized that goodness. The important link here is that the Native-American is the real steward of the land; it was the Native-American who knew the land when it was "young" and was "astounded" by her love. The personification of the land is important in clarifying the intensity of the Native-American's relationship to the land. Unfortunately, that relationship is in the past and now seems to her all that is real, because of the encroachments of civilization represented by fever, paved-over forests, and foul air. What Sainte-Marie does is wrest the symbol of home out of the Irving Berlin tradition as haven for democratic principles and raison d'être for manifest destiny, and replace it with a more "primitive" vision where people establish an I/Thou relationship with the land. Her message seems to be that if we can learn from the Native-American, we can reestablish that "love" that exists between the land and her people and preserve ourselves and have a real home.

Although not Native-Americans, the rock group Kansas provided one of the most eloquent and powerful statements about the role of the land in the myth of America in their "Song for America" (1975). They engage in a retelling of the whole myth beginning, as Katherine Lee Bates did, with the image of the "virgin" land. Where the songwriter of the eighteenth century saw the paradise emerge once a path had been cut through the wilderness, the songwriter of the 1970s sees paradise existing before civilization arrived on the shore. Like Buffy Sainte-Marie, they portray the land as though it has a personality; it is an abundant paradise, who in her innocence is ready to confer her treasure, gifts, and "milk and honey" on those seeking a utopia and the freedom that "they crave." In short, the songwriters are consciously employing the traditional symbols of the myth.

The song then shifts, describing how, because we saw no wonder, we have ravaged and plundered the land by chopping trees and plowing the earth. Eventually the mountains are "seared" by highways, leaving us with rows of houses endlessly stretching from "sea to shining sea." Recall here that Bates's vision was that God, by shedding His grace on us, would "crown thy good with brotherhood" across the country. In the 1970s, materialism has replaced the more ineffable quality of brotherhood, and good hardly seems to have been crowned. In fact, instead of having achieved a country where the goodness of the beautiful skies and amber waves of grain are wedded to goodness in brotherhood, we have a land which is "ruled" and where, as the song concludes, a "weary race" stands on its paradise and dreams of a place and is ready to rise. But, as a result of what we have done to the land, that dream is partially undermined by the nagging feeling that, "We blew it."

If there is a general theme we can draw from the songs of the seventies, it is that line of Paul Simon: "I wonder what's gone wrong." The songwriters sincerely seem to present a picture of a culture that is totally confused, a culture that has abandoned the certainty of its mythology out of necessity, but does not have an alternative direction in which to move. Readers may recall the last frames of *The Graduate* where Benjamin has "rescued" Elaine from marriage and ostensibly the shallow life that faced her; as they ride in the bus and the glow of the rebellion wears off, they take on wistful looks that remind us that now they must live with the decision. Similarly, through the sixties and into the early seventies, America's songwriters attacked the old myth and attempted to show us that it was an anomaly all along; it wasn't the thing that made America great but the thing that actually brought us down.

Ever so tentatively then, a new myth of America begins to take shape. However, if it is an America whose destiny does not lie beyond its shores in a never-ending spiral of expansion and whose materialism has blinded us to more significant things in life, what are we to believe? The country, like its people, begins to look at "me," and it asks who am I? The songs imply that we made a tentative attempt at answering that: God did not place us here with a special mission to bring freedom and democracy to all the world; what strength and character we may have resides in the land (which must be preserved and not plowed—no more clearing paths through the thicket so Paradise can show its face); freedom and opportunity remain our reason for being, but they have become elusive goals, with African/Americans slowly losing confidence in the dream and almost everyone losing confidence in the efficacy of work to ennoble and empower them.

There were those, such as Billy Swan, who could say that our incredible diversity (from rock, jazz, and soul to hamburgers and hot dogs with a little protesting and a lot of TV thrown in) was "America to Me." And there were those such as David Byrne, who in his "The Big Country" (1978), views a landscape rich with its baseball diamonds, farmlands, friends, and neighbors from an airplane but must conclude that he wouldn't live there if "you paid me." Even he, however, says that he is weary of traveling and wants to be "somewhere." It seemed that he and almost everyone else just didn't know where that place was. There were some, however, who could still see John Winthrop's "citie on the hill," and they would raise their voices in the eighties.

CHAPTER X   **"Born in the U.S.A."**

The 1980s

When Ronald Reagan took the oath of
office in January of 1981, there were
those who believed that we might
be on the verge of a "renaissance of
wonder" or, at least, that our second
American nightmare was over. With
Reagan assuming the presidency, there
was a feeling that the old values and
verities would once again have currency.
He did—actually, he said—much to encourage these beliefs. And so
it is with Reagan as symbol that we begin this final look at the
myth of America in popular song. We will look as well at the other
side of the Reagan years, the side which attempted to give the lie
to his rhetoric by latching on to the realities and, for some, the historical necessity of American decline.

As these conflicting perspectives simultaneously inspired and ex-
asperated Americans, songwriters became more vocal in their concerns about America's future. We may not have experienced a total
cultural renaissance, but a renaissance of socially concerned music
made its way onto the airwaves and stereos of Americans in the
eighties. In fact, many mainstream artists not only dealt with the
theme of America but simultaneously enjoyed popular success. Thus
this chapter is important in our examination of the myth.

Reagan symbolized Jay Gatsby's belief that you could go back, that you could recapture something of greatness or magic or whatever it was that made your life meaningful in the past. Reagan brought to the office of the presidency and, by extension, to American culture more than a promise of new leadership. He brought a battery of tried and true myths along with him. He was associated, first of all, with that most durable and "American" of heroes, the cowboy; he was remembered for other roles in films dealing with sports heroes (George Gipp, Grover Cleveland Alexander) and with war (*Hellcats of the Navy, This Is the Army,* which, by the way, featured Kate Smith reprising "God Bless America"). For many Americans his association with GE meant he was sympathetic to the goals of the capitalist system. Finally, he symbolized the outsider; he took the rather unfashionable stand that government was not the solution to our problems, but, in fact, may be *the* problem. This struck a responsive chord with a number of individuals, who had watched their personal fortunes and expectations dissipate while the government grew. And we still couldn't wrest hostages away from outlaw foreign terrorist groups. Reagan confirmed the rather inchoate sentiment that this would never have happened to John Wayne in the movies, and it shouldn't be happening to us.

These last points, the convergence of Reagan's rhetoric and our cultural expectations grounded in popular myths, are particularly important in terms of the treatment of the myth in the 1980s. What Reagan symbolized cut deep to the core of our national identity, of what we wanted to believe about ourselves. What he said cut deeper even still. He was called the Great Communicator. It was the one thing about him almost everyone could agree on: He had an ineffable quality of speaking in glaring generalities, making mistakes, saying dumb things, being ignorant of facts he should have known—and not having to pay the price. Hence, he earned the title "The Teflon President." What made things work for him was partly *how* he delivered the message and partly *what* was in the message.

Reagan was able to recycle the myth of America and reify it for almost all the generations. William F. Lewis describes the myth that emerged in his speeches:

> America is a chosen nation, grounded in its families and neighborhoods, and driven inevitably forward by its heroic working people toward a world of freedom and economic progress unless blocked by

moral or military weakness. Reagan portrays American history as a continuing struggle for progress against great obstacles imposed by economic adversity, barbaric enemies, or Big Government. It is a story with great heroes—Washington, Jefferson, Lincoln, Roosevelt—with great villains—the monarchs of pre-Revolutionary Europe, the Depression, the Communists, the Democrats—and with a great theme—the rise of freedom and economic progress. (1987, 282).

One can immediately identify in Reagan's vision of America the mythemes we have been examining throughout this book. He was able to give Americans a perfectly articulated, intelligible, and significant vision of America. It was a vision that focused on goals, so that means never got in the way of the transcendental vision. Walter Mondale tried to get us to focus on means and forge a "new reality," and he paid the price, much as Carter had for telling us that we were in the grip of a "malaise" in the 1970s. Reagan sold us the promise, he was able to deliver a message that people wanted to hear; it was a message, moreover, that drew powerfully on what had made the myth a potent force in the culture prior to the 1960s: the will to believe wedded to the desire for significance. The message, as we shall see, inspired songwriters.

With such a powerful message then, how do we account for the voices of dissent. One will not hear this message in the songs of Jackson Browne, John Cougar Mellencamp, Neil Young, Lou Reed, Living Colour, and Public Enemy. John Mellencamp, in fact, stated in his 1989 song "Country Gentleman" that the country gentleman (Reagan) isn't going to help the poor but only his rich friends; his narrator concludes by saying that the country gentleman "prayed" [sic] on our weakness and it's a good thing he's gone back to the country.

The spirit of protest was still alive in the 1980s. These people saw a different America. They saw an America that faced a surfeit of positive hero figures—in fact, saw in Reagan all that might be wrong with heroes: He really had not engaged in heroic acts; he just had acted heroically in the movies. Paul Simon had asked in 1968, "Where have you gone, Joe DiMaggio?" We found out in the 1980s: He had been replaced by high-priced talent of dubious moral integrity, à la Pete Rose and Wade Boggs.

Those who raised their voices in dissent also saw an America that seemed to have lost the ability to face the future with confidence. We seemed to be falling behind Japan and Germany as a technological leader in the business world. They saw American students who knew little of the past and who, because of weaknesses in the educational system, seemed to offer little hope for the future. They faced the realities of the Global Village, which meant that nothing—literally nothing—happened in isolation anymore. Like the Butterfly Effect in chaos science, if a minor head of government in the Third World country abdicated his/her position of power, it could have global consequences, consequences which, moreover, America could do little or nothing about. Finally, as the eighties drew to a close, Americans witnessed first the spectacle of the Wall Street "meltdown" as the bullish young turks who had dominated the middle years of the decades were either indicted or sent packing, and, second, the near collapse of our banking institutions. This last event was particularly difficult, because ever since the Great Depression Americans had blithely assumed that the banks would forever be safe and that we would never again witness failures on the magnitude of 1930–1933. Americans had good reason to feel that they were up against the ropes.

It is not surprising, then, to see in many recent polls that 40 percent or more of those in questioned said they had little confidence in the future of the United States and assumed that our best days were over.

As the decade wore on, in spite of the Reagan rhetoric, there was the growing feeling that America was in decline. The theme was trumpeted forcefully and effectively by Paul Kennedy, who wrote in his 1987 book *The Rise and Fall of the Great Powers:*

> The United States now runs the risk, so familiar to historians of the rise and fall of previous Great Powers, of what might roughly be called 'imperial overstretch': that is to say, decision-makers in Washington must face the awkward and enduring fact that the sum total of the United States' global interests and obligations is nowadays far larger than the country's power to defend them all simultaneously. (515)

This was not the first time that America's ability to be an effective world leader had been questioned, but in light of Reagan's rhetoric, it was a dire portent. America seemed faced with redefining its role in the world.

This was difficult, however, because, coincidental with the sense of decline, the culture still faced the problem that had plagued it during the 1970s: an inability to define a cultural vision and purpose. The 1985 book *Habits of the Heart* brought into clear focus the fuzziness at the center of our national vision. The authors, Robert Bellah et. al., noted, that in the very definition of our notions of individualism, there were troubling undercurrents. They note that almost everyone has a difficult time reconciling individual needs with concerns about "public good." In short, in spite of the Reagan rhetoric, the ability to articulate a meaningful vision of America remains elusive.

This inability to forge a telos is also part of the postmodern condition. Paul Johnson (1983) locates in the theory of relativity the genesis for decline and chaos in the twentieth century. We have observed over the last ten to fifteen years that the lines between popular culture and "high" culture continue to blur. In popular music, for instance, the notion that rock 'n' roll performers are "artists" gains strength as the years roll by. But then there is MTV, a programming format that almost completely eliminates linearity (you can tune in anytime and not worry that you have missed something), and whose product quite often seems less concerned about the fit between lyric and visual message than with just syncing the edits effectively to the beat. The songwriter who would deal with the myth of America, then, faces an awesome challenge.

The relational and the relativistic are important factors in the songs dealing with the myth. They reflect the reality of and, in some cases, the necessity for the relational in our contemporary world. They also show the songwriter, trying to transcend the purely relational by occasionally grounding experiences in something more transcendental and meaningful. It becomes a difficult task.

Songwriters in the eighties had to demonstrate an ability to cross over (produce songs showing movement on more than just one of the *Billboard* or *Cashbox* charts simultaneously). Consequently, a composer might write a song that would strike a responsive chord among adult listeners but might not show any movement on the Top 100 or Country charts. If, however, writers craved the "platinum" success associated with crossover, they would have to find sentiments that cut across demographic, ideological, regional, and racial boundaries—an increasingly difficult task in the eighties. This occasionally seemed to happen as in the case of Bruce Springsteen and, to a lesser extent, John Mellencamp. Just as often, however, writers seemed content to follow a more relational approach by speaking to one audience and hoping that sales would be enough to move his or her effort up that particular chart as was the case with performers such as Jackson Browne and many country artists. In addition to dealing with crossover, songwriters had to deal with the continuing fragmentation of rock and musical styles that had begun in the late sixties and early seventies. In the eighties, however, there was a minor shift. After the breakup of disco and punk, the "trend" wave abated slightly and gave way to the super-star phenomenon. Thus, instead of seeing the dominance of, let us say, art-rock or heavy metal in a given year, we experienced the explosion of individual talent. We saw the triumph of Michael Jackson, Madonna, Bruce Springsteen, U2, Prince, and so forth.

The approach to the myth reflects both this shift in the star-making machinery of the industry and the shift to a strongly relational and relativistic approach to ideology. For what we generally will be dealing with here are a series of very individual responses to the idea of America. There are some similarities. For instance, the work of most of the songwriters and performers shows the influence of the folk-protest movement and, especially with Mellencamp and Springsteen, Woody Guthrie. Many of the songwriters also see the solution to our problems in recapturing whatever was good in the past; although what is perceived as good varies from artist to artist. Another similarity they share is a deadly seriousness and sense of urgency in defining the kind of country in which they wish to live. Their songs fly in the face of ideology—although a serious ideology is still important and sought after. These songs show us at a juncture where myth and ideology are in conflict. The myth is still important to these songwriters. Their songs clearly demonstrate that we indeed cannot abide chaos and that the country and what it represents is crucial in how we define who we are as individuals.

The myth of America in the 1980s is not a single vision but instead is proving to be a pluralistic vision featuring a classic struggle between the forces of the present and the forces of the past. The new myth, articulated in the music of the 1960s and 1970s and attempting to eschew the mythemes of the past, is the most popular, but, in keeping with the traditions of the myth in popular song, it continues to evolve and undergo change. Let us begin by looking at those songs that reaffirm the classic myth and seem to say, as Gatsby did, that you *can* recapture the past.

It is not terribly surprising that most of the songs that hearken to the classic myth of America were written during the first term of Reagan's presidency. As these tunes made their way onto the nation's airwaves and record players, there was something almost shocking about them in their unabashed evocation of the old mythemes. The songwriter was summoning the vision of past glories in hopes of animating new visions of greatness. Among the earliest voices were those of country artists, primarily Charlie Daniels with his "In America" (1980). Apparently good and irritated at the beating the United States had been taking abroad, especially in the wake of the Iran embassy takeover, Daniels wrote and sang a song that went straight to the racial memory and the patriotic solar plexus. It begins ominously with a devilish fiddle solo, and Charlie declares that it looks like America's been "fixin' to fall," a nice inversion of "fixin' to fight." But he tells us that for him and some people from Tennessee, the Russians can just go "to hell" if they think we are weak just because the Statue of Liberty has stumbled a little bit. One might be reminded here of Paul Simon's Statue of Liberty clearly adrift; in Daniels' song she is anchored firmly.

The narrator in this song portrays himself in the role of the underdog: This is no member of a silent majority; in fact, he seems to be declaring, "There may only be a few of us who still believe in the myth, but we don't give a damn." There are few things we love more than the underdog, and so Charlie is pretty much assured of everyone identifying with him.

But what is the antidote to this problem that he observes? To evoke the theocratic ideal, naturally; as we put America back on a course of righteousness, then God will bless America again. The song resonates with the mythemes and attendant sentiments of the Revolutionary War times, as well as those from before World War II. He also draws upon the mytheme of the land and yokes it with another powerful theme, that of home, noting that everything between Long Island Sound and San Francisco is "our home." And he goes on to say that because the vast land is home, the little fighting we've done among ourselves should not be an invitation to anyone from the outside to dare interfere. One may be reminded here of those early songs that declared we were a world unto ourselves and would not be subject to outside threats. Daniels, rather than show the individual in isolation as earlier songwriters do, uses the idea of communal isolation to strengthen feelings of purpose: In short, we are alone only as in so far as we are all Americans. He seems to be addressing himself to our enemies when, in the chorus, he states that we sure fooled those enemies because they never thought they'd see us united again, but now we're walking and talking with pride again.

In a similar vein is Lee Greenwood's "God Bless the U.S.A." (1984), which shamelessly rips off Irving Berlin for its title and almost every other major song and songwriter for its sentiments. He too begins ominously by suggesting images of isolation and disenfranchisement. He notes, for instance, that if all the things he worked for were taken away, and he had to start over again, he'd thank his "lucky stars" that he was living in America because here our flag represents freedom, and that is something that no one can take away. Notice how Greenwood's reference to work, unlike Simon's, reaffirms the efficacy of work and its ability to earn things worth having. Like some previous songwriters, Greenwood draws together the themes of freedom and God's beneficence, and like previous songwriters he, in subsequent verses, states he "won't forget the men who died" to make him free and that he will defend "her" still today. Finally, in the last stanza he evokes the land mytheme by alluding to major cities. In a sense, he is drawing a compromise between Chuck Berry's vision and Charlie Daniels's, for as he sings about each city, he gives a sense of sweep and breadth to the country, and then he adds that in each of the cities "there's pride in every American heart."

In the final analysis, one may be more shocked by this song than perhaps moved by it, because the sentiments seem so archaic. The song, however, is also illuminating because it, along with Daniels's song, illustrates the persistence of the theocratic-enlightenment myth. It also makes the Reagan presidency and the power of his rhetoric easier to understand. Greenwood's and Daniels's songs cannot merely be dismissed as a bit of jejune revisionism on the part of some Deep South country music "crackers." Through the seventies and eighties, country music has broken out of its regional niche and won many adherents throughout the country, especially among working class adults, who find in its sentiments a connection to past traditional values that seem to be eroding or have been ground under by wrongheaded liberalism—a liberalism which they see as endemic to much contemporary rock music. The feeling is deep and more widespread than some would like to admit.

One, in fact, sees in country songs that wave the flag less enthusiastically an abiding faith in the myth. "America's Farm" (1980) by

Ronnie Rogen and performed by Levon Helm states that in spite of ominous signs such as the "Red, White and Blue" being mixed up and confused and that the train has seemingly jumped the track, we can find a solution on America's farm. In other words, with hard work and land we don't have to be headed down a "dead-end road." Similarly, David Lynn Jones's songs, such as "Living in the Promiseland" (1985) and "Tonight in America" (1983) reaffirm the hope symbolized by the Statue of Liberty that there is room enough for everyone and that the sacrifices made in wars have made it possible for us to say that it is good to be alive in America today. Both songs contain strong echoes of the Hutchinsons' songs, especially "Uncle Sam's Farm," which showed how important the land was to achieving equality and opportunity.

There were also songs written in the pop-rock and Tin Pan Alley traditions which perpetuated the traditional myth. Alan and Marilyn Bergman's and John Williams's "America . . . The Dream Goes On" (1982, 1984) is in a direct line of descent from the national anthem. It begins by expressing the now-familiar belief that if we remember how the country began, we can be our best. They use the controlling metaphor of the song sung or whistled by our fore-bears to unify the mythemes. The mythemes of the land and the patriot's sacrifice are evoked and linked in their lines about the song echoing in the dust, the farms and factories and how it asks us to remember Washington, Jefferson, Lincoln, Roosevelt, Kennedy, and Martin Luther King. One can see that the pantheon of heroes has added two figures to keep the succession current and egalitarian. The final image in the song is that, even though voices may change, the song remains the same from "sea to sea." The only element missing here is that of God' providential role and the attendant theme of manifest destiny, although the latter is strongly suggested in the sentiment that, if we recall our birth, we can then discover how to be the best we can. In other words, we still are evolving and in a state of becoming, and the song will remain a constant even into the future.

The "jazz-rock" group Chicago also penned an "America" song in 1980, which offers a critique and a solution. This is one of the first political statements from this group, since their somewhat humorous "Harry Truman" from the midseventies. Their tentative approach to solutions is typical of groups who took strong stands in the late sixties (they were McGovern supporters and became extremely disillusioned after the 1972 election) but who felt they had to modify their political expectations through the seventies. They begin by describing apocalyptic portents in the country: We do not trust one another, some mistakenly think everything is "cool" in the White House, Capitol Hill seems ready to "crumble" and come "apart at the seams." Later they add that people going insane and "preaching" about freedom is done in vain. Their conclusion is that we are tired of seeing "you stumble" (that referent is not very clear) and that the American Dream is being crushed. They also state that here may be hope for the future and the red, white, and blue if we trust one another. They conclude by saying that there is so much more that we can do. Their call for solidarity, achieved through trust, reinforces the conviction that a new collective consciousness is necessary if the country is going to fulfill its promises of freedom, opportunity, and equality.

Finally, Neil Diamond's "America" (1980, 1982) from his film remake of *The Jazz Singer* is similar to Neil Sedaka's "The Immigrant" from the seventies in that it focuses on the immigrant experience. (Is it just ironic that they both worked out of the Brill Building area in the sixties?) The images are pretty shopworn by now: People seeking the dream of freedom and finding a home where freedom's light burns bright. Diamond literally quotes "My Country! 'Tis of Thee" at the end but punctuates the lines with "today," which is to say that the dream is still alive and is as viable now as it was a hundred years ago. Both songs attempt to reify the mytheme of manifest destiny in the dream-of-freedom motif. In place of God, the songwriters suggest that it is the principles of freedom, opportunity, equality that drive us; our history is rooted in the pursuit of these principles, and our future is in the preservation of them for people to share if they choose to come to these shores.

By 1985 the positive approach to the myth seems to have played itself out. Reagan's second term seemed less filled with promise. The country, moreover, found out how deep its disillusionment ran when Bruce Springsteen's *Born in the U.S.A.* climbed inexorably up the charts. Springsteen's album proved to be the lightning rod for the voices of dissent. From 1985, the message about America that graces the album and singles charts is one in marked contrast to that presented by country musicians and pop-rock artists of the early eighties.

Basically, the songwriters present us with a myth of alienated individuals cut off from their land and its promise; nevertheless, these individuals have remained true to the promise and continue to seek an affirmation of their "Americanness." We have seen in the past that, during times of crisis, the myth was used to explain why we stood in opposition to or were being assailed by an alien force. The new myth of America also identifies "enemies." Some, like the Plugz in their song "American" (1981), see the enemy as materialism symbolized in part by TV; others, like Jimmy Barnes ("Working Class Man," 1985) and Little Steven ("Voice of America," 1983) basically point out that the common ordinary individual, who has steadfastly done his/her duty, has been compromised by Uncle Sam (recall John Prine's song) or betrayed by his "own kind."

These images of America owe a great deal to the ideas of Bob Dylan, Paul Simon, and the other members of the folk-protest tradition. Songwriters and musicians such as Bruce Springsteen, John Cougar Mellencamp, Jackson Browne, U2, Neil Young, Don Henley, and Los Lobos best typify this tradition, and they, almost without exception, approach the subject, Guthrielike, from the perspective of the common person. The outline of the basic myth that these songwriters articulate consists of the following points: The American dream is dead, and the theocratic paradise of opportunity is no longer viable; the land is no longer a New Eden with the power to regenerate the individual; work has become the central symbol for the dream, and at the same time, it symbolizes the spoiled idealism of the dream; opportunity has given way to mere survival and is now nothing more than a sad remnant of what was once a vital, animating force; finally, the image of the working person that emerges is that of the American Cain, a wanderer who is alienated from the promise of the new land, but who has nonetheless kept faith even though the country has not.

In their treatment of the myth, Springsteen and Mellencamp use symbols associated with materialism and the myth of success as points of departure. Springsteen, for instance, does not extol the dynamic energy and potentiality of the city; he does not see alabaster cities on a shining hill. Instead, he sees the city as the sad detritus of the "runaway American dream," as he declares in "Born to Run" (1976); the city and its industry are symbols, in "Born in the U.S.A." and "My Hometown," of bad faith on the part of the powers that be. Nonetheless, the Springsteen hero proclaims proudly, against those clanging and slightly dissonant open-fourth chords, that he is "Born in the U.S.A."

All of Springsteen's heroes are looking to move; mobility is potential salvation and perhaps transcendence. They have that Huck Finn and Gatsbylike restless energy, but the quest is ill-defined and the object, according to "Born to Run," is somewhere besides the city. They are representative of twentieth-century Americans who see mobility as synonymous with opportunity. They do believe, in some cases, that "out there" is something worth grabbing for; in most cases, however, the only consolation the heroes (especially of the middle period albums) have is the love of the girl, who is a partner. Love, Springsteen seems to say at times, is the only force that may save the hero from the fate of the characters we encounter in *Nebraska* (an album which, in terms of its bleak and desolate images of Americans, may be the logical conclusion for the ideas suggested by Paul Simon and Randy Newman). For Springsteen, the common man is the locus of the American experience. His common man fought in Nam and was kicked around, but he still proclaims proudly that he is "Born in the U.S.A."; he continues to drive down the sad streets that once offered promise and a future, but which now offer none, and tells his children that this is their hometown, as though the mere admission of that fact will offer them a brief transcendent moment of hope and pride.

John Cougar Mellencamp became one of the most vocal critics of the myth of America in the 1980s, and as the decade progressed, his voice grew more strident. In general, he paints a bleak portrait of the country where individuals are ground down to a point where to hope is too painful. Like Springsteen he sees what hope there might be in the people. It is for this reason that *Rolling Stone* cartoonist C. F. Woodruff included him in "Mr. Guthrie's Homeroom" along with Springsteen and Bob Dylan (*Rolling Stone* 25 January 1990). The strength of the people can be seen in one of his first hits, "Pink Houses" (1983), where he uses the symbol of the pink house as locus of the myth of America. In the song, he juxtaposes images of unrealized potential in the verses with the somewhat affirmative sentiment, expressed in the chorus: "Ain't that America for you and me." For instance, in the second verse he sings of a young man who listens to rock 'n' roll music and believes that will be his "destination"; in this image is an echo of past regenerative images and ideas, which suggested that there was hope for the future for the individual. He then adds that when he was younger, they told him he'd be president, but he adds that the dream vanished as quickly as it came. The use of understatement is most effective in communicating the stolid faith of the common person. In the last verse, Mellencamp sings about those who work in high rises and vacation in the Gulf of Mexico, but, he reminds us, that it is the "simple man" who pays for "the thrills, the bills, the pills that kill."

Much like Springsteen, Mellencamp employs a common image, centered mainly around classic notions of the American Dream, to help us understand his version of the myth. The pink house is a haven and possession that symbolizes what it means to be an American. But it is not an image that leads to transcendence and hope, only one which, by its tackiness, suggests a stolid determination and resignation to the "way it is." Like Paul Simon's working day and Bruce Springsteen's hometown, the pink house is at once an ineluctable force and vestigial remnant of the dream, the only remaining symbol of the quest.

The themes that were suggested in "Pink Houses" were given fuller play in his albums *Scarecrow* (1985) and *The Lonesome Jubilee* (1987). The songs on *The Lonesome Jubilee* are very Guthriesque in their depiction of the disenfranchised. Throughout there runs the theme that the promise is dead; in "Empty Hands," for instance, he depicts people standing in lines with no plans for the future. The tragedy of the situation is highlighted in the next refrain, where he states that at one time he had "great expectations" and thought he knew the plan. But this has come to nought. If one will recall Woody's "This Land Is Your Land," one can see an important difference: Where Woody held out hope for the future via the image of the land, Mellencamp sees the poor as inheritors of nothing but empty hands. Similarly, in "Down and Out in Paradise" (the title of which almost says it all), he evokes the image of the land of milk and honey as well as that of Paradise to show how the reality has not kept pace with the promise for opportunity.

Finally, in his "Hotdogs and Hamburgers" from the same album, he attacks the mytheme of the patriots and manifest destiny. The song tells the story of a young man who picks up a hitchhiking Indian girl and makes a pass at her. She tells him that he is no better than the Pilgrims from "olden days," who tried to get something for nothing. He is embarrassed and somewhat repentant, which opens the door for her to tell him the story of the Indian nation, which, in turn, explains why she cannot trust him. When he drops her off, there is an old Indian man waiting for her; once the old man gets a look at the narrator he "sees right through" him, and the narrator feels further shame about the way the old west was actually won. When he finally arrives in Los Angeles, he declares with great irony that the City of Angels is about the best we can do, and he asks the Lord for forgiveness, echoing Christ's words on the cross, for we know not what we do.

The mytheme of the patriot's sacrifice has always been the source of the regenerative aspect of the myth: Through successive eras, by recalling and emulating their acts and perpetuating their vision, the best in us would be reified. But contemporary songwriters view this historical pageant differently. They show that the sacrifice was really that of the Native Americans, who gave up lands and a life-style of grace, beauty, and rootedness to the land. By destroying them to build our alabaster cities, we have gutted the heart of what the real America is all about.

Like Steinbeck's and Guthrie's characters, Mellencamp's narrators are individuals abandoned by the collective forces of government, business, and the very institutions (i.e., marriage, parents) which should be nurturing our dreams of freedom and opportunity. And like Woody's narrators and characters, they see that the only possible hope, the only possible way to transcend the grinding oppression of their daily lives, lies in a faith in the collective power of the people. In his "We Are the People"—which echoes almost verbatim Ma Joad's line from the film version of *The Grapes of Wrath*—he affirms the transcendent nature of the experience of the common person when he states that the people "live forever," and that if anyone should try to divide and conquer them, they will rise up in opposition. He concludes by reiterating the great New Testament message of social justice, as he quotes Christ's words about the meek inheriting the earth. One can see here the same impulses that animated Guthrie and the other members of the folk-protest movement, all the way down to looking to the work and words of Christ. For both Springsteen and Mellencamp the only salvation, the only transcendence possible, is through a system or collective effort that reaffirms the integrity of the individual. They have been able to strike a responsive chord in listeners, as is seen in the refrains to their biggest hits, by asserting a pride in their Americanness, and that the simple Americans they depict in their songs can take a measure of pride in the fact that they have been true to the promise. Thus, in a sense, they have risen above the meanest aspects of the system and have found significance in their lonely individualism and their abiding faith in the promise.

Jackson Browne's version of the myth of America in "For America" (1986) is a bit different from Springsteen's or Mellencamp's view of America. It is closer to Simon's vision in that he senses that underlying our current cultural-political malaise is moral failure. In "American Tune" Simon stated that he could not help but wonder what has gone wrong; Browne, similarly, uses words like "conscience" and "truth" throughout his song. His basic thesis is that the United States needs to wake up to itself; the problem is what "itself" is. The opening stanza vaguely recalls Randall Jarrell's "Death of a Ball Turret Gunner" as the narrator describes himself as not really understanding that he was part of some sort of larger plan, and so he continued to believe in the country and went off "looking for the promise"; secure in his dreams and his own mind, he looked ahead and could speak of the future with confidence. When he wakes, however, it is not "to black flak and the nightmare fighters" but to the reality that the freedom he sought wasn't nearly as "sweet" after the "truth" was finally known. He suggests that we have been lied to and that the country is asleep (or perhaps has been hypnotized by the lies) and needs to have its conscience awakened. But to what must our collective conscience be awakened?

The answer seems to lie for him in "The Star-Spangled Banner"; he utilizes fragments from the national anthem in each chorus of the song. There is an element of ambiguity here, however, as he seems to suggests that the real meaning of America is contained in the anthem. For instance, in the first chorus he states that "By the dawn's early light" and by everything he knows to be right, we are going to reap what we sow. One might read in the allusion to "The Star-Spangled Banner" a suggestion that the roots of our current crises might well lie in the anthem. It is the sentiments in the anthem that illuminate the dream and animate our best impulses as a country. In the second and third choruses, he sandwiches the line about the "rockets' red glare" between a line about seeing the country's "shining dream" in his mind and a line about the blank stare of the current generation. In short, the rockets seem to illuminate both the promise of America and our current apathy; his final line is a warning that we had better wake "her" up, which suggests that we need to recapture something from the past, something that once animated our dreams.

The irony in this song, however, is that by evoking the sentiments of "The Star-Spangled Banner," he is actually alluding to the song that animated the very myth he deplores and that he suggests is anomalous with what America really means. In one stanza he castigates those who haul out the old cliché of "My country wrong or right" and adds that he doesn't think that that sentiment has anything to do with finding out the truth about things. In short, he seems to share Springsteen's sentiments that people have bought the old myths, and that has blinded them to wrongs perpetrated in its name. He, nonetheless, equates the national anthem with truth—maybe the true meaning of America, that is, the patriot's dream—and this leads him, like Springsteen and Mellencamp, to reaffirm his faith in the country.

In Browne's song there's something fuzzy at the core, something inherently contradictory. He worries about the next war but seems to suggest that the country's vision of itself is illuminated by an anthem that glorifies war and the old myths. The irony here is that Browne seems to see us finding a higher purpose (that sense of transcendence) in the ideals of the forefathers (so he keeps alive the archetype of the Pilgrim/patriot mytheme) as represented in "The Star-Spangled Banner" while forgetting that those self-same ideals were partially responsible for leading us into Vietnam and, more recently, Central America—the issue he rails at most vociferously in the whole album. On the other hand, in his *World in Motion* (1989) album, he approaches the whole myth from a different vantage point. He establishes the necessity for taking a high moral stance by stating in the very opening of the title song that the sun is setting on the United States, and we are in decline. Therefore, renewal is necessary—but only if we are not deluded by the images of abundance perpetuated on TV screens and billboards, and will take an active role in eliminating hunger, greed, and hatred. He states that he will volunteer himself, so we can achieve that world he knows the world can be. One may be reminded of the searing self-righteousness of Dylan's early music as one listens to these lines. Browne, like Dylan in "A Hard Rain's A-Gonna Fall," has assumed the prophetic,

Cassandralike stance of one who will sing about what he sees wrong, so all people can see it.

In his "How Long" from the same album, he asks us to focus on the home front to see the dangers lurking internally. To focus this theme he begins by asking us to imagine looking at the earth from a satellite. He states that we would see a beautiful sight with its greens and blues and whites, so beautiful that we might think it a veritable "paradise." However, as we focus on the streets below, we see hungry people who should be fed with the money that is now going for defense. The ultimate symbol of the perversion of the promise of Paradise is found in "The Word Justice." Here, in a not too thinly veiled allusion to Oliver North, he rails against a man who would defend democracy behind closed doors. The fear expressed in this song is that the freedoms and rights guaranteed by the idea of democracy will become the province of political dealers working out of the sight of the common people. To demonstrate further the level of internal corruption, he notes that the drugs and wars that are killing our children are not really being fought by gangs like the Crips and the Bloods, but by the CIA which protects the sources. This last leads him to declare that the battlefield is inexorably coming home, and democracy faces falling through. He waits, however, with some sort of faith for a time when the world "will be real" for everyone, and the only way for this to happen is if there is justice for everyone.

Jackson Browne also believes that individuals make a difference. People must become aware of the problems and do whatever they can to achieve the dream of freedom, opportunity, and equality— all of which are lumped loosely under his call for justice. He sees the government as having failed and as continuing to pervert the ideals of the country. He does not offer a strong message of hope or transcendence; his hope that the world will become real is mercurial at best, and in the final analysis, even if individuals become involved, what they will finally produce is vague. In Jackson Browne's treatment of the myth there is a great deal of portent and little promise.

The Oliver North affair also prompted a musical response from 10,000 Maniacs. Their album *Blind Man's Zoo* (1989) demonstrated a growing political edge on the part of this group. In their "Please Forgive Us" they imply that news about our going to war gets buried in the last pages of the newspaper. They continue this critique of covert warmongering when they talk about people wrapping themselves in the Stars and Stripes and calling themselves heroes. In actuality, they declare, all this does is validate murder in the name of freedom. The message here is similar to that of the 1960s. There is a skepticism about America's role in the world. We are not seen as liberators, and we need to keep asking the people of other countries to forgive us for we know not what we do. The not-too-subtle allusion to Christ's words on the Cross continues the tradition of trying to locate in Christian mythology some sort of moral center for our behavior. Other songs on the album such as "Big Parade" and "Dust Bowl" draw upon images from popular culture to show us failing in our mission. "Big Parade" inverts the heroic images of war by talking of a procession past the Vietnam War Memorial. It casts doubt on the notions of God's role, manifest destiny, and the patriot's sacrifice, by suggesting that the tales told in school about war—even the Civil War—being "honest" wars may not be so. The message is similar to Tom Paxton's classic "What Did You Learn in School Today" from the 1960s. In short, the heroic dimension is gone from our history; instead, we seem to be a country, as "Hateful Hate" implies, which in pursuing God's will has engaged in little more than genocide; in this case the allusion is to Africa and to our treatment of African-Americans. These ideas are all presaged in the song "Dust Bowl," which portends that, rather than achieve a sense of renewal, we may again be facing a disaster on the scale of that which afflicted us in the 1930s. The Dust Bowl for them is more than just the ravaged land, but is a symbol for our ravaged culture and politics.

Don Henley and Lou Reed also produced albums within the last two years of the decade, which had portentous overtones. Like Browne's and Mellencamp's albums, individual songs deal with different aspects of the myth. Thus, we will see them dealing with the manifest destiny mytheme and perhaps the patriot mytheme in one song, while in another they will deal with the land and the attendant mythemes of freedom and opportunity. And like Browne and Mellencamp, they lock in on key cultural icons and symbols to assess the state of the myth. Henley, for instance, in his "Gimme What You Got" sees our materialistic drift as being a major problem; he shows the pathetic level of excess that we have reached in his description of a baby whose first word is "more" and who is able to discard her plate because she is in the "home of the brave and land of the free." The materialism carries over into his "If Dirt Were Dollars" but with wider-ranging ramifications. He begins with a cautionary tale—the kind that we are getting more used to hearing—wherein he states that the brave new world has gone bad, and we may think that we are the finest things that God has put on earth, but in reality we are just whistling past the graveyard. He then proceeds to indict the mythemes of manifest destiny and God's role as he rails at the "old men" spouting the same old fears while they quote scripture and wrap themselves in Old Glory (note the similarity to the image used by 10,000 Maniacs). He does a nice inversion of Thoreau by describing them as hearing "phantom" drums and pipes, an allusion to leaders following old dreams of glory and leading us to war. He then immediately adds, however, that these same leaders will not take the blame, the "buck stops nowhere," as he says, and evil remains. Like Jackson Browne's songs, Henley is quick to point out that we lack a core of values that sustains a sense of right and good, but in this song he cannot find an alternate to the current system.

His fine title song from the album, "The End of the Innocence," is equally problematic. This song focuses on the symbol of the land as a controlling metaphor and yokes that with the theme of seduction. The opening stanza describes a pastoral utopian vision of long days, deep skies, where there were no cares, and he had the security of Mom and Dad; he adds very quickly, however, that happily ever after ultimately fails, and we realize that we have been "poisoned" by these fairy tales, leaving the lawyers to work out details since "Daddy had to fly." The chorus describes a place untouched by human hands, where tall grasses wave gracefully in the wind, and where he and his girl can go, and she can let her hair down; but, he reminds her, she will have to put up her best defense because this will be the end of the innocence.

The second verse is the one that bears most directly on the myth of America. He begins by quoting directly the lines from "America the Beautiful," "O beautiful, for spacious skies," and then adds that the skies have become threatening. He states that "they" are making swords out of plowshares for the "tired old man" that we made our "king." Finally, he states that we have been poisoned by the fairy tales of "armchair warriors" and now all we have is lawyers cleaning up details left since Daddy lied.

As with Jackson Browne's songs, I find a fuzziness at the core here. Is Henley saying that we cannot possibly hope to recapture the innocence of the past? Is he saying that we have been seduced by the land and the promise of it, and in the seduction we destroyed it? Or is he saying that there still is a place free of war and greed where two people can go, commune with nature, engage in lovemaking (i.e., lose their innocence), and be absolved of the sins of civilization? All of these questions are further complicated by the final image in the song where it appears the narrator is leaving; is he a wanderer engaged in a perpetual pursuit to reconcile innocence and experience? Can they be reconciled?

Lou Reed in his album *New York* (1989) sees nothing in the past. The image that perhaps epitomizes his approach to the past is his appellation for the Statue of Liberty as the Statue of Bigotry. Reed uses New York as a metaphor for the entire American experience, with each song dealing with some aspect of the corruption of the country. He basically concludes that our vision has been perverted primarily by materialism; in "Strawman," for instance, he asks a series of rhetorical questions, such as do we need another million dollar movie, another racist preacher, or another blank skyscraper. He concludes as well that there is no opportunity or equal rights; on "Dirty Boulevard" the Statue of Bigotry says, in echo of the actual words on the base, "give me your tired and your poor," but she adds that she'll piss on them. In a later stanza, he states that the huddled masses are all clubbed and then dumped on the dirty boulevard where no one dreams of being a doctor or a lawyer. It is also considerably more savage in its indictment of the gulf that exists between the promise embodied in the symbolism of the Statue and the reality than Neil Sedaka's, Don McLean's, and Paul Simon's treatment of the same theme. It does, in this regard, reflect a disillusionment and cynicism about the myth of America.

Reed, as opposed to some of the other songwriters, does talk about solutions, but the answers may be less than satisfying to some listeners. In "Strawman" he thinks that it probably will take a "minor miracle to turn things around," and then he offers two images of how this might manifest itself: one a flaming sword, the other a golden ark floating up the Hudson. The flaming sword suggests an image of war or perhaps of a crusade, and the flaming sword at the Gates of Eden. The ark implies a covenant or a ship that might preserve survivors. In both cases there is an ironic twist on the original vision and divine mandate articulated by the founders, because Reed does not believe that the tree of life is available to us and that the ark, taking a somewhat less heroic voyage up the Hudson than the *Mayflower*'s voyage across the ocean, will only deposit those seeking the blessings of democracy at the foot of the Statue of Bigotry, and the covenant will be one formed out of despair.

Reed, in short, sees no solution in the past. This is made most evident in his songs "There Is No Time" and "Busload of Faith," where he warns us not to depend on God ("Busload of Faith") and on the old clichés ("my country right or wrong") and symbols (the flag); he says that we must not let the past become our destiny, and that only a busload of faith will help us get by. As we have noted with previous songs, the same problems and questions arise: What do we place our faith in if not God and country? He says not to bother engaging in inner searches and says nothing about trusting one another. Finally, "Good Evening, Mr. Waldheim" is as good reminder as we will get not to trust our leaders. In his own way, he reaffirms the new myth that has also been articulated by Springsteen and Mellencamp, and that is that in a world where faith seems to be dying one still must strive to believe. The tragedy is that all that faith may yield is the ability to get by; Reed like other songwriters of the 1970s and 1980s sees in mere survival something of a minor triumph. To believe, even if it means that you believe that you cannot depend on anyone or anything to get by, is finally all we can ask. Welcome to the 1990s.

Finally, we come to Neil Young's "Rockin' in the Free World" (1989) from his excellent *Freedom* album. His song, like those of Browne, Mellencamp, Henley, Reed, and Springsteen, goes after those in power and points up their failure to make the system work for everybody. His song opens with the evocation of the flag as he states the "Red white and blue" are out on the street just shuffling along as though they were asleep. The flag functions almost as a metonymy for the homeless. He asks us to see in the plight of the homeless the reflection of ourselves, they are only a symptom of the internal rot afflicting the nation. We have a culture where there is no opportunity, where a woman will dump her kid to "get a hit," and where, as the third stanza suggests, we have rhetoric instead of real solutions. The triumph of rhetoric over significant action is symbolized in his attack on Bush's thousand points of light, which for him are not beacons of hope but symbolic of the homeless, and his attack on the kinder, gentler "machine gun hand." He illustrates an anomaly of the abundance of land by noting that our landscape is now dominated by department stores and toilet paper and styrofoam boxes, which do nothing but destroy the ozone. We are, in short, our own worst enemy. Finally, he attacks the myth of opportunity when he states that the elected officials (men of the people) say we have reason to hope, because we have fuel and roads to drive— ironic blessings, since both are yoked in the destruction of the environment. The point is that the old campaign clichés are dead; the people just have to keep on going and grab some sense of integrity during hard times.

One of the positive benefits of the 1980s phenomenon of crossover has been the wonderful infusion of minority music into the musical mainstream. Throughout the 1970s, with the exception of Stevie Wonder and a few disco artists, many wondered if rock would ever again see the easy mixture of white and black styles of music coexisting on the charts that they had seen in the 1960s. Thanks in great measure to Michael Jackson's *Thriller* (1982) album and Prince's extraordinary success with *Purple Rain* (1984)—the movie and the album—early in the decade, the audience for black and other minority musical styles has grown. This, of course, has been aided as well by steady growth in minority populations throughout the decade. The music of these minority groups has followed the pattern of that of white musicians by concentrating more and more of its energies on social issues. African-American musicians began including protest or social awareness in their music throughout the seventies, but in the eighties, with the arrival of rap, it has grown in intensity. This spirit of protest has also inspired others, and it is with them that we begin before turning to developments in African-American music.

Chris Williamson sings often of the condition of the Native-American. Continuing the tradition of Buffy Sainte-Marie, she focuses her songs on the Indian heritage to try to establish the meaning of America for her audience. For example, in her song "Grandmother's Land" (1984), she uses the tale of Chief Joseph's flight toward Canada in 1877. This story allows her to make some ironic observations about the notions of freedom for Native-Americans. The story itself deals with Chief Joseph's tribe being driven off their land and being forced to seek freedom in Canada.

In the song the narrator sings of wanting to be restored to their "Glory Land." Earlier in the song she observes that anyone who comes to America is a foreigner—thus, the poignancy and irony of the true Americans being driven to a foreign soil to reclaim their freedom.

From the Mexican-American community came the sounds of Los Lobos, perhaps the most popular of the groups bringing together the sounds of rock with Spanish and Mexican influences. In their album, *By the Light of the Moon* (1986), they made some of their most trenchant statements concerning the state of Mexican-Americans in America. Like other minority artists—and white artists for that matter—they see a terrible disparity between the promise and the reality. In yet another song alluding to "The Star-Spangled Banner," their song, "One Time One Night," has the narrator recalling a "quiet voice" who sang an old song about "the home of the brave" and the "land of the free." This reverielike chorus, however, is juxtaposed with verses that catalog scenes from the lives of the people. There are senseless deaths, a housewife's wasted life, and, in general, scores of people who have a lot of faith but die before their time. Similarly, in "Is This All There Is" they speak of the search for the promised land made by people who have "tired souls" and empty hands. They climb mountains, sail the seas, come here to work for fifteen years on a sewing machine, only to end up with a baby crying for more food and asking, "Is this all there is?" In general, their protest about the "mess" that America is in centers around issues that have been part of the minority approach to the myth, that is, economic opportunity and freedom. If there is a solution, it lies within the individuals trying to find a way out of the "mess," which, may lie in recapturing the real meaning of that long-ago song about the "land of the free and the home of the brave."

One other song from Latin-American culture bears notice here, and that is Ruben Blades's "Buscando America." The title of the song means "Searching for America." Blades, then, continues the Dylan-Simon tradition. His song implies that there is an America (i.e., some country that will fulfill the promises implicit in the idea of America) that he is looking for, but he fears that he will not find it. What has happened to create this sense of doubt? He states that there are people afraid of the truth who "have made her disappear" and that justice seems not to exist there. In the final stanza he declares that America has been kidnapped and gagged, and it is now up to us to free her. He continues to call out for America, because it is there that his future lies. One can see a similar feeling as in the songs of Springsteen, Mellencamp, and Chris Williamson. The people are steadfast in their faith in spite of the failure of the system. Like Mellencamp, he implies that the return of America or her release from bondage will only be made possible by the efforts of ordinary people.

The minority group that has most consistently examined the myth is the African-American. Black treatment of the myth in the 1980s oddly enough parallels the white treatment. Some largely support the old myth of opportunity and promise, and some rage at the system for failing to provide opportunity and promise. Of this first group we have the contributions of two of the most famous and popular black musicians: James Brown and Prince. Both, somewhat surprisingly, reaffirm the mytheme of America as the land of opportunity. One can understand this from James Brown, who is the embodiment of the myth of success, but his "royal badness's" (Prince) perspective is somewhat incongruous.

Brown's contribution to "Living in America" (1985) is primarily that of singer and interpreter as the song was written by Dan Hartman and Charlie Midnight. The song is reminiscent of Chuck Berry's "Living in the U.S.A." as it extols the urban experience as being an archetypally American experience; in the bridge, for instance, he sings that even though you're not looking for the promised land, you might find it in any one of a number of cities. One notices, as well, that for the writers the dream is still alive; in the song they, like the songwriters of the nineteenth century—and even Guthrie to a certain extent—equate a journey over America with a journey to self-discovery: They suggest the openness of the land with references to superhighways (metonymy for opportunity) and add that any destination is within reach, and one may find out who one is on the way. Finally, they recall the mytheme of brotherhood as they describe us living "eye to eye" and "hand to hand." In this section they also invert Simon's and Springsteen's resigned attitude toward work as merely part of survival in the country these days. In the last stanza, when they refer to everybody working overtime, it seems to suggest vitality as they preface the line with references to all night diners and all night radio and railroad tracks. It seems to suggest that the country never sleeps and is most alive when everyone is working.

Prince's "America" (1985) attempts in each of its stanzas to have it both ways: He seems to want simultaneously to criticize and to affirm the traditional myth. For instance, early in the song he pictures "aristocrats" climbing mountains to make money but, he adds, they are losing time. Next he refers to communism, implying that for some it is just a word; however, if the government should fall, he warns, it will be the "only word" that we hear. By introducing the specter of communism, he is able to stress an "appreciate what you've got" mentality in the lyric. This is especially true in stanzas where he addresses the attitude of the oppressed or deprived; in one verse he notes that "little sister" lives in a hovel, and even though she's not "in the black" she is happy that she "ain't in the red." And for those who would doubt that this is a great country and do not respect it, he tells the tale of Jimmy, who never went to school and thought saying the pledge of allegiance wasn't cool. He adds that nothing made him proud, but he's living on a "Mushroom cloud." The song's ultimate message is "keep the children free." For Prince, the American experience is freedom, evidenced in his verbatim quotation of "America the Beautiful" in the chorus. His is a song which seems to want to protest social conditions, but ultimately states that, even though we have problems, they are small compared to what we would have under Russian domination.

That two African-American artists would be associated with the Reagan hardline (Brown through *Rocky IV* and Prince through his song) may strike some as peculiar, to say the least. The message about America in these songs by these most popular black musicians has seemingly changed little from the time of Chuck Berry, which may strike some people as irritating. One might assume that because African-Americans have only marginally been part of the dream and that the myth of opportunity oftentimes rang false for them, they would have taken a harsher, more critical view of it.

Other African-American artists have taken a different approach to the myth. One I would describe as the healing approach. It owes much of its spirit to the memory and philosophy of Dr. Martin Luther King, Jr. Bobby Womack's "American Dream" (1984) uses King's "I Have A Dream" speech as subtext (as well as the actual recording of the speech). Womack's song somewhat keeps the dream at bay by reminding listeners that this vision of America will be difficult to achieve. He states that for him it is a "fantasy" that this country of rainbows, hills, and blue skies will light up the hope that someday kids can experience freedom in the "home of the brave." Once again, the national anthem is the touchstone for what America is all about, but it is interesting that he has referred to some of the traditional aspects of the land mytheme to highlight the hope and promise of the myth.

Janet Jackson's recent phenomenally popular *Rhythm Nation 1814* (1989) also attempts to spread a message of hope. Songs, such as the title tune and "State of the World," engage in what has become a standard practice in popular songs of diagnosing cultural ills and evils, but in both songs, she also prescribes antidotes. Judging from the popularity of the albums, besides providing killer grooves that one can dance to, the message seems to have found an appreciative audience. She declares in "Rhythm Nation" that things may be getting worse but that by working together we can improve the way we live. She believes that these hard times may be "a test," and that if we do not struggle against the odds, we will not experience progress. Similarly, her "State of the World" paints a picture of the culture where it seems no one has time for goals or dreams; she illustrates this with a description of the fifteen-year-old runaway mother, the spread of drugs and crime, kids not being able to play outside, and, in general, a pervasive feeling of worthlessness that is infecting many people. Her solution is not to escape through drugs but to become educated; it is only through knowledge that we can battle the evils of prejudice, ignorance, bigotry, and illiteracy. Finally, she has a message for adults in her "Livin' in a World (They Didn't Make)" by James Harris III and Terry Lewis. She warns adults that they cannot teach kids rules that they don't abide by themselves; this sort of hypocrisy will only perpetuate a world filled with hate. Jackson's image of America is one of hope. It may remind some of Sly Stone prior to *There's a Riot Going On* and other African-American artists of the 1970s in its tacit assumption that the world imagined by Dr. King is still possible, that the American Dream is a dream for all people.

Vernon Reid of Living Colour takes a somewhat different view than Jackson. His "Which Way to America" (1988) proposes that there are two Americas: There is "your" America, an America we see on TV and which is doing quite well; and there is his America, the America he sees when he looks out the window and reads the newspaper headlines. That America is not doing well, in fact, it is "catching hell" and "doing time." Then he asks which way he must go to get to "your" America. Should he follow the mythic advice that animated so many previous generations of Americans and go west? He says, however, that he would rather not "crossover," but he also does not want to "go under." Finally, he asks where he can find all those things we associate with contented middle class life, such as picket fences, lemonade, VCRs, stereos, and TV. At the end of the song he still wants to know how to get to "your" America. In the printed lyric the last America is turned upside down (and consequently is backward), which is the typographical correlative for the experience of the African-American—that is, their America is the antithesis of "your" America.

The notion of two Americas has become increasingly popular as the eighties has worn on. Younger African-Americans, convinced that little progress has been made in the thirty years since the Civil Rights movement took center stage in American culture, are finding that whatever hope may exist for them is not contained in the dreams of heroes such as Martin Luther King but, instead, in the dreams of Malcolm X and, more recently, Louis Farrakhan. Perhaps it is impossible to "cross over" and retain one's identity and integrity as an African-American. Perhaps the only solution is a separate station. This is the message that is being broadcast with greater frequency in rap (or hip-hop) music in the late eighties. Some groups, such as Public Enemy, are overtly political and tentatively working out a vision of America for their audiences; others engage in casual ills-cataloging but largely support the quest for part of the existing dream.

The myth that is perpetuated in rap music is that America is a country whose destiny is to perpetuate a legacy of inequality that has been part of our history since the founding of the country. The ghetto symbolizes the country's destiny in its ability to grind people into oppression and abject despair by reminding them of their inability to share in freedom, opportunity, and equality. De La Soul in their "Ghetto Thang" (1989), for instance, point out that the option of freedom or death is just a joke to those experiencing the "ghetto thang." They add that there are no dreams in the ghetto. The only response to this situation is, for some rap groups, to fight the powers even if it means becoming an outlaw.

One of the earliest rap hits to question the myth was "The Message" (1982) by Grandmaster Flash and the Furious Five. The narrator of the song is clearly on the edge as he wonders how he has not gone under living in this "jungle." He catalogs a number of social ills, most of which center around him not having any choices or opportunity (symbolized by having his car repossessed, which, in turn, limits his ability to get away). He states that he skips school and gets a job as a street sweeper. This, however, creates a greater conflict because he knows that what it is all about in the "land of milk and honey" is money, and he is going to be excluded from that portion of the dream by merit of his menial job. He lives in a deterministic world where he feels like an outlaw. Earlier in the song he has warned us not to push; this last sentiment explains why: He is the outsider with nothing to lose. Were we to take this character and allow him to evolve over time, he would become the narrator of N.W.A.'s "Straight Outta Compton" and "F———the Police," who boldly brandishes a firearm and warns people to just stay the hell out of the way, because he will off someone with little or no compunction. It may be a pose, but the rhetoric is compelling.

The inheritors of Grandmaster Flash's message are Public Enemy. Their very name bespeaks the persona they have adopted for their audience. Their link to the "Godfather of Soul" is almost purely stylistic, for their politics are revolutionary and exclusionary. But, in this way, they are consistent with mythogenesis in American culture. Our traditional myth accrued power as we were able to use it to set ourselves apart, and so it is with Public Enemy, as they articulate a vision of the world that is intelligible and significant for African-Americans. In their song, "Fight the Power" (1989), they do not dream, they do not hope, *they demand*—telling the powers-that-be that they have to give African-Americans what they "want" and "need." They show how the myth has failed by pointing out that freedom of speech for them is just "freedom of death," because if they speak their minds, they will be perceived as a threat and eventually eliminated. They see nothing in our heritage to give them hope for the future. The succession of patriots are, for them, just 400 years of "rednecks." Their destiny lies in uniting to fight the power structure. Only by restoring power to the people will rights be ensured and will they enjoy real freedom. A perverse sort of transcendence is communicated in the level of hatred that is contained in the songs. They are at that juncture Langston Hughes saw where the "dream deferred" does not just wither but explodes.

Throughout the eighties songwriters continued to perpetuate that belief that the country has been cast adrift from its moorings. The dilemma is that the home harbor of the theocratic ideal is riddled with problems—it is too much the myth (in the negative sense of the term), we know too much now; we know that God has not willed our direction in the world, the land is not a source of regeneration and transcendence, we question the patriot's sacrifice, and we remain awash in the solipsistic aftershocks of the "me decade." In short, for the songwriter, the country has failed; it is not an individual failure but more like a collective failure of will and faith, and the only recourse is for the individual either to wander, Ulysseslike, in search of a newer and better world, or to hold on doggedly to the last material remnants of the myth of success: work and home. In each case, however, a basic part of the American dream remains viable, and that is faith. It is on this point that the songs of the 1980s differ from the previous decades.

Where little hope or sense of transcendence was offered—except in only rare cases—at all in the 1970s, the spirit of transcendence, so crucial to our myths, remains an animating force in the myth in the 1980s. We have traveled from faith in a God who, in Augustinian terms, has willed the direction of history, to a simpler ideal: It is important, in and of itself, to be an American and to believe in the country's promise. The constant allusions to "The Star-Spangled Banner" and other icons of the past confirm the belief that somewhere in the foundations of the Republic, there is an ideal for all to live by and be renewed through. That ideal always seems to elude our grasp, and so we reaffirm our faith in the integrity and the efficacy of the individual. To have faith in the individual, to believe in the basic goodness and spirit of the common person (either as individuals or as a collective body), will lift one above the mundane and above the forces that would sap us of our individualism and carry us to a meaningful fulfillment of our destiny which becomes murkier as the decades progress.

However, the songwriters seem to suggest that a risk attends holding on to this faith; one may have to settle for less, one may be left with only survival or faith itself. In our contemporary popular songs, the feeling is that one nowadays may be entitled to little besides survival, and to do that is in itself an achievement. Survival, however, may not necessarily be a trial that will purify and regenerate individuals, but will instead find them, like Springsteen's American, "ten years burning down the road/Nowhere to run ain't got nowhere to go."

CONCLUSION "A Deathless Song"

*But America's always
been the best and worst
rolled into one, and it's
going to be very
interesting to see how it
goes in the next couple
of years.*
—The Edge (U2), 1988

*I think that voice held
him most, with its
fluctuating, feverish
warmth, because it
couldn't be over-
dreamed—that voice
was a deathless song.*
—F. Scott Fitzgerald,
The Great Gatsby

There are those in our culture who believe that the American Revolution is not yet completed, that the promises contained in the land itself and the charters we drafted to establish the republic have not been realized. In a sense, this survey of popular songs dealing with the myth of America has offered graphic evidence that the revolution is not complete.

As we stand on the brink of a new decade and a new century, we seem to be looking back in search of some sort of meaningful core to our national identity. But where are the songs that might play a role in moving us in that direction? Have they been written by Springsteen, Henley, Mellencamp, Public Enemy? If we think back on the songs we have surveyed here and recall especially those which have been most memorable and most durable, we need to ask what it was they said that struck a responsive chord?

First, they almost without exception affirmed that we are *one* nation. They did this by offering symbols that reconciled the contradictions and disparate strands that often threatened to divide us. Every American, the myth said, valued freedom, opportunity, and equality (even if only nominally for this last mytheme); every American saw in the land a seedbed, where the above mentioned qualities could flourish; they saw in it a reflection of their own goodness and their belief in the future; every American looked with pride on the accomplishments and sacrifices of our patriotic forebears, and every American saw our history moving in a well-defined direction; our conflicts and trials regenerated us and gave proof that there was a teleology at work in our history; every American, moreover, believed that God willed that destiny for *His* people. I purposely used the term "every American" to reinforce the hegemonic character of this mythic narrative in our culture. The myth of America addressed one of the basic needs of our culture by providing, to quote Leszek Kolakowski, answers to "ultimate questions" and addressing our need for "faith in the permanence of human value" (1972, 4).

This last point leads us to the second need that this myth fulfilled. Throughout this study we have seen how the songs—at least up until the last twenty years—have reaffirmed a transcendental vision. The songs have shown us a people caught up in events that are greater than their narrowly personal concerns or individual needs. Even looking at the landscape, we see something greater than the mere aggregate of flora, fauna, water, and rock. Those rocks and rills and fruited plains fill one with wonder, they are the avenue to the "throne of Liberty" and to the alabaster cities of our future. They help us realize universal brotherhood by uniting us in a celebration of our shared link to the soil, which is, after all, the one thing that we truly have in common.

We have also seen that the individual mythemes are but pieces in a cosmic tapestry. Our patriot's sacrificed for freedom, opportunity, and equality for the community, and so each individual could enjoy his/her individuality within that larger community. They were guided in their pursuit of these qualities by their faith in the providential vision. When today (whether "today" is 1862, 1918, 1930, 1942, or 1966) we are called upon to serve (and not just militarily), we have the assurance that our sacrifice is only part of a larger plan.

Do we have this today? It seems not. Our songs do not speak with the same assurance that those in the past did—even those that espoused protest or revolution or repudiation of the myth. This should not surprise us. This is not the America of 1790 or even 1890. This, in fact, is not the America of 1960. The songs of the 1970s and the 1980s have revealed a new America. It is a more complicated place, and one whose vision of the future is predicated on different perceptions of the values contained in our myth. We are experiencing a mythic paradigm shift. We are in a transition stage where the vision of the future is cloudy. Chaos researcher Robert Shaw made a statement that captures where we are right now in regards to forging a new mythic vision: "You don't see something until you have the right metaphor to let you perceive it" (Quoted in Gleick 1987, 262). We have not as yet found that metaphor or that conglomeration of symbols that will generate or regenerate mythemes to animate a new myth. The mythemes that songwriters create will have to account for this changing America. What are some of the issues the new myth will have to confront?

One of those changes deals with pluralism. We saw a brief recognition of this issue in Harry Chapin's "What Made America Famous" of the seventies, but the eighties and the nineties have emphasized even more the changing face of the national community. The presence on the musical scene of more minority artists has made the biggest difference. They present us with "minority" opinions and sometimes images of "another" America that force us to reexamine the premises of our national monomyth.

The dilemma for songwriters is where to stand. If they are going to use the myth to reconcile contradictory impulses and speak to the need for transcendence, they will have to find a common ground for all of us. This, difficult today. Look at this quote from George Bancroft in 1854: "Our country stands, therefore, more than any other, as the realization of the unity of the race. . . . Finally, as a consequence of the tendency of the race towards unity and universality, the organization of society must more and more conform to the principle of FREEDOM" (Quoted in Boorstin 1965, 371). Or this from Studs Terkel's *The Great Divide*, in which he quotes Sherwood Anderson's *Puzzled America* (1934): "Anderson found a 'hunger for belief, a determination to believe in one another, in the leadership we're likely to get out of democracy'" (1988, 11). This is not the case today. Robert Dahl notes that today we are "less prone to draw a veil of idealization over the politics of everyday life" (1989, 301) than we would have perhaps thirty years ago. We are inundated with massive amounts of information, facts, details, and statistics, which seem to militate against mythopoesis, and we are increasingly worried about leadership. The songs reveal that the future looks less sure; we are less willing to offer answers and new visions. Those who do offer a vision, like Public Enemy, speak of the world being a "terrordome," and they confront us with, as the album title states, our *Fear of a Black Planet*. We have lost our moral vision. The Madisonian concept of civic virtue seems to have vanished and with it the belief that we can function as *one* nation.

However, this is not to say that the quest is finished or that we have given up hope. Ever since the Bicentennial, songwriters have been intent upon finding some meaning for the country's existence and a vision for its future. Randy Newman humorously helped put to rest the idea that we could bomb the world into accepting us as a world power in his "Political Science" and others have built upon that by asking us to look first to ourselves (a theme, oddly enough, enunciated in songs of the forties) and take care of things at home. Therefore, at the end of the twentieth century, we seem less willing to look beyond our shores for an affirmation of our greatness and a transcendental vision. History has shown us that the pursuit of manifest destiny might indeed jeopardize that one crucial aspect of our myth that may be the only common ideological ground we share: freedom. We seem less willing to believe that individuals can be empowered through a community (whether a community of labor, protest, or even ethnic origin). We seem less willing to hope for a utopian vision where the country achieves some moral or material perfection. Thus, the anger of Lou Reed or Neil Young or Public Enemy can be seen as a transitional stage in the evolution of new myth. We need to recall the anger in the early songs of the Revolution and those of the abolitionists and of the folk-protest movement to understand the hope that lies underneath any reevaluation of the myth.

In spite of what history has seemingly "taught" us and in spite of our occasional attempts to repudiate the myth, there is a belief that somewhere in our past or in our people is the kernel for a great republic. Robert Dahl states: "Yet the nature of the democratic idea, and its origins, prevent the hope from ever dying out that the limits can be transcended by creating new (or recreating ancient) democratic forms and institutions" (1989, 225). There are those who believe that by recalling and reliving the dream of our patriotic forebears, we can have a better America and achieve greatness in the future. Some seek clues to our future in the sentiments of past songs, such as "The Star-Spangled Banner," "America the Beautiful," or "God Bless America." John Mellencamp, Bruce Springsteen, and Don Henley have all alluded to the small town of the past as a place where community, people, freedom, and opportunity still can be found. There is a danger of invoking the past to look into the future. Perhaps quite without knowing it, the songwriters, by evoking these symbols, may indeed be calling for a return to a condition which can never be, if it ever was. The ironic—maybe tragic—aspect of this return to the past is that it creates an ideological "black hole": Sentiments that have been rejected are summoned forth under the guise of symbols, which seem to fulfill a need for a moral vision. Once the symbol is "read," however, the sentiment collapses into itself, because it cannot reconcile the contradiction created by being, at once, the thing that we desire and the thing that has brought us to this undesirable place in history. The songwriter and audience find themselves impaled on the horns of the dilemma.

Nonetheless, we keep writing the songs. We keep searching for America. And this is the most significant aspect of this whole study: in Paul Simon's phrase, in our most "uncertain hours" we still look to the "idea" of America for some sustenance. We seem to resist aggressively the thought that our lives can be controlled by facts and historical determinism. We seem to want to resist the "culture of separation" suggested by modernity. And so we continue to seek a myth of America. We currently are in the diagnostic stage: Songwriters are cataloging those things that seem to be "not America." We may see in time a prognostic stage where songwriters will offer ideas and hope for the future.

Although mythopoesis is fraught with dangers, we need it to transcend our great capacity for folly and insignificance. If indeed the myth can help us achieve that higher awareness, can bring the realities of the world into conformity with our capacity to wonder and dream, then it will be serving the culture well. Songwriters in the eighties and the nineties may wish to avoid the pitfalls of the old myth, but everyone from Ruben Blades and Los Lobos, to Prince, to Living Colour, to Neil Young, to Public Enemy recognize the country's responsibility to its destiny. Currently our songs seem—at least on the surface—to divide over conflicting versions of what is the public good, and what is a national community, and what is our destiny. There are those who see the public good and our national vision best served by a renewal of values and there are those who see the public good best served by empowering of the individual through economic parity. What this basically means is that we just haven't found that "metaphor" yet that will restore the teleological dimension of the myth. The myth may have undergone some revision, but we haven't lost it.

The myth of America is, indeed, a deathless song. It is a song we cannot let go of. It haunts us, it inspires our anger, our hope, our distrust, our longing, our greatness, and our shame, but like all myths it is ever-present and ubiquitous. So indeed, it may be true: The revolution is not completed. Songwriters may focus on different particulars: They may even strive for a new vision. They may ask us to repudiate the old "lies" (which, in essence, is an acknowledgment of their hold on our consciousness), but they almost universally seem to agree on some basic things: This is a country where everyone should enjoy the blessings of freedom, equality, and opportunity; this is a country blessed with a bountiful natural landscape (materially and aesthetically); and this is a country that needs to continue the quest to find itself, to find a true moral vision, to fulfill its revolutionary destiny, and to be a place where it really means something when we sing "Born in the U.S.A."

BIBLIOGRAPHY

Alexander, Michael. "The Impressions." In *Side Saddle on the Golden Calf: Social Structure and Popular Culture in America*, edited by George Lewis. Pacific Palisades, Calif.: Goodyear, 1972.

Allen, Frederick Lewis. *Only Yesterday: An Informal History of the 1920s.* New York: Harper Perennial Library, 1931.

American War Songs. Philadelphia: National Committee for the Preservation of Existing Records of the National Society of the Colonial Dames of America, 1925. (Privately printed)

Anderson, Gillian B. *Freedom's Voice in Poetry and Song.* Wilmington: Scholarly Resources Inc., 1977.

Arnett, Hazel, ed. *I Hear America Singing: Great Folksongs from the Revolution to Rock.* New York: Praeger Publishers, 1975.

Auerbach, Nina. *Woman and the Demon: The Life of a Victorian Myth.* Cambridge: Harvard University Press, 1982.

Bailyn, Bernard, David Brion Davis, David Herbert Donald, John L. Thomas, Robert H. Wiebe, and Gordon S. Wood. *The Great Republic: A History of the American People.* Boston: Little, Brown and Co. 1977.

———. *The Ideological Origins of the American Revolution.* Cambridge: Harvard University Press, 1967.

Baker, Houston A. *Blues, Ideology, and Afro-American Literature: A Vernacular Theory.* Chicago: The University of Chicago Press, 1984.

Baraka, Imamu Amiri. *Blues People: Negro Music in White America.* 1963. Reprinted, Westport, Conn. Greewood Press, 1980.

Barol, Bill " 'Myths Keep Us Strangers': Springsteen On Love, Fear and Rock and Roll." *Newsweek* 2 November 1987: 76–78.

Barthes, Roland. *A Barthes Reader.* Edited by Susan Sontag. New York: Hill & Wang, 1982.

Becker, Ernest. *The Denial of Death.* New York: The Free Press, 1973.

Bellah, Robert, and Richard Madsen, William Sullivan, Ann Swidler, and Steven M. Tipton. *Habits of the Heart: Individualism and Commitment in American Life.* New York: Harper & Row, 1985.

Bennett, Tony, and Graham Martin, Colin Mercer, Janet Woollacott, eds. *Culture, Ideology and Social Process: A Reader*. London: The Open University; B.T. Batsford Ltd., 1981.

Bercovitch, Sacvan. *The American Puritan Imagination: Essays in Revaluation*. Cambridge: Cambridge University Press, 1974.

———. *The Puritan Origins of the American Self*. New Haven: Yale University Press, 1975.

Bode, Carl. *Ante-Bellum Culture*. Carbondale: Southern Illinois University Press, 1959.

The Book of Popular Songs: Being a Compendium of the Best Sentimental, Comic, Negro, Irish, Scotch, National, Patriotic, Military, Naval, Social, Convivial and Pathetic Songs, Ballads and Melodies. Philadelphia: G. G. Evans Publisher, 1860.

Boorstin, Danial. *The Americans: The Colonial Experience*. New York: Vintage Books, 1958.

———. *The Americans: The National Experience*. New York: Vintage Books, 1965.

Bordman, Gerald. *American Musical Theatre: A Chronicle*. 2d ed. New York: Oxford University Press, 1986.

Bowman, Kent. *Voices of Combat: A Century of Liberty and War Songs, 1765–1965*. Contributions to the Study of Music and Dance, No. 10. Westport, Conn.: Greewood Press, 1987.

Branch, Taylor. *Parting the Waters: America in the King Years, 1954–1963*. New York: Simon & Shuster, Touchstone Books, 1988.

Brown, William R. "Attention and the Rhetoric of Social Intervention." *Quarterly Journal of Speech*, 60 (1982): 16–27.

———. "Ideology As Communication Process," *Quarterly Journal of Speech* 64 (1978): 123–40.

Burke, Kenneth. *Language As Symbolic Action: Essays on Life, Literature, and Method*. Berkeley: University of California Press, 1966.

———. *A Rhetoric of Motives*. New York: Prentice-Hall, 1950.

Campbell, Joseph with Bill Moyers. *The Power of Myth*. New York: Doubleday, 1988.

Cassirer, Ernst. *The Myth of the State*. New Haven: Yale University Press, 1946.

Cawelti, John. *Adventure, Mystery, and Romance: Formula Stories as Art and Popular Culture*. Chicago: The University of Chicago Press, 1976.

———. *The Six-Gun Mystique*. Rev. ed. Bowling Green, Ohio: Bowling Green State University Popular Press, 1986.

Charters, Samuel. *The Poetry of the Blues*. New York: Oak Publications, 1963.

Chase, Richard. *The American Novel and Its Tradition*. Garden City, N.Y.: Doubleday Anchor Books, 1957.

Chase, Gilbert. *America's Music: From the Pilgrims to the Present.* 3d ed. New York: McGraw Hill, 1987.

Chesebro, James W., Davis A. Foulger, Jay E. Nachman, and Andrew Yanelli. "Popular Music as a Mode of Communication, 1955–1982."*Critical Studies in Mass Communication* 2 (1985): 115–35.

Clarke, Garry E. *Essays on American Music.* Westport, Conn.: Greenwood Press; Contributions in American History, No. 62, 1977.

Commager, Henry Steele. *The American Mind: An Interpretation of American Thought and Character Since the 1880's.* New York: Bantam Books, 1950, 1970.

Cook, Albert. *Myth and Language.* Bloomington: Indiana University Press, 1980.

Cooper, B. Lee. *The Popular Music Handbook: A Resource Guide for Teachers, Librarians, and Media Specialists.* Littleton, Colo.: Libraries Unlimited, 1984.

————. *A Resource Guide to Themes in Contemporary American Song Lyrics, 1950–1985.* Westport, Conn.: Greenwood Press, 1986.

Cords, Nicholas, and Patrick Gerster. *Myth and the American Experience.* 2 vols. New York: Glencoe Press, 1973.

Courlander, Harold. *Negro Folk Music.* New York: Columbia University Press, 1963.

Cowell, Henry, ed. *American Composers on American Music: A Symposium.* Stanford: Stanford University Press, 1933.

Cox, Harvey. *The Secular City: Secularization and Urbanization in Techological Perspectives.* Rev. ed. New York: MacMillan, 1965, 1966.

Craig, Warren. *Sweet and Low Down: America's Popular Song Writers.* Metuchen, N.J.: The Scarecrow Press, 1978.

Crawford, Richard, ed. *The Civil War Songbook.* New York: Dover, 1977.

Curtis, Jim. *Rock Eras: Interpretations of Music and Society, 1954–1984.* Bowling Green, Ohio: Bowling Green University Popular Press, 1987.

Dahl, Robert A. *Democracy and Its Critics.* New Haven: Yale University Press, 1989.

Dane, Barbara, and Irwin Silber, eds. *The Vietnam Songbook.* New York: Monthly Review Press; Guardian Book, 1969.

Daniel, Ralph T. *The Anthem in New England Before 1800.* Evanston, Ill.: Northwestern University Press, 1966.

Davis, David Brion. "Expanding the Republic, 1820–1860." In *The Great Republic: A History of the American People.* Boston: Little, Brown & Company, 1977.

Denisoff, R. Serge. *Great Day Coming: Folk Music and the American Left.* Urbana: University of Illinois Press, 1971.

————. *Sing a Song of Social Significance.* Bowling Green, OH: Bowling Green University Popular Press, 1972.

————. *Solid Gold: The Popular Record Industry.* New Brunswick, N.J.: Transaction Books, 1975.

————, comp. *Songs of Protest, War, and Peace: A Bibliography and Discography.* Santa Barbara, Cal.: American Bibliography Center–CLIO Press, 1973.

Détienne, Marcel. *The Creation of Mythology.* Translated by Margaret Cook. Chicago: The University of Chicago Press, 1981.

Dickstein, Morris. *Gates of Eden: American Culture in the Sixties.* New York: Basic Books, 1977.

Donald, David Herbert. "Uniting the Republic, 1860–1890." In *The Great Republic: A History of the American People.* Boston: Little, Brown and Co. 1977.

Eaklor, Vicki L. *American Anti-Slavery Songs: A Collection and Analysis.* Westport, Conn.: Greenwood Press, 1988.

Eco, Umberto. *A Theory of Semiotics.* Bloomington: Indiana University Press, 1976.

Eliade, Mircea. *Myth and Reality.* Translated by Willard R. Trask. New York: Harper Torchbooks, 1963.

Ellinwood, Leonard. "Revolutionary Hymnody." *Journal of Church of Music* November 1975: 2–5.

Ellison, Mary. *Lyrical Protest: Black Music's Struggle Against Discrimination.* New York: Praeger, 1989.

Engel, Lehman. *Their Words Are Music: The Great Theatre Lyricists and Their Lyrics.* New York: Crown Publishers, 1975.

Ewen, David. *All the Years of American Popular Music.* Englewood Cliffs, N.J.: Prentice-Hall, 1977.

Ferlinghetti, Lawrence. *A Coney Island of the Mind.* New York: New Directions, 1955.

Fisher, Miles Mark. *Negro Slave Songs in the United States* (reprint). New York: Russell & Russell, 1968.

Fisher, William Arms. *Ye Old New-England Psalm Tunes, 1620–1820.* Boston: Oliver Ditson Co., 1930.

Fitzgerald, F. Scott. *The Great Gatsby.* New York: Scribners, 1925.

Fraser, Barbara Means. "The Dream Shattered: America's Seventies Musicals." *Journal of American Culture* 12 (1989): 31–37.

Frith, Simon. *Music for Pleasure: Essays in the Sociology of Pop.* Cambridge, England: Polity Press, 1988.

————. *Sound Effects: Youth, Leisure, and the Politics of Rock 'n' Roll.* New York: Pantheon, 1981.

Fussell, Paul. *The Great War and Modern Memory.* New York: Oxford University Press, 1975.

Geertz, Clifford. *The Interpretation of Cultures: Selected Essays.* New York: Basic Books, 1973.

Gershwin, Ira. *Lyrics on Several Occasions*. New York: Viking, 1953, 1973.

Gillett, Charlie. *The Sound of the City: The Rise of Rock and Roll*. Rev. and expanded. New York: Pantheon, 1983.

Ginsburg, Allen. *Howl and Other Poems*. San Francisco: City Lights Books, 1956.

Gitlin, Todd. *The Sixties: Years of Hope, Days of Rage*. New York: Bantam Books, 1987.

Gleason, Harold, and Warren Becker. *Early American Music: Music in America from 1620–1920*. 2d ed. Music Literature Outline Series III. Bloomington, Ind.: Frangipani Press, 1981.

Gleick, James. *Chaos: Making a New Science*. New York: Viking, 1987.

Gramsci, Antonio. "Antonio Gramsci" and "Section Four: Class, Culture and Hegemony" in *Culture, Ideology and Social Process: A Reader*, edited by Tony Bennett et al. London: B. T. Batsford Ltd, 1981.

Green, Stanley. *Ring Bells! Sing Songs!: Broadway Musicals of the 1930s*. New York: Galahad Books, 1971.

Green, Suzanne Ellery. *Books for Pleasure: Popular Fiction, 1914–1945*. Bowling Green, Ohio: Bowling Green University Popular Press, 1974.

Greenway, John. *American Folksongs of Protest* (Reprint). New York: Octagon Books, 1970.

Grossberg, Lawrence. "Another Boring Day in Paradise: Rock and Roll and the Empowerment of Everyday Life." *Popular Music* 4 (1984); 225–60.

Guralnick, Peter. *Sweet Soul Music: Rhythm and Blues and the Southern Dream of Freedom*. New York: Harper & Row, 1986.

Hague, Eleanor, compiler. *Spanish-American Folk Songs* (reprint). 1917, New York: Kraus Reprint Co., 1969.

Halpern, Ben. "'Myth' and 'Ideology' in Modern Usage." *History and Theory* 1 (1961): 129–49.

Hamm, Charles. *Yesterdays: Popular Song in America*. New York: Norton, 1979.

Haralambos, Michael. *Right On: From Blues to Soul in Black America* (reprint). New York: DaCapo Press, 1979.

Hart, Dorothy, and Robert Kimball, eds. *The Complete Lyrics of Lorenz Hart*. New York: Alfred A. Knopf, 1986.

Hart, James D. *The Popular Book: A History of America's Literary Taste*. Berkeley: University of California Press, 1963.

Harwell, Richard B. *Confederate Music*. Chapel Hill: The University of North Carolina Press, 1950.

Hawkes, Terence. *Structuralism and Semiotics*. Berkeley: University of California Press, 1977.

Heaps, Willard, and Porter W. Heaps. *The Singing Sixties: The Spirit of Civil War Days Drawn from the Music of the Times*. Norman: University of Oklahoma Press, 1960.

Higginson, Thomas Wentworth. *Army Life in a Black Regiment* (reprint). New York, Collier Books, 1962.

Hille, Waldemar, ed. *The People's Song Book*. New York: Boni and Gaer, 1948.

Hirsch, Paul M. "Sociological Approaches to the Pop Music Phenomenon." *American Behavioral Scientist* 14 (January–February 1971): 371–88.

Hitchcock, H. Wiley. *Music in the United States: A Historical Introduction*. 2d ed. Englewood Cliffs, N.J.: Prentice-Hall, 1974.

Hoare, Ian, ed. (with Clive Anderson, Tony Cummings, and Simon Frith). *The Soul Book*. New York: Dell Publishing Co.; Delta Books, 1975.

Hodgson, Godfrey. *America in Our Time*. Garden City, N.Y.: Doubleday, 1976.

Horstman, Dorothy, ed. *Sing Your Heart Out, Country Boy*. New York: E.P. Dutton, 1975.

Jackson, George Stuyvesant, ed. *Early Songs of Uncle Sam, 1825–1850* (reprint). Boston: Bruce Humphries, 1964.

Jameson, Frederic. *The Political Unconscious: Narrative As a Socially Symbolic Act*. Ithaca: Cornell University Press, 1981.

Jasen, David. *Tin Pan Alley: The Composers, the Songs, the Performers and Their Times*. New York: Donald I. Fine, 1988.

Jehlen, Myra, and Sacvan Bercovitch, eds. *Ideology and Classic America Literature*. Cambridge, Eng.: Cambridge University Press, 1986.

Johnson, Paul. *Modern Times: The World from the Twenties to the Eighties*. New York: Harper & Row, 1983.

Kaplan, E. Ann. *Rocking Around the Clock: Music Television, Postmodernism, and Consumer Culture*. New York: Methuen, 1987.

Keil, Charles. *Urban Blues*. Chicago: The University of Chicago Press, 1966.

Kennedy, David M. *Over Here: The First World War and American Society*. New York: Oxford University Press, 1980.

Kennedy, Eugene. "Earthrise: The Dawning of a New Spiritual Awareness." *New York Times Magazine*, 15 April 1979, 14–15, 51–56.

Kennedy, Paul. *The Rise and Fall of the Great Powers: Economic Change and Military Conflict from 1500 to 2000*. New York: Random House, 1987.

Kinkle, Roger D. *The Complete Encyclopedia of Popular Music and Jazz, 1900–1950*. 4 vols. New Rochelle, N.Y.: Arlington House 1974.

Klein, Joe. *Woody Guthrie: A Life*. New York: Ballantine Books, 1980.

Kolakowski, Leszek. *The Presence of Myth*. Translated by Adam Czerniawski. Chicago: The University of Chicago Press, 1972, 1989.

Krehbiel, Henry Edward. *Afro-American Folksongs: A Study in Racial and National Music* (reprint). New York: Frederick Unger, 1962.

Kroker, Arthur and David Cook. *The Postmodern Scene: Excremental Culture and Hyper-Aesthetics*. Montreal: New World Perspectives, 1986.

Lacan, Jacques. *Ecrits: A Selection*. Translated by Alan Sheridan. New York: W. W. Norton, 1977.

Langer, Susanne K. *Philosophy in a New Key: A Study in the Symbolism of Reason, Rite, and Art*. 3d ed. Cambridge: Harvard University Press, 1957.

Lasch, Christopher. *The Culture of Narcissism: American Life in An Age of Diminishing Expectations*. New York: W. W. Norton, 1978.

Lawrence, Vera Brodsky. *Music for Patriots, Politicians, and Presidents: Harmonies and Discords of the First Hundred Years*. New York: MacMillan, 1975.

Lax, Roger, and Frederick Smith. *The Great Song Thesaurus*. 2d ed. New York: Oxford University Press, 1989.

Lerner, Max. *America As A Civilization: Life and Thought in the United States Today*. New York: Simon & Shuster, 1957.

Levi-Strauss, Claude. *Myth and Meaning*. New York: Schocken Books, 1978.

————. *Structural Anthropology*. Translated by Claire Jackson and Brooke Grundfest Schoepf. Garden City, N.Y.: Doubleday Anchor Books, 1963, 1967.

Levy, Lester. *Give Me Yesterday: American History in Song, 1890–1920*. Norman: University of Oklahoma Press, 1975.

————. *Grace Notes in American History: Popular Sheet Music from 1820 to 1900*. Norman: University of Oklahoma Press, 1967.

Lewis, William F. "Telling America's Story: Narrative Form and the Reagan Presidency." *Quarterly Journal of Speech* 73 (1987): 280–302.

Lieberman, Robbie. *"My Song Is My Weapon": People's Songs, American Communism, and the Politics of Culture, 1930–1950*. Urbana: University of Illinois Press, 1989.

Lomax, Alan (compiler), Woody Guthrie, and Pete Seeger. *Hard Hitting Songs for Hard-Hit People*. New York: Oak Publications, 1967.

London, Herbert I. *Closing the Circle: A Cultural History of the Rock Revolution*. Chicago: Nelson-Hall, 1984.

Lord, Albert B. *The Singer of Tales*. Cambridge: Harvard University Press, 1960.

Lowens, Irving. *Music and Musicians in Early America*. New York: Norton, 1964.

MacDougall, Hamilton C. *Early New England Psalmody: An Historical Appreciation, 1620–1820*. Brattleboro, Vt.: Stephen Daye Press, 1940.

Mackan, Bob, Peter Forntale, and Bill Ayres. *The Rock Music Source Book*. Garden City, N.Y.: Doubleday Anchor Books, 1980.

Mailer, Norman. "The White Negro." *The Long Patrol: 25 Years of Writing from the Work of Norman Mailer*. Edited by Robert F. Lucid. New York: World Publishing Co., 1971.

Makay, John J., and Alberto Gonzalez. "Dylan's Bibliographical Rhetoric and the Myth of the Outlaw Hero." *The Southern Speech Communication Journal* 52 (1987): 165–80.

Malone, Bill. *Country Music, U.S.A.* Rev. ed. Austin: University of Texas Press, 1985.

Malone, Bill, and Judith McCulloh, eds. *Stars of Country Music: Uncle Dave Macon to Johnny Rodriguez.* Urbana: University of Illinois Press, 1975.

Marcus, Greil. *Mystery Train: Images of America in Rock 'n' Roll Music.* Rev. and expanded. New York: E. P. Dutton, 1982.

Marrocco, W. Thomas, and Harold Gleason. *Music in America: An Anthology from the Landing of the Pilgrims to the Close of the Civil War, 1620 –1865.* New York: W. W. Norton, 1964.

Marx, Leo. *The Machine in the Garden: Technology and the Pastoral Ideal in America.* New York: Oxford University Press, 1964.

———. *The Pilot and the Passenger: Essays on Literature, Technology, and Culture in the United States.* New York: Oxford University Press, 1988.

May, Henry F. *The End of American Innocence: A Study of the First Years of Our Own Time, 1912–1917.* New York: Alfred A. Knopf, 1959.

———. *The Enlightenment in America.* New York: Oxford University Press, 1976.

McCarthy, John, Richard Peterson, and William Yancey. "Singing Along with the Silent Majority" in *Side Saddle on the Golden Calf: Social Structure and Popular Culture in America*, edited by George Lewis. Pacific Palisades, Calif.; Goodyear, 1972.

McCue, George, ed. *Music in American Society, 1776–1976: From Puritan Hymn to Synthesizer.* New Brunswick, N.J.: Transaction Books, 1977.

McGee, Michael Calvin. "The 'Ideograph': A Link Between Rhetoric and Ideology," *The Quarterly Journal of Speech* 66 (1980): 1–16.

McPherson, James M. *Battle Cry of Freedom: The Civil War Era.* New York: Oxford University Press, 1988.

Mellers, Wilfrid. *A Darker Shade of Pale: A Background to Bob Dylan.* New York: Oxford University Press, 1985.

Miller, Perry. *The New England Mind: From Colony to Province.* Vol. 2. Boston: Beacon Press, 1953.

Moseley, Caroline. "The Hutchinson Family: The Function of Their Song in Ante-Bellum America." In *American Popular Music: Readings from the Popular Press, Volume I: The Nineteenth Century and Tin Pan Alley*, edited by Timothy E. Scheurer. Bowling Green, Ohio: Bowling Green State University Popular Press, 1989. pp. 63–64

Myers, Gordon. "Songs of Early Americans." *Music Journal*, September 1969: 36–37.

Nimmo, Dan and James E. Combs. *Subliminal Politics: Myths and Mythmakers in America.* Englewood Cliffs, N.J.: Prentice-Hall, 1980.

Nozick, Robert. *Anarchy, State, and Utopia.* New York: Basic Books, 1974.

Nye, Russel. *The Unembarrassed Muse: The Popular Arts in America*. New York: Dial, 1970.

Oliver, Paul. *The Meaning of the Blues*. New York: Collier Books, 1972.

Orman, John. *The Politics of Rock Music*. Chicago: Nelson-Hall, 1984.

Oster, Harry. *Living Country Blues*. Detroit: Folklore Associates, 1969.

Palmer, Robert. *Deep Blues*. New York: Penguin Books, 1982.

Parrington, Vernon I. *Main Currents in American Thought: An Interpretation of American Literature from the Beginnings to 1920*. 3 Vols. New York: Harcourt, Brace & Co., 1927.

Patai, Raphael. *Myth and Modern Man*. Englewood Cliffs, N.J.: Prentice-Hall, 1972.

Pattison, Robert. *The Triumph of Vulgarity: Rock Music in the Mirror of Romanticism*. New York: Oxford University Press, 1987.

Pichaske, David. *A Generation in Motion: Popular Music and Culture in the Sixties*. New York: Schirmer, 1979.

Porter, Cole. *The Complete Lyrics of Cole Porter*. Edited by Robert Kimball. New York: Vintage Books, 1984.

Pratt, Waldo Selden. *The Music of the Pilgrims: A Description of the Psalmbook Brought to Plymouth in 1620*. Boston: Oliver Ditson, 1921.

Rabson, Carolyn. *Songbook of the American Revolution*. Peaks Island Maine: NEO Press, 1974.

Reynolds, David S. *Beneath the American Renaissance: The Subversive Imagination in the Age of Emerson and Melville*. New York: Alfred A. Knopf, 1988.

Richardson, Robert D. *Myth and Literature in the American Renaissance*. Bloomington: Indiana University Press, 1978.

Robertson, James Oliver. *American Myth, American Reality*. New York: Hill & Wang, 1980.

Rodnitzky, Jerome L. *Minstrels of the Dawn: The Folk-Protest Singer as a Cultural Hero*. Chicago: Nelson-Hall, 1976.

Ruppersburg, Hugh. "Subverting the American Dream: *Country, The River,* and *Places in the Heart.*" *Journal of American Culture* 9 (Winter 1986): 25–29.

Rushing, Janice Hocker. "Mythic Evolution of 'The New Frontier' in Mass Mediated Rhetoric." *Critical Studies in Mass Communication* 3 (1986): 265–96.

Rybczynski, Witold. *Home: A Short History of an Idea*. New York: Viking, 1986.

Sackheim, Eric. *The Blues Line: A Collection of Blues Lyrics from Leadbelly to Muddy Waters*. New York: Schirmer Books, 1969.

Scheurer, Timothy, ed. *American Popular Music: Readings from the Popular Press*. 2 vols. Bowling Green, Ohio: Bowling Green State University Popular Press, 1989

Silber, Irwin, ed. *Songs of the Civil War*. New York: Columbia University Press, 1960.

———. *Songs of Independence*. Harrisburg, PA: Stackpole Books, 1973.

Silverman, Jerry, ed. *Folk Blues*. New York: Oak Publications, 1958, 1968.

Slotkin, Richard. *The Fatal Environment: The Myth of the Frontier in the Age of Industrialization, 1800–1890*. New York: Atheneum, 1985.

———. "Myth and the Production of History." *Ideology and Classic American Literature*, edited by Sacvan Bercovitch and Myra Jehlen. Cambridge: Cambridge University Press, 1986.

———. *Regeneration Through Violence: The Mythology of the American Frontier, 1600–1860*. Middletown, Conn.: Wesleyan University Press, 1973.

Songs of the Workers: To Fan the Flames of Discontent. 34th ed. Chicago: Industrial Workers of the World, 1973.

Southern, Eileen. *The Music of Black Americans: A History*. 2d ed. New York: W. W. Norton, 1983.

Stevenson, Robert. *Protestant Church Music in America: A Short Survey of Men and Movements from 1564 to the Present*. New York: W. W. Norton, 1966.

Stokes, Geoffrey. *Starmaking Machinery: Inside the Business of Rock and Roll*. New York: Vintage, 1976.

Stone, Michael. "Heav'n Rescued Land: American Hymns and American Destiny." *Journal of Popular Culture* 10 (1976): 133–141.

Strenski, Ivan. *Four Theories of Myth in Twentieth Century History*. Iowa City: University of Iowa Press, 1987.

Sturrock, John, ed. *Structuralism and Since: From Levi-Strauss to Derrida*. New York: Oxford University Press, 1979.

Sussman, Warren I. *Culture as History: The Transformation of American Society in the 20th Century*. New York: Pantheon Books, 1973, 1984.

Taft, Michael. *Blues Lyric Poetry: An Anthology*. New York: Garland Publishing Inc., 1983.

Tawa, Nicholas E. *A Sound of Strangers: Musical Culture, Acculturation and the Post-War Ethnic American*. Metuchen, N.J.: Scarecrow Press, 1982.

Taylor, Joshua C. *The Fine Arts in America*. Chicago: University of Chicago Press, 1979.

Terkel, Studs. *American Dreams: Lost and Found*. New York: Pantheon, 1980.

———. *"The Good War": An Oral History of World War II*. New York: Pantheon, 1984.

———. *The Great Divide: Second Thoughts on the American Dream*. New York: Pantheon, 1988.

Thomas, John L. "Nationalizing the Republic, 1890–1920." In *The Great Republic: A History of the American People*. Boston: Little, Brown &

Co. 1977.

Titon, Jeff Todd. *Early Downhome Blues: A Musical and Cultural Analysis.* Urbana: University of Illinois Press, 1977.

Todorov, Tzvetan. *Symbolism and Interpretation.* Translated by Catherine Porter. Ithaca: Cornell University Press, 1978, 1982.

Ward, Ed, Geoffrey Stokes, and Ken Tucker. *Rock of Ages: The "Rolling Stone" History of Rock and Roll.* New York: Rolling Stone Press/ Summit Books 1986.

Warner, Anne. *Traditional American Folk Songs: From the Anne and Frank Warner Collection.* Syracuse: Syracuse University Press, 1984.

Weiss, Richard. *The American Myth of Success: From Horatio Alger to Norman Vincent Peale.* New York: Basic Books, 1969.

Whitcomb, Ian. *After the Ball: Pop Music from Rag to Rock.* New York: Simon & Schuster, 1974.

———. *Rock Odyssey: A Musician's Chronicle of the Sixties.* Garden City, NY: Doubleday Dolphin Books. 1983.

White, Hayden. "Structuralism and Popular Culture." *Journal of Popular Culture* 7 (Spring 1974): 759–75.

Whitman, Wanda Willson, ed. *Songs That Changed the World.* New York: Crown, 1969.

Wiebe, Robert H. "Modernizing the Republic, 1920 to the Present." In *The Great Republic: A History of the American People.* Boston: Little, Brown & Co. 1977.

———. *The Search for Order, 1877–1920.* New York: Hill & Wang, 1967.

Wilder, Alec. *American Popular Song: The Great Innovators, 1900–1950.* New York: Oxford University Press, 1972.

Wilk, Max. *They're Playing Our Song.* New York: Atheneum, 1973.

Wills, Garry. *Inventing America: Jefferson's Declaration of Independence.* New York: Vintage Books, 1978.

Woll, Allen L. The Hollywood Musical Goes to War. Chicago: Nelson-Hall, 1983.

———. *Songs from Hollywood Musical Comedies, 1927 to the Present: A Dictionary.* New York: Garland Publishing, Inc., 1976.

Wood, Gordon S. "Framing the Republic, 1760–1820." In *The Great Republic: A History of the American People.* Boston: Little, Brown & Co. 1977.

DISCOGRAPHY

The following is a selected discography. Included are only those items which I was able to listen to during my research. The format of the recording will follow the entry and will be designated by the following symbols: long-playing record (LP); 45 rpm record (45): 78 rpm record (78); cassette (C); cassette single (CS); compact disc (CD).

Allison, Luther. "Bad News Is Coming." *Bad News Is Coming*. Gordy B964L. (LP)

Anderson, Bill. "Where Have All Our Heroes Gone?" Decca 32744. (45)

Andersen, Eric. "My Land Is a Good Land." *The Best of Eric Andersen*. Vanguard VRS-9206. (LP)

Autry, Gene. "God Must Have Loved America." Okeh 06359. (78)

Bales, Richard. *The Confederacy* (Based on Music of the South During the Years 1861–1865). Richard Bales, cond. With essays by Bruce Catton and Clifford Dowdey. Columbia LS 1004. (LP)

———. *The Union* (Based on Music of the North During the Years 1861–1865). Richard Bales, cond. With essays by Bruce Catton, Clifford Dowdey, and Allan Nevins. Columbia LS 1006. 2 (LP)

Bare, Bobby. "God Blessed America Again." RCA 74-0264. (45)

Barnes, Jimmy. *Jimmy Barnes*. Geffen Records GHS 24089. 1985 (LP)

Berry, Chuck. *Chuck Berry's Golden Decade*. Chess 1514. (LP)

———. "Promised Land." *St. Louis to Liverpool*. Chess 1488. (LP)

Berkeley, Roy. *Folk and Country Songs of the FDR Years*. Longview L241. (LP)

Bernstein, Leonard. *West Side Story* (Original Broadway Cast). Columbia JS 32603. 1957. (LP)

Blondell, Joan. "Remember My Forgotten Man." *The Golden Age of the Hollywood Musical*. (Songs by the original artists.) United Artists UA-LA215-H. (LP)

Britt, Elton. "There's A Star Spangled Banner Waving Somewhere." Bluebird B-9000-B. (78)

Brown, James. "Living in the U.S.A." *Rocky IV* (Soundtrack). CBS ZK 40203. (CD)

———. "Say It Loud (I'm Black and Proud) [1968]." *The Best of James Brown.* Polydor PD-1-6340. (LP)

Browne, Jackson. *Lives in the Balance.* Asylum 9 60457-1-E. 1986. (LP)

———. *World in Motion.* Elektra 9 60830-2. 1989. (CD)

Burke, Solomon. "*I Have a Dream.*" ABC DSX-50161. 1974. (LP)

Cagney, James and Frances Langford. "Over There." *Yankee Doodle Dandy* (Silver Screen Soundtrack Series). Curtain Calls 100/13. (LP)

Canova, Judy, and the Riders of the Purple Sage. "Stars and Stripes on Iwo Jima." Decca 23447. (78)

Carter, Maybelle. "I Told Them What You're Fighting For." *A Living Legend.* Columbia CS-9275. (LP)

Chapin, Harry. "What Made America Famous." *Verities and Balderdash.* Elektra 1012. (LP)

ChiLites. "Give More Power to the People [1971]." *Give More Power to the People. Brunswick 7541.* Also on *Greatest Hits,* Brunswick 754184.

Crosby, Bing. "Brother, Can You Spare A Dime?" *Songs of the Depression.* Book-of-the-Month Club Records 21-5406. (LP)

Daniels, Charlie. "In America." *Full Moon.* Epic EK 36571. 1980. (CD) Also on *A Decade of Hits,* Epic EK 38795. (CD)

Deer, John. "Battle Hymn of Lt. Calley." Royal American RA 34. (45)

De La Soul. "Ghetto Thang." Tommy Boy TBC 7943. 1989. (CS)

The Del-Lords. *Frontier Days.* EMI America ST-17133. 1984. (LP)

The Doors. "The Unkown Soldier." Elektra 45628. 1968. (45)

Dudley, Dave. "Vietnam Blues." Mercury 72550. (45)

Dylan, Bob. *Bringing It All Back Home.* Columbia KCS 9128. 1965 (LP)

———. *The Freewheelin' Bob Dylan.* Columbia KCS 8786. 1963. (LP)

———. *The Times They Are A-Changin'.* Columbia KCS 8905. 1964. (LP)

Early American Vocal Music: New England Anthems and Southern Folk Hymns. The Western Wind Vocal Ensemble. Nonesuch H-71276. (LP)

Earth Opera. "American Eagle Tragedy." *The Great American Eagle Tragedy.* Elektra 74038. (LP)

Farina, Richard, and Mimi Farina. "House Un-American Blues Activity Dream." *Best of Richard and Mimi Farina.* Vanguard VDS 21/22. (LP)

The Fifth Dimension. "Save the Country." *Portrait.* Bell 6045. 1970. (LP)

Foley, Red. "Smoke on the Water." *Red Foley's Gold Favorites.* Decca 74107. (LP)

Foster, Stephen. *Songs by Stephen Foster, Vol. II.* The Camerata Chorus of Washington (with guest soloists). Nonesuch H-71333. (LP)

Garland, Judy, and Mickey Rooney. "God's Country." *Soundtracks from "Babes in Arms" and "Babes on Broadway."* Curtain Calls 100/6-7. (LP)

Gaye, Marvin. *What's Going On.* Tamla T5—310. 1971. (LP)

Gershwin, George, and Ira Gershwin. *Of Thee I Sing* and *Let 'Em Eat Cake*. Michael Tilson Thomas, cond. Columbia M2K 42522. (CD)

Grandmaster Flash and the Furious Five. "The Message." *Grand Master Flash & The Furious Five*. Sugar Hill SH 2568 B. 1982. (LP) Also available on *Rapmasters: The Best of the Street*, Priority Records 4XL 7958. (C or CD)

Greenwood, Lee. "God Bless the U.S.A." *Greatest Hits*. MCAD-5582 DIDX-385. (CD)

Guthrie, Arlo. "Patriot Dream." *Amigo*. Reprise 2239. (LP)

Guthrie, Woody. *Columbia River Collection*. Rounder 1036. (CD)

———. *Dust Bowl Ballads*. Rounder CD 1040. (CD)

———. And Huddie Ledbetter (Leadbelly). *Folkways: The Original Vision*. Smithsonian Folkways SF 40001. (CD)

———. *Library of Congress Recordings*. Rounder CD1041/2/3. (CD)

———. *Woody Guthrie: Original Recordings, 1940–1946*. Warner Bros. (by arrangement with Asch Folkways Records) BS 2999. 1977. (LP)

Haggard, Merle. "Fightin' Side of Me." Capitol 2719. (45)

———. "Okie from Muskogee." Capitol 2626. (45)

Hall, Tom T. "America the Ugly." *I Witness Life*. Mercury SR-61277. 1972. (LP)

Hamblen, Stuart. "Old Glory." Columbia 20779. 1942. (78)

The Hand That Holds the Bread: Progress and Protest in the Gilded Age, Songs from the Civil War to the Columbian Exposition. Cincinnati University Singers, Earl Rivers, dir. New World Records NW267. (LP)

Harrison, Don. "American Dream." *Not Far from Free*. Mercury SRM-1-1185. 1977. (LP)

Helm, Levon. "America's Farm." *American Son*. MCA Records MCA-5120. 1980. (LP)

Henley, Don. *The End of the Innocence*. Geffen 9 24217-2. 1989. (CD)

Horton, Johnny. "Johnny Freedom." *Johnny Horton Makes History*. Columbia CS 8269. 1960. (LP)

The Impressions. "This Is My Country." *This Is My Country*. Curtom CRS 8001. 1968. (LP)

Jackson, Aunt Molly. *Aunt Molly Jackson*. Library of Congress Recordings. Rounder Records 1002. (LP)

Jackson, Janet. *Rhythm Nation 1814*. A&M Records CD 3920. 1989. (CD)

Jackson, Stonewall. "The Minute Men (Are Turning Over in Their Graves)." *All's Fair in Love 'n' War*. Columbia 4-43552. (LP)

Jenkins, Bobo. "Democrat Blues." *Classic Blues: Country Blues Classics, Vol. 2*. Blues Classics BC 6 A. (LP)

Johnson, Robert. "Stones in the Passway." *King of the Delta Blues*. Columbia CL 1654. (LP)

Kansas. *Song for America*. Kirshner PZ-33385. (LP)

Kaplan, Artie. *Confessions of a Male Chauvinist Pig.* Hopi VHS 901. (LP)

Kaye, Sammy. "Let's Bring New Glory to Old Glory." RCA Victor 27949. (78)

————. "Remember Pearl Harbor." RCA Victor 27738 (78) or ABC Paramount ABCS-250 (LP)

King, Albert. "Born Under a Bad Sign." *King of the Blues Guitar.* Atlantic SD 8213. 1968 (LP)

Lenoir, J.B. "Eisenhower Blues." *The Best of Chess Blues, Volume One.* MCA-Chess CHD-31315. (CD)

Living Colour. "Which Way to America?" *Vivid.* Epic EK 44099. 1988. (CD)

Mack, Warner. "Pray For Your Country." Decca 50157. (45)

Mayfield, Curtis. "Underground." Curtom CRS-8009. 1974. (LP)

McLean, Don. "The Statue." *Prime Time.* Arista AB 4149. (LP)

Mellencamp, John. *The Lonesome Jubilee.* Mercury 832 465-2 Q-1. 1987. (CD)

————. "Pink Houses." *Uh-Huh.* Riva Records RVL 7504. 1983. (LP)

Melvin, Harold, and the Blue Notes. "Where's the Concern for the People." *Now Is the Time.* ABC AA-1041. 1977. (LP)

Miller, Jody. "Home of the Brave." *Home of the Brave.* Capitol ST-2412. 1965. (LP)

The Steve Miller Band. *Living in the U.S.A.* Capitol STBB 11114. (LP)

Moore, Melba, and others. "Lift Every Voice and Sing." Capitol 4JM-44500. 1990. (CS) Includes a track with the Rev. Jesse Jackson talking about the writing and development of the song.

Negro Songs of Protest. Collected by Lawrence Gellert. Rounder Records 4004. (LP)

Newbury, Mickey. "An American Trilogy." *Frisco Mabel Joy.* Elektra EKS-74107. 1971. (LP)

Newman, Randy. *Sail Away.* Warner Reprise MS 2064. 1972. (LP)

N.W.A. "Straight Outta Compton." Priority Records 4V7207. 1989. (CS)

Nyro, Laura. *New York Tendaberry.* Columbia PC-9737. (LP)

Ochs, Phil. *Chords of Fame.* A&M SP-4599. 1976(?). (LP)

————. *There But For Fortune.* Elektra 9 60832-2. (CD)

Payne, Freda. "Bring the Boys Home." Invictus 9092.

Pittsburgh Phil. "Vietnam." Bob Cat 1022. (45)

Plugz. *Better Luck.* Restless Records 7-72624-1. 1981 (LP)

Popular Music in Jacksonian America. The Yankee Doodle Society. Musical Heritage Society MHS 834561. (LP)

Prince. "America." *Around the World in a Day.* Paisley Park 9 25286-2. 1985. (CD)

Prine, John. "The Great Compromise." *Diamonds in the Rough.* Atlantic SD 7240. (LP)

————. "Your Flag Decal Won't Get You into Heaven Anymore." *John Prine.*

Atlantic SD 8296. (LP)

Public Enemy. "Fight the Power." *Music from "Do the Right Thing."* Motown MOTD-6272. 1989. (CD)

———. *It Takes a Nation of Millions to Hold Us Back.* Def Jam FCT 44303. 1988. (C)

———. "911 Is A Joke b/w Revolutionary Generation." Def Jam/Columbia 38T 73309. 1990. (CS)

———. "Welcome to the Terrordome." Def Jam/Columbia 44T 73135. 1989. (CS)

Reed, Lou. *New York.* Sire 9 25829-2. 1988. (CD)

Reeves, Del. "The Private." United Artists 50157. (45)

Ritter, Tex. "Message from the Alamo." Capitol 5966. (45)

Rivers, Johnny. "Come Home America." *L.A. Reggae.* United Artists 5650. (LP)

Robeson, Paul. "Ballad for Americans." RCA Victor 26516 and 26517. (78)

Robison, Carson. "We're Gonna Have to Slap the Dirty Little Jap" b/w "Remember Pearl Harbor." Bluebird 11414. (78)

Sainte-Marie, Buffy. *Best of Buffy Sainte-Marie.* ABC Vanguard 314. (LP)

———. *Sweet America.* ABC D-929.

Scott, Earl. "G.I." Decca 32177. (45)

Sedaka, Neil. "The Immigrant." *Sedaka's Back.* Rocket BXLI-3046. (LP)

Short, J. D. "Fighting for Dear Old Uncle Sam." *Delta Blues.* Folkways FTS 31028. (LP)

Simon, Paul, and Art Garfunkle. *Bookends.* Columbia KCS 9529. 1968. (LP)

Simon, Paul. *There Goes Rhymin' Simon.* Columbia KC 32280. 1973. (LP)

Sinatra, Frank. "The House I Live In." *Frank Sinatra: A Man and His Music.* Reprise 2FS 1016. (LP)

Songs of the Civil War. New World Records NW 202. (LP)

Songs of Liberty. Various Ensembles. Book-of-the-Month Club Records 61-7634 (two disc set). (CD)

Songs of Liberty: Music of the Revolutionary War. James S. Darling, director. Colonial Williamsburg Foundation WS-106. (LP)

Songs That Got Us Through WW II. Various Artists. Rhino R2 70960. 1990. (CD)

Son House. "American Defense." *The Legendary Son House, 1941–42 Recordings.* Roots Special Edition RSE 1. 1942. (LP)

Springsteen, Bruce. *Born in the U.S.A.* Columbia CK 38653. 1984. (CD)

———. *Born to Run.* Columbia PC 33795. 1975. (LP)

Steppenwolf. "Monster." *16 Greatest Hits.* ABC Dunhill X-50135. (LP)

Swan, Billy. "That's America For Me." *You're OK, I'm OK.* A&M 4686. (LP)

Talking Heads. "The Big Country." *More Songs About Buildings and Food.* Sire SRK 6058. 1978. (LP)

The Temptations. "Ball of Confusion (1970)." *The Temptations Anthology*

10th Anniversary Special. Motown M 782A3. 1973. (LP)

———. "Cloud Nine (1969)." *The Temptations Anthology 10th Anniversary Special.* Motown M 782A3. 1973. (LP)

"There's A Good Time Coming" and Other Songs of the Hutchinson Family. The Smithsonian Collection N 020. (LP)

"There's No Business Like Show Business": The Magical Songs of Irving Berlin. Various Artists. Book-of-the-Month Club 60-5256. (LP)

They Come to America. Various Artists. A&M WC 98334. 1986. (C)

Tubb, Ernest. "The Soldier's Last Letter." *Ernest Tubb Favorites.* Decca DL 8291. *(78)*

War. "The World Is a Ghetto"(1972). *Greatest Hits.* United Artists UA-LA648-G. 1976. (LP)

Waters, Muddy. *I'm Ready.* Blue Sky ZK 34928. 1978. (CD)

The Weavers. *Greatest Hits.* Vanguard VCD-15/16. (CD)

Womack, Bobby. "American Dream." *The Poet II.* Beverly Glen Music BG-10003. 1984. (LP)

Wonder, Stevie. "He's Mista Know It All." *Innervisions.* Tamla T-326V1. 1973. (LP)

———. "Living for the City." *Innervisions.* Tamla T-326V1. 1973. (LP)

Work, Henry Clay. *Who Shall Rule This American Nation?: Songs of the Civil War Era.* The Camerata Chorus of Washington (with guest soloists). Nonesuch H-71317. (LP)

Wright, Johnny. "Hello Vietnam." Decca 31821. (45)

Young, Neil. *Freedom.* Reprise 9 25899-2. 1989. (CD)

INDEX

References to all songs, except "The Star Spangled Banner," are only to the pages where the song is initially discussed.

a Beckett, Thomas, 57
"Abe Lincoln," 153
Abolition, 57, 60–63
Acuff, Roy, 161, 166, 190
"Adams and Liberty," 44–45
Adamson, Harold, 131
African-American music, 80–81, 98, 135, 140–46, 202–09, 240, 242–46
"After the War is Over (Will There Be Any Home Sweet Home)," 111
Allen, Lewis, 124, 134–35
"America" (Bernstein-Sondheim), 168
"America" (Billings), 33–35
"America" (Diamond), 228
"America" (Prince), 243
"America" (Simon), 186–87
"America, I Love You," 97, 101–02
"America My Home," 215
"America the Beautiful," 93–96
"America . . . The Dream Goes On," 227
"America the Ugly," 193–94
"America Today," 104
American Communist Party, 146, 147
"American Defense," 143
"American Dream" (Harrison), 209
"American Dream" (Womack), 243–44
"The American Dream" (Kaplan), 198
"The American Dream" (Pankow), 227–28
"American Eagle Tragedy," 176
"American Prayer," 130
American Society of Composers, Authors and Publishers (ASCAP), 129, 148

"American Tune," 187–89
"America's Farm," 226
"Anacreontic Song," 44
Andersen, Eric, 179
Anderson, Bill, 192
Anderson, Sherwood, 115, 250
Andrieu, Harry, 111
Anomaly-masking/anomaly-featuring, 6, 63, 124, 139, 159–60, 182–84, 212
"Are You Bombing with Me Jesus," 175
"Are You Walking There for Me?," 178
Arlen, Harold, 122
Ash, Frances, 136
Autry, Gene, 163, 192

Babes in Arms (movie musical), 122
Bache, Anna, 73
"Back in the U.S.A.," 169
Baez, Joan, 181
Baldwin, James, 214
"Ballad for Americans," 123–24
"Ballad of You and Me," 159
Bancroft, George, 250
Bare, Bobby, 190
Barlow, J., 191
Barlow, Joel, 27, 41
Barnes, Jimmy, 229
Baskette, Billy, 105
Bates, Katherine Lee ("America the Beautiful"), 12, 49, 75, 93–95, 108, 125, 156, 179, 216, 237, 243, 252
"Battle Cry of Freedom," 76
"Battle Hymn of Lt. Calley," 190
"Battle Hymn of the Republic," 69

"The Battle Song of Liberty," 107
Bay Psalm Book, 18, 19, 22
Beat Poets, 168, 184
Bedlow, Henry, 79
The Beggar's Opera (1728), 26
Bergman, Alan and Marilyn, 227
Berlin, Irving, 10, 12, 15, 28, 35, 49, 55, 87, 93, 122, 123, 124–25, 127–28, 136, 161, 167, 183, 186, 190, 194, 207, 210, 216, 225
Bernstein, Leonard, 168
Berry, Chuck, 59, 169, 209, 226, 243
"Better Go Down and Join the Union," 152
"Better World," 153
"The Big Country," 217–18
"Big Parade," 236
Bierstadt, Albert, 12, 94
Billings, William, 22–23, 33–36, 70
"Black, Brown and White Blues," 144
Blackmar, A. E., 71
Blades, Ruben, 241–42, 252
Blake, Eubie, 134
Blind Man's Zoo, 235–36
Bliss, Phillip Paul, 84
"Bob Dylan's Dream," 183–84
"Bob Dylan's 115th Dream," 184
"Bonnie Blue Flag," 74
"Bonnie Blue Flag" (Northern parody), 74
"Born in the U.S.A.," 229–30
Born in the U.S.A., 228
"Born to Run," 230
"Bourgeois Blues," 145
Boyden, George, 110
Boyden, Ian, 175
Bradbury, William B., 73, 81
Bradford, William, 17, 19, 34, 38, 54, 58
Brandon, Joseph, 151
"Bring Back My Daddy to Me," 107
Broadside, 145, 160, 171
Broadside ballad, 26–27
Broonzy, Big Bill, 140, 144
"Brother, Can You Spare a Dime?," 118
Brown, Al W., 104
Brown, James, 242–43
Brown, John, 159, 177
Browne, Jackson, 7, 221, 224, 229, 233–35, 237
Bryan, Alfred, 100
Bryan, William Jennings, 89, 100
Buck Privates, 132

Burke, Joseph, 102, 104
Burt, Ed (Edith Berbert), 163
Burton, Nat, 132
"Buscando America," 241
Bush, George, 239
"Busload of Faith," 239
By the Light of the Moon, 241
Byrne, David, 217–18

"Can I Go Dearest Mother," 61
Carr, Benjamin, 41
Carr, Howard ("Kid"), 105
Carter, Jimmy, 198, 221
Catch-22, 172, 207
Chaos Science, 222, 250
Chapin, Harry, 213–14, 250
Chaplin, Ralph, 152, 153
Chapman, M.W., 26
Charlieres, Nathan, 159
"Chester," 33
Chicago (rock group), 227–28
Chief Joseph, 240–41
The Chi-Lites, 207
"Christians at War," 149
The Civil War, 46, 65–85, 130, 190
Clark, J.G., 67
Clements, Zeke, 163–64
"Cloud Nine," 205
Cobb, George L., 107
Cohan, George M., 97, 101, 102, 116, 118, 120, 121, 129, 132, 173
"Colored Volunteer," 81
"Columbia," 41–42
"Columbia, The Gem of the Ocean," 57–58
Columbia River Project, 156
"Come Home America," 213
Comer, Ethel, 152
"Comin' in on a Wing and a Prayer," 131
"The Commonwealth of Toil," 152
Composers Collective, 147
"The Conscript's Mother," 79–80
"Convention," 61
Cooke, Charles, 134
"Cops of the World," 176
"Coulee Dam," 156
Covert, Bernard, 69
Crevecoeur, Michel-Guillaume-Jean, 12, 45, 58
Culture, defined, 4
cummings, e.e., 75, 120

Dale, Ralph, 175
Daniels, Charlie, 225–26
Darnell, Shelby. *See* Bob Miller
Dasher, C. D., 83
Davis, Bennie, 105
"Declaration of Independence," 25, 42, 44, 50, 67, 70, 75, 81, 153
The Deer Hunter, 136
De La Soul, 245
Deloria, Vine, 197
Dempsey, J.E., 102, 104
Depression (The Great Depression), 114, 117–20, 121, 123, 128, 143, 146, 200, 222
Diamond, Neil, 228
Dickinson, John, 30–33
DiMaggio, Joe, 192, 221
"Dirty Boulevard," 238
"Dixie's Land" (parody by Albert Pike), 69–70
"Dixie's Land" (Northern parody), 73
"The Dixie Volunteer," 106
Dodge, H.C., 92
Donnelly, Dorothy, 134
"Do Re Mi," 154
Douglass, Frederick, 150, 159, 209
"Down and Out in Paradise," 231
"Down the Street We Hold Our Demonstration," 154
Dreslane, Jack, 97
Dresser, Paul, 86–87, 96, 101, 193
"The Drummer Boy of Shiloh," 71–72
Dubin, Al, 118–19, 135
Dudley, Bide, 111
"Dust Bowl," 236
"Dust Bowl Refuge," 156
Dwight, Timothy, 41–43, 45
Dylan, Bob, 52, 128, 140, 158, 168, 171, 173, 179–86, 194–95, 215, 229, 234

Earth Opera, 176
Easy Rider, 166, 197
Edenic Myth, 79, 188, 211–12
Emancipation Proclamation, 14, 72, 77, 135
Emerson, L. O., 78
"The End of the Innocence," 237–38
"Empty Hands," 231
The Enlightenment, 22–24

"The Faded Coat of Blue," 82
Fairman, George, 112
Farina, Mimi, 210
Farina, Richard, 210
Farrakhan, Louis, 245
"The Fatherhood of God and the Brotherhood of Man," 91
Ferlinghetti, Lawrence, 168, 187, 200
Field, James T., 73
Fields, Dorothy, 117
"Fight the Power," 246
"The Fightin' Side of Me," 192–93
"The First Gun Is Fired," 75
Foley, Red, 163
Folk-protest movement, 48, 119, 147–61, 164–65
Folk Revival, 172–74
"A Fool There Was," 151
"For America," 233–34
Foreman, Gladys, 204
Foster, Stephen, 10, 58, 147
Freedom, 239–40
Friedland, Anatole, 110
"The Future America" (parody of "My Country! 'Tis of Thee"), 92

Garden, John, 155
Garrison, William Lloyd, 62
Gaye, Marvin, 207, 208
Gellert, Lawrence (*Negro Songs of Protest*), 141, 143
Gershwin, George, 55
Gershwin, Ira, 55, 117, 120, 137
"Ghetto Thang," 245
Gilbert, L. Wolfe, 110
"Gimme What You Got," 236–37
Ginsberg, Allan, 168, 187, 200
"Give More Power to the People," 207
Glazer, Tom, 152
Glogau, Jack, 103
"God Bless America," 124–25
"God Bless the U.S.A.," 226
"The God of the Fathers," 63–64
"God Must Have Loved America," 163
"God's Country," 122–23
"God Save the South," 72
"God Save the Thirteen States," 37
Gold Diggers of 1933, 119
"Goodbye Broadway, Hello France," 105
"Good Evening, Mr. Waldheim," 239
"The Good Old U.S.A.," 97

"Good Morning, Mr. Zip-Zip-Zip," 108
Gordon, Mack, 133
Gorney, Jay, 118–19
Gottler, Archie, 97, 101
The Graduate, 172, 217
Graff, George, 103
Grandmaster Flash and the Furious Five, 245–46
"Grandmother's Land," 240
Grant, Freddy, 166
Grant, Shurli, 175
The Grapes of Wrath (novel), 127, 138–39
The Grapes of Wrath (film), 127, 151, 232
Gray, Thomas, 18, 54
"The Great Compromise," 210
The Great Awakening (1740s), 25
The Great Gatsby, 3, 219–20, 224, 248
Greenwood, Lee, 49, 226
Grossman, Bernie, 104, 110
Gunning, Sara Ogan, 154
Guthrie, Arlo, 213
Guthrie, Woody, 14, 35, 55, 59, 78, 122, 123, 133, 135, 144, 146, 147, 149, 150–51, 152, 153, 154, 155–57, 158, 160, 164–65, 166, 168, 179, 181, 182, 183, 184, 186, 187, 190, 194, 224, 229, 231, 232, 242

Haggard, Merle, 192–93
"Hail Columbia," 46
Hall, Matthew, 160
Hall, Tom T., 191, 193–94
Hamblen, Stuart, 164
Hammerstein, Oscar, 129, 132
"The Hand That Holds the Bread," 92
Harburg, E.Y., 117, 118–19, 122, 135, 188
"A Hard Rain's a Gonna Fall," 181
"Hard Time Killin' Floor Blues," 142
"Hard Times Ain't Gone No Where," 142
Harris, Charles K., 90, 96, 116, 117
Harris III, James, 244
Harrison, Don, 209
Harold Melvin and the Blue Notes, 208
Hart, Lorenz, 117, 120, 129
Hartman, Dan, 242
"Hateful Hate," 236
Havens, Jimmie, 105
Hayes, Alfred, 153
Hays, Hoffman, 155
Hays, Lee, 149, 158, 164

Hays, Will S., 71
Hellerman, Fred, 149
Helm, Levon, 227
"Hello Central, Give Me No Man's Land," 110
"Hello Vietnam," 191
Henry, Roslyn, 158
Henley, Don, 229, 236–38, 248, 252
Henry, Patrick, 27, 28
"Here's to You MacArthur," 132
"The Hero's Grave," 83
"The Hero of Fort Sumter," 73
"He's My Uncle Sam," 129
Hewitt, James, 41, 47–48
Hicks, Robert, 142
Higginson, T.W., 14–15, 60
"Higher Ground," 208
Hill, Joe, 148, 150, 154, 165
Hoier, Thomas R., 104
"Hold the Fort," 84
"Home of the Brave," 180
"Honor Our Commitment," 176
Hootenanies, 158, 173
Hopkinson, Francis, 44
"Hotdogs and Hamburgers," 231–32
"The House I Live In," 134
"The House I Live In" (parody), 174
"House Un-American Blues Activity Dream," 210
Howard, H., 191
Howe, Irving, 147
Howe, Julia Ward, 71
Howe, T. H., 83
"How Long," 235
"How Long? How Long?," 204
Hughes, Langston, 246
Hutchinson Family, 53, 57–59, 227
Hutchinson, John, 91

"I Ain't Marchin' Any More," 177
"If Dirt Were Dollars," 237
"If I Am Free," 160
"If I'm Not at the Roll Call (Kiss Mother Goodbye For Me)," 110
"I Have a Dream" (Solomon Burke), 208
"I'm Gonna Love That Guy (Like He's Never Been Loved Before)," 136
"The Immigrant," 212–13
"In America," 225–26
Innervisions, 207
"The International" (IWW version), 153

International Workers of the World (also Wobblies), 148, 149, 154
"Is This All There Is," 24
"It's All Over Now," 112
"I Still Love the Red, White and Blue," 120–21

Jackson, Andrew (Jacksonian Democracy), 49, 54
Jackson, Janet, 161, 243
Jackson, Stonewall (country singer), 191
Jacobs, Al, 133
James, Skip, 142
"Jefferson and Liberty," 48
Jefferson, Thomas, 7, 24, 27, 29, 48–49, 120, 132, 157, 159, 191, 221, 227
Jerome, M.K., 110
Jesus Christ, 150–51, 178, 208, 232, 236
"Jesus Christ," 150
John Henry, 150–51
"Johnny Freedom," 189
Johnson, Cliff, 163
Johnson, Howard, 106, 107
Johnson, James Weldon, 98
Johnson, J. Rosamond, 98
Johnson, Lonnie, 142
Johnson, Robert, 140, 203
Johnston, Jack, 164
Jones, David Lynn, 227
Jones, Isham, 107
Jones, Maggie, 142
"Just a Baby's Letter (Found in No Man's Land)," 110
"Just a Baby's Prayer at Twilight," 110
"Just Before the Battle, Mother," 69
"Just Like Washington Crossed the Delaware (General Pershing Will Cross the Rhine)," 106–07

Kansas (rock group), 216–17
Kaplan, Artie, 198
"Keep the Trench Fires Going for the Boys Out There," 107
Kendrick, John F., 149
Kennedy, John F., 169, 171, 172, 227
Kent, Walter, 132
Key, Francis Scott, 51–52
King, Dr. Martin Luther, 145, 202, 208, 209, 227, 243–44, 245
"Kingdom's Coming," 81
The Kingston Trio, 170, 171

Knights of Labor, 84, 89, 147
Kristofferson, Kris, 191

"A Laborer You See, and I Love Liberty," 92
Labor-protest songs, 91–93
"Lafayette (We Hear You Calling)," 105
"Lamentation Over Boston," 22–23
"The Land of Opportunitee," 137
Latouche, John, 122, 123–24, 134
Lawrence, Ray, 110
Leadbelly (Huddie Ledbetter), 141, 146, 166
Leave It to Me, 120–21
Lee, Robert E., 66, 106, 108, 132, 159
Lenoir, J.B., 144
Leslie, Edgar, 97, 101, 106
"Let's Bring New Glory to Old Glory," 133
"Let's Have a New Deal," 143
Lewis, Sam, 110
Lewis, Terry, 244
The Liberator, 61, 62
"Liberty Song," 30–32
Liberty Tree, 31–32, 38, 46, 53, 72, 83
"Life Saver Blues," 142
"Lift Every Voice and Sing," 98
Lincoln, Abraham, 120, 123, 132, 150, 153, 163, 221, 227
Lindbergh, Charles, 120, 192
Livernash, Will, 164
"Livin' in a World (They Didn't Make)," 244
Living Colour, 161, 221, 244–45, 252
"Living in America," 242
"Living in the City," 207
"Living in the Promiseland," 227
"Living in the U.S.A.," 209
Lloyd, George W., 92
Lloyd, Henry Demarest, 149
Loesser, Frank, 131
Lomax, Alan, 146, 148
The Lonesome Jubilee, 231–32
Los Lobos, 229, 241, 252
Lowenfels, Walter, 159
Lozier, John Hogarth, 72
Luther, Frank, 162

MacArthur, Douglas, 132, 192
MacCarthy, Harry, 74
Mack, Warner, 190

Mailer, Norman, 167, 194
Malcolm X, 209, 245
Manifest Destiny, 50, 57
Mann, Barry, 180
"Marching Along," 81
"Marching Through Georgia," 75
Martin, Carl, 143
Massachusetts Bay Colony, 16, 18, 24, 25
Mather, Cotton, 13, 19
Mayfield, Curtis, 204, 205, 209
McGee, Willie, 153, 160
McLean, Don, 212, 238
McHugh, Jimmy, 131
McPherson, Warren, 190
"Me Decade," 200–01
Mellencamp, John (Cougar), 221, 223,
  224, 229–32, 234, 242, 248, 252
"The Message," 245–46
Meyer, George W., 106, 107
Midnight, Charlie, 242
Miller, Bob (Shelby Darnell), 162–63
Miller, Jody, 180
Miller, Steve, 209
"The Minutemen Are Turning Over in
  Their Graves," 191
"Monster," 176
Moore, Herbert, 104
Moran, Edward, 107
Morse, Theodore, 97, 109
Munzinger, C., 73
Music Television (MTV), 223
"My Belgian Rose," 112
"My Country! 'Tis of Thee," 54–57, 60
"My Country! 'Tis of Thee" (Abolition-
  ist parody), 61–63
"My Country 'Tis of Thy People You're
  Dying," 215
"My Hometown," 229–30
"My Land Is a Good Land," 179
Myth: defined, 4–5; functions, 6–7; of
  America, 5, 26, 113, 139, 209, 217, 229,
  246–47, 249, 253; of the Frontier, 94;
  of Success, 4, 20, 95, 116, 203, 229,
  242; of war, 100, 110, 130–31, 159, 176;
  megafunctions, 7–9, 130; reconciling
  opposites and/or contradictions, 24,
  25–26, 33–34, 40–41, 42, 57, 61, 66,
  68, 82, 91, 94, 99, 108, 130, 149–50,
  162, 174, 194, 249–50, 252; transcendence, 38, 40, 46, 48–49, 52–53, 54–56,
  59–60, 71–72, 80, 83, 94, 98, 99, 102,

104, 107, 125, 130, 151–52, 162, 182,
185, 194–96, 212, 223, 231–32, 234–
35, 246, 247, 249, 251, 252
Mytheme: defined, 11–12; of freedom/
  liberty/equality/opportunity (of democracy and democratic principles),
  13–14, 21–22, 28–29, 33, 36, 37, 38, 44,
  47, 48–49, 51–52, 54, 55–57, 59, 60–
  63, 67–68, 75–78, 81, 82, 92, 93–94, 98,
  102, 108, 118, 122, 123–24, 126–28,
  131, 132, 133, 134, 135, 139, 141–45,
  152, 154–55, 156, 157, 159, 164,
  176, 178–79, 180, 183, 186–87, 188,
  189, 190–92, 193–94, 203, 204–05,
  207, 208–09, 211–12, 213, 214, 215–16,
  217, 226, 227–28, 229, 230–32, 235,
  236, 238, 239–40, 241, 242, 243, 244,
  245–46, 251; of destiny (or manifest
  destiny), 13, 20, 35, 36, 37, 42–43, 45,
  48, 57, 58, 64, 68–72, 82, 83, 91, 94,
  96, 97, 98, 102, 103, 105, 106–07, 118–
  19, 126, 131, 132, 133, 135, 149, 151–
  53, 156, 158–59, 162–63, 164, 175–76,
  177, 180, 182–83, 190, 191, 194–95,
  211–12, 214, 216, 217, 229, 231–32,
  233, 236, 237, 245, 249, 251; of God
  (theocratic vision), 12–13, 19–20, 29–
  30, 31–32, 34–35, 36, 37–38, 45, 46, 52,
  55–57, 59–60, 62, 68–72, 91, 92, 93–
  95, 97, 98, 102–03, 125, 127, 131, 133,
  134, 135, 139, 142–43, 144, 149–50,
  151–53, 162–63, 175–76, 177, 179,
  182–85, 187, 190, 195, 203, 207, 209,
  210, 217, 225, 226, 227, 228, 229, 236,
  239, 249; of land, 12, 14, 19, 20–
  21, 34–35, 36, 40, 42, 44, 45–46, 48–
  49, 53–54, 55–57, 58–59, 63–64, 78–
  80, 92, 93–94, 107, 118, 122, 123, 124,
  125, 126–27, 133, 135, 142, 144, 155–
  57, 179–80, 186–87, 193, 203, 205–06,
  209, 214–17, 225, 226, 227, 229, 231,
  236–37, 242, 243–44, 246, 249; of
  pilgrims/patriots, 11, 12, 13, 30,
  31, 36, 38, 44–45, 46, 47–48, 52, 55–56,
  59–60, 62, 63, 72–75, 80–81, 84, 95,
  96, 97, 98, 105–06, 118, 120, 123, 124,
  132, 133, 137, 153–55, 157, 159, 162–
  63, 176, 177–78, 183, 184, 187, 190,
  191–92, 205, 213, 215–16, 226, 227,
  231–32, 234, 237, 246, 249, 251–52; of
  regeneration, 21, 30, 33, 36, 38, 46–47,

52–53, 62, 78–79, 82–84, 91, 94, 111–
12, 136–37, 153, 179, 182, 185–86,
187, 205, 211–12, 214, 215, 230–32,
234, 236, 249

"National Anti-Slavery Hymn," 60–61
"National Jubilee," 82
Native-Americans, 215–16, 232, 240–41
Nebraska, 230
New Left, 174
"The New Massachusetts Liberty Song,"
36
"New Yankee Doodle," 47–48
Newman, Randy, 211–12, 230, 251
New York (Lou Reed), 238–39
"The New York Volunteers," 72
"North Bound Blues," 142
Nunn, Earl, 163
N.W.A., 246
Nyro, Laura, 180

Ochs, Phil, 140, 158, 166, 171, 173–74,
175–76, 177, 180, 192, 215
"Ode on Science," 39, 41
Of Thee I Sing, 114, 137
"Of Thee I Sing," 120
"Okie from Muskogee," 192
Old Left, 172, 174
Old Glory, 11, 14, 51–52, 73, 74–75, 76,
83, 97, 103, 106, 109, 120, 121, 132–
33, 134, 135, 137, 152, 162–63, 164,
192, 210, 236, 237, 239
"Old Glory," 164
"The Old Granite State," 59–60
"Old Sawbucks," 150
"Old Stonewall," 83
"The Old Union Wagon," 72
Oliver, William, 204
Olson, Ole, 107
"One Big Union," 152
"150 Million," 159
"One Time One Night," 241
"On Independence," 36–37
"Original Hymn," 62
"Our Country May She Always Be Right
(But Our Country, Right or Wrong)," 96
"Over There," 102

Paine, Thomas ("Adams and Liberty"), 45
"The Palmetto State Song," 77
Park Avenue, 137

"Pastures of Plenty," 151
"The Patriot's Banner. A Parody," 76–77
"Patriot's Dream," 213
Paxton, Tom, 177, 236
"Peace, It's Wonderful," 159
"The People's Rally Cry," 92
The People's Song Book, 146–47, 160
Peter, Paul and Mary, 170, 171
Piantadosi, Al, 100
"Pie in the Sky," 154
Pierpoint, James, 73–74
Pike, Albert, 69–70
"Pink Houses," 230–31
Platoon, 192
"Please Forgive Us," 235–36
Pledge of Allegiance, 133, 134, 243
Plugz, 229
Plymouth Plantation, 16, 24, 25
Popular Front, 153
Populism, 88, 91, 94, 127, 128
Porter, Cole, 117, 120–21, 129
Pourmon, E.J., 111
"Power and the Glory," 180
"Praise the Lord and Pass the Ammuni-
tion," 131
"Pray for Your Country," 190
"Prayer for Peace," 175
Prince, 240, 242–43, 252
Prine, John, 177, 210–11
"The Private," 191
Progressives, 88, 107
"Promise Land," 169
"The Promised Land," 54
Public Enemy, 221, 245–46, 248, 251

"Rally, 'Round the Flag Boys," 73
Raye, Don, 133
Razaf, Andy, 134
Reagan, Ronald, 219–223, 226, 228, 243
"Red Cross Store," 141
Reed, Lou, 221, 236, 238–39, 251
Reid, Vernon, 244–45
Reisner, C. Francis, 105
"Remember My Forgotten Man," 118
"Remember Pearl Harbor," 162
Remington, Frederick, 12, 94
Revolutionary War, 24–38, 70–71, 129,
152, 159, 190, 213, 225
Reynolds, Malvina, 158, 178
"Rhythm Nation," 244
Rhythm Nation 1814, 244

Rivers, Johnny, 213
Roberts, Paul, 162
Robeson, Paul, 123, 149, 158
Robinson, Carson, 162
Robinson, Earl, 122–24, 134–35, 143,
    149, 153, 158, 160, 174–75, 213
"Rockin' in the Free World," 239–40
Rodgers, Jimmie, 161
Rogen, Ronnie, 226–27
"Roll On Columbia," 157
Romberg, Sigmund, 132, 134
Roosevelt, Franklin Delano, 133, 151,
    159, 221, 227
Root, George F., 68, 75, 76, 92
Rose, Fred, 163
Rose, Vincent, 131
Ruby, Harry, 106
Russell, Harry, 105

"Sail Away," 211–12
Sainte-Marie, Buffy, 214–15
St. John, Peter, 27, 29
Satire, 118, 119–21
"Save the Country," 180
Sawyer, Charles C., 75
"Say a Prayer for the Boys Out There,"
    108
Scarecrow, 231
Schwartz, Jean, 110, 116
Schwartz, Arthur, 137
Second Great Awakening, 41, 42, 43
Sedaka, Neil, 212–13, 228, 238
"Seaman Three," 153
"See America First," 117
Seeger, Charles, 147
Seeger, Pete, 146, 149, 158, 164, 171, 174
"Send Me Away with a Smile," 103
Sewall, Jonathan Mitchell, 36–37
Sewall, Samuel, 16, 19, 25, 36
Shapiro, Vic, 159
Sharpe, Jacqueline, 176
Silber, Irwin, 149, 158
"Silver Dew on the Blue Grass Tonight,"
    163
Simon, Norman, 198
Simon, Paul, 140, 173, 179–80, 184, 186–89,
    191, 197, 206, 217, 225, 229, 230, 231,
    233, 238, 252
Simpson, Joshua, 61
Sinatra, Frank, 123, 134–35

Sing Out!, 48, 145, 158, 160, 161, 171–
    72
Sir Lancelot, 144–45
Smith, Lonnie, 140
Smith, Samuel Francis, 54–56
"Smoke on the Water," 163
"A Soldier's Rosary," 102
"Solidarity Forever," 153
"Somebody Ought to Wave a Flag," 121
Sondheim, Stephen, 168–69
"Song for America," 216–17
"Song for the 4th of July," 43–44
"Song of the 'Aliened American'" (par-
    ody of "My Country! 'Tis of Thee"),
    61
"Song of the West Virginia Miners," 154
"A Song Made Upon the Foregoing Occa-
    sion," 28–30
Son House, 143
"Sons of Liberty," 32–33
Sousa, John Phillip, 173
"The South," 77–78
"The Southern Cross," 79
"Southern Soldier," 77–78
"Southern Song of Freedom," 69, 77
"Southron's Chaunt of Defiance," 71
"So What's the Big Blonde Boy of Freedom
    Doing Now," 179
Spanish-American War, 87, 95
Springsteen, Bruce, 59, 128, 168, 188,
    223, 224, 228–30, 231, 233, 234, 242,
    247, 248, 252
"Stand Up! Ye Workers," 152
"The Star Spangled Banner," 7, 47, 51–
    53, 76, 84, 97, 121, 145, 154, 160, 163,
    233–34, 241, 244, 247, 252
"Stars and Stripes on Iwo Jima," 163
"State of the World," 244
"The Statue," 212–13
Statue of Liberty, 9, 14, 110, 132, 134,
    188, 197, 210, 225, 227, 238–39
"Strawman," 238
Steppenwolf, 15, 169, 176
Stillman, Albert, 131
Stock, Lawrence, 131
Stone, Sly, 204–05, 244
"Stouthearted Men" (U.S. Navy version,
    1943), 132
Styne, Jule, 189
Sumner, Jezeniah, 39, 41

Swan, Billy, 217–18
"Sweet America," 215
"Sweet Liberty Land," 155

Taylor, Tell, 107
The Temptations, 205–06
10,000 Maniacs, 235–36, 237
Themes: alienation, 174, 180–81, 182–
  88, 212; brotherhood, 46–47, 94, 208,
  213, 214, 216–17, 242, 249; home, 10,
  52, 70, 78–79, 96, 99, 109, 111, 125,
  133–34, 186, 191, 192, 212, 216, 225,
  247; individualism, 92, 119, 122, 123–
  24, 126–28, 139, 144, 149–50, 159,
  180–85, 194, 198–99, 211–12, 232,
  241, 247, 249; mother, 10, 70, 79–80,
  96, 99, 101–02, 109–10, 111; peace,
  103–04, 159; unionism, 151–53, 158,
  180; work, 14, 59, 74, 139, 144,
  154–55, 186–89, 207, 217, 226, 229,
  242, 247
"There Is No Time," 239
"There Is Power in a Union," 149
"There's a Service Flag Flying at Our
  House," 104
"There's a Star Spangled Banner Waving
  Somewhere," 162
"They Call It America" (But I Call It
  Home), 166
"They Tell Us to Wait," 154–55
"This Is My Country" (Mayfield), 205
"This Is My Country" (Raye-Jacobs),
  133–34
"This Land Is Your Land," 125–27
Tin Pan Alley, 87, 88, 89–90, 116, 129,
  170
"'Tis Finished! or Sing Hallelujah," 82
"Tom Joad," 156
"Tonight in America," 227
Tracey, William, 107
Tree of Liberty. See Liberty Tree
Treuer, Konrad, 82
Tubman, Harriet, 159
Tucker, Henry, 75

Uncle Sam, 9, 58, 97, 163, 175, 176, 193,
  229
"Uncle Sam's Farm," 58
"Underground," 209
"Union Feeling," 154

"Vietnam," 173
"Vietnam Blues," 191
The Vietnam War, 136–37, 173, 175–76,
  178–79, 190–92, 198, 210, 234
"Visions," 208
Von Tilzer, Harry, 90, 107, 116

"Wake Up, America," 106
"Walk in Peace," 144–45
Ward, S.A., 93
Warren, Harry, 118–19, 133
Warren, Joseph, 27, 35–36
Washington, George, 14, 75, 120, 123,
  132, 159, 163, 177–78, 191, 221
Watson, Frederic, 111
Wayne, John, 192, 220
"We Are Americans Too," 134
"We Are Coming Father Abra'am," 78
The Weavers, 123
"We Don't Want the Bacon (What We
  Want Is a Piece of the Rhine)," 105
Weems, Parson, 14
"Weeping, Sad and Lonely or When This
  Cruel War Is Over," 75–76
Weil, Cynthia, 180
Weiss, George, 189
Weldon, Will, 142
"Welfare Blues," 143
"(We'll Write) The Last Page of Mein
  Kampf," 164
"We're Gonna Have to Slap the Dirty Lit-
  tle Jap," 162
"We're in the Army Now," 107
"We Sure Got Hard Times Now," 142
"We've Always Welcomed Strangers," 158
"What Made America Famous," 213–14
What's Going On, 207
"When Our Boys Come Marching
  Home," 108
"When the War Is Over I'll Return to
  You," 111
"Where Have All Our Heroes Gone," 191
"Where There's A Will, There's A Way,"
  177
"Where's the Concern for the People?,"
  208
"Which Way to America," 244
"While You're Away," 110
"White Boots Marching in a Yellow
  Land," 175–76

"The White Cliffs of Dover," 136
White, Joshua, 143
Whitfield, Norman, 205–07
Whitman, Walt, 86, 183
Whittier, John Greenleaf, 62
"The Whole Wide World Around," 152
"Who Shall Rule This American Nation?," 65
"Who's in Charge of Killing in Vietnam," 178
Wieder, Judith, 179
Williams, W. R., 104
Williamson, Chris, 240–41, 242
Wills, Bob, 163
Wilcox, Carlos, 82
Winthrop, John, 19, 95, 218
"With God on Our Side," 182–83
Wolf, Bill, 159
Wonder, Stevie, 205, 207–08
Woodruff, Joseph, 111

"The Word Justice," 235
Work, Henry Clay, 65, 69, 75, 81, 82
"The Workingman's Army," 91–92
World in Motion, 234
World War I, 46, 68, 70, 99–113, 129–30, 133, 136
World War II, 51, 68, 70, 128–37, 143, 225
"W.P.A. Blues," 142

Yankee Doodle Dandy (film), 129
"(I'm a) Yankee Doodle Dandy," 97
Yellen, Jack, 107
Younker, F., 83
Young, Joe, 110
Young, Neil, 221, 229, 239–40, 251, 252
"You're a Grand Old Flag," 97
"You're a Lucky Fellow Mr. Smith," 132
"Your Flag Decal Won't Get You into Heaven Anymore," 177
"Your Land and My Land," 134